Lecture Notes of the Institute for Computer Sciences, Social Informatics and Telecommunications Engineering

436

More information about this series at https://link.springer.com/bookseries/8197

Muhammet Nuri Seyman (Ed.)

Electrical and Computer Engineering

First International Congress, ICECENG 2022
Virtual Event, February 9–12, 2022
Proceedings

 Springer

Editor
Muhammet Nuri Seyman (iD)
Bandırma Onyedi Eylül University
Bandirma, Turkey

ISSN 1867-8211   ISSN 1867-822X (electronic)
Lecture Notes of the Institute for Computer Sciences, Social Informatics
and Telecommunications Engineering
ISBN 978-3-031-01983-8   ISBN 978-3-031-01984-5 (eBook)
https://doi.org/10.1007/978-3-031-01984-5

This Springer imprint is published by the registered company Springer Nature Switzerland AG
The registered company address is: Gewerbestrasse 11, 6330 Cham, Switzerland

Preface

This volume contains the papers presented at ICECENG 2022, the first International Congress of Electrical and Computer Engineering, which was held online during February 9–12, 2022, in Bandirma, Turkey. It is a great privilege for us to present the proceedings of ICECENG 2022 to the authors and delegates of the event. We hope that you will find it useful, exciting, and inspiring.

The aim of ICECENG is to bring together researchers, developers, and students in computing, technology trends, artificial intelligence, and security who are interested in studying the application of formal methods to the construction and analysis of models describing technological processes at both micro and macro levels. ICECENG also aims to provide a platform for discussing the issues, challenges, opportunities, and findings of computer engineering research. The ever-changing scope and rapid development of engineering create new problems and questions, resulting in the real need for sharing brilliant ideas and stimulating good awareness of this important research field. Our conference seeks to provide some answers and explore the processes, actions, challenges, and outcomes of learning and teaching.

In response to the call for papers, the Program Committee received 48 submissions and selected 17 of them to be included in the conference program. Unfortunately, many manuscripts from prestigious institutions could not be accepted due to the reviewing outcomes and our capacity constraints. Each paper was reviewed, on average, by three referees and the selection was based on originality, quality, and relevance to the conference. The scientific program consisted of papers on a wide variety of topics, including IoT, machine-to-machine, biometrics, and, more generally, deep learning and machine learning.

We would like to thank the people, institutions, and companies that contributed to the success of this first edition of ICECENG 2022. We would like to extend our thanks to the keynote speakers, Ali Can Karaca, Yildiz Teknik University, and Ilyas Ozer, Bandirma Onyedi Eylul University, for their hard work. We would also like to express our gratitude and appreciation for all of the reviewers for their constructive comments on the papers. We acknowledge Springer for publishing the proceedings of ICECENG 2022 and Microsoft CMT management system for providing a useful platform for conference administration.

We hope this first edition of the conference will serve as a springboard for collaborations, projects, and all future editions of ICECENG 2022.

March 2022   Muhammet Nuri Seyman
                                                                   Adem Dalcali

Organization

Steering Committee

Muhammet Nuri Seyman   Bandirma Onyedi Eylul University, Turkey
Adem Dalcali   Bandirma Onyedi Eylul University, Turkey

Organizing Committee

General Chair

Muhammet Nuri Seyman   Bandirma Onyedi Eylul University, Turkey

General Co-chair

Adem Dalcali   Bandirma Onyedi Eylul University, Turkey

Technical Program Commitee Chairs

Muhammet Nuri Seyman   Bandirma Onyedi Eylul University, Turkey
Adem Dalcali   Bandirma Onyedi Eylul University, Turkey

Local Chairs

Necmi Taşpınar   Erciyes University, Turkey
Ilyas Özer   Bandirma Onyedi Eylul University, Turkey
Harun Özbay   Bandirma Onyedi Eylul University, Turkey

Workshops Chair

Mahmut Ünver   Kirikkale University, Turkey

Publications Chairs

Muhammet Nuri Seyman   Bandirma Onyedi Eylul University, Turkey
Adem Dalcali   Bandirma Onyedi Eylul University, Turkey
Feyzullah Temurtaş   Bandirma Onyedi Eylul University, Turkey
Onursal Cetin   Bandirma Onyedi Eylul University, Turkey

Web Chair

Fatma Kebire Bardak   Bandirma Onyedi Eylul University, Turkey

Technical Program Committee

Feyzullah Temurtaş	Bandirma Onyedi Eylul University, Turkey
Necmi Taşpınar	Erciyes University, Turkey
Serhat Duman	Bandirma Onyedi Eylul University, Turkey
Ilyas Özer	Bandirma Onyedi Eylul University, Turkey
Mahmut Unver	Kirikkale University, Turkey
Onursal Çetin	Bandirma Onyedi Eylul University, Turkey
Yalçın Işık	Selçuk University, Turkey
Harun Özbay	Bandirma Onyedi Eylul University, Turkey
Evren İşen	Bandirma Onyedi Eylul University, Turkey
Gökçe Nur Yılmaz	TED University, Turkey
Abdullah Gökyıldırım	Bandirma Onyedi Eylul University, Turkey
Rustem Yılmazel	Kirikkale University, Turkey
Aykut Diker	Bandirma Onyedi Eylul University, Turkey
Ali Durmuş	Kayseri University, Turkey
Rafet Durgut	Bandirma Onyedi Eylul University, Turkey
Abdullah Yeşil	Bandirma Onyedi Eylul University, Turkey
Abdullah Elen	Bandirma Onyedi Eylul University, Turkey
Kadir İleri	Karabuk University, Turkey
Serhat Berat Efe	Bandirma Onyedi Eylul University, Turkey

Contents

Computing

Security

Technology Trends

User Reactions About Wildfires on Twitter

Ridvan Yayla(✉) [iD] and Turgay Tugay Bilgin [iD]

Bursa Technical University, Yildirim, Bursa 16310, Turkey
{ridvan.yayla,turgay.bilgin}@btu.edu.tr

Abstract. Forests are the most important part of nature that provides the global balance within the ecosystem. Therefore, wildfires are one of the natural disasters that mostly affect the ecological balance. As an interdisciplinary study, the aim of this study is to measure the reactions of users by classifying comments about wildfires on Twitter with machine learning methods and to investigate the measures against wildfires. In the study, the user comments on wildfires were used on Twitter, which is used by all segments of the society and provides data analysis. A pre-processing has been firstly made for the comments about wildfires by performing word-based text analysis. Sentiment analysis has been realized as positive, negative, and neutral. Moreover, each sentiment group has been evaluated by dividing into four mostly expressed categories. The classification model accuracies have been compared by analyzing with the standard statistical scales. In the study, 58% of Twitter users wish that the wildfires would be ended immediately, approximately 34% of users think that firefighting related to government is enough, 7% of users think that the firefighting is insufficient. Moreover, all Twitter users have frequently referred to firefighting, global warming, support, and sabotage probability in their comments for wildfires. This research supported with sentiment analysis, reveals that wildfires create an alarming situation for all segments of society and it is necessary to act together against wildfires.

Keywords: Wildfires · Machine learning · Sentiment analysis

1 Introduction

The forests that create the energy dynamic within the ecosystem are one of the most important elements that provide global balance. The ecological effect of fires, when combined with the human factor, leads to irreversible hazards for forest health. These hazards merged with the human factor have spread to large areas with the effector the abiotic factors in especially the areas that have high-temperature risk. The deficiency to the response of the emergency, sabotage probability, the effect of the wind and temperature are seen as the main factors. The wildfires that especially start in July 2021 in Turkey left a deep mark on society and led to tangible and spiritual loss. In this period, wildfires all over the world became the most spoken topic on Twitter that is a social media platform. While some users support to responding the wildfires, some thought of the sabotage probability. All users specified that the forest sources should be protected

© ICST Institute for Computer Sciences, Social Informatics and Telecommunications Engineering 2022
Published by Springer Nature Switzerland AG 2022. All Rights Reserved
M. N. Seyman (Ed.): ICECENG 2022, LNICST 436, pp. 3–14, 2022.
https://doi.org/10.1007/978-3-031-01984-5_1

by all society in this period. In this study, the opinions of the Twitter users on wildfires are analyzed in three main sentiments and 4 categories, and the performance of the model accuracies are compared within three different classifiers.

Forest resources are used in many areas from furniture to paper production with a rich usage source in the ecosystem. In addition, many studies such as waste paper, low-cost fiber production are being done for the protection of these resources. İmamoğlu et al. analyzed the waste paper problems for avoiding of decrease of forest sources [1]. However, forests can become beneficial and convenient with controlled usage of the resources when they are protected in ecological balance. On the other hand, uncontrolled wildfires that create with unknown reasons significantly restrict the usage of forest resources. The unfavorable results of the wildfires within the ecosystem have caused the destruction of the settlement areas, the death of human and alive organisms, air pollution, and disruption of ecological balance [2]. Beşli & Tenekeci contributed to avoiding the wildfires by using decision trees that predicted higher accuracies from satellite data [3]. Çoşkuner determined that future wildfires will cause forest protection problems for region-forests by analyzing with long-term meteorological parameters to Eastern Black Sea forests [4]. Küçükosmanoğlu made a statistical analysis of wildfires that existed between 1960 and 1987 in Turkish Republic [5]. The wildfires can be quickly detected with the development of information technologies in nowadays. Moreover, the wildfires are followed by all sections of the society.

Twitter is a social media platform used by all ages and walks of society all over the world [6]. The wildfires that existed on July 2021 in Turkey were observed by all segments of society and Twitter users showed different reactions about a lot of topics from wildfire fighting to global warming. As an interdisciplinary approach, the Twitter user comments during wildfires were classified by sentiment analysis in our study, and the traces of the wildfires on society were examined.

2   Materials and Methods

2.1   Feature Extraction

In our study, the Turkish tweets on wildfires of the Twitter users between July and August 2021 are examined and a classification approach based on sentiment analysis is proposed. Initially, tweets are extracted based on Python language by a free Twitter developer account. Secondly, the tweets are divided into three main sentiments as positive, neutral, and negative. At the same time, the sentiment analysis is evaluated by three different classifiers. Thirdly, each divided tweet with sentiment analysis is divided into 4 categories by the most reaction expressions. Finally, according to the category topics, the most reaction expressions are analyzed by each sentiment group.

2.2 Sentiment Analysis

Sentiment analysis has been performed based on three main emotions as negative, positive, and neutral [7]. The sentiment analysis is basically made by English language. In the literature, there are a few non-English sentiment analysis algorithms such as Spanish or German language but these non-English sentiment analysis algorithms don't reflect sentiments as English as due to the word limitation. Instead of usage of the non-English sentiment analysis, sentiment analysis based on English language is useful for reflecting sentiments. In this study, the Turkish tweets are firstly translated to English and sentiment analysis is made by English translation text. The original Turkish tweets are evaluated by 4 categories for the user reaction in each sentiment group.

2.3 Baseline Algorithm

Sentiment analysis is examined based on three baseline algorithms. The classifiers are determined three main baseline models. The models are used for the sentiment accuracy and all tweet text are performed three classifier models as below:

1. Linear Support Vector Machine (Linear-SVM)
2. Logistic Regression
3. Naïve Bayes

In machine learning, support vector machines (SVMs support vector networks) are supervised learning models with associated learning algorithms that analyze data used for classification and regression analysis. SVM, which is a binary classification model, is basically divided into two classes. For multi-class classification, the same principle is utilized after breaking down the multi-classification problem into smaller subproblems, all of which are binary classification problems [8]. It is called as Linear SVM. In this study, Linear SVM is used for three sentiment analysis in the tweet texts.

Logistic Regression analysis is a method that provides the opportunity to make classification according to probability rules by calculating the estimated values of the dependent variable as probabilities [9]. Regardless of the fact that linear regression is a binary classification method, logistic regression is a useful method for multi-class classification. Because three sentiment analysis is examined in this study, logistic regression analysis is used as multi-class classification.

Naïve bayes is a supervised learning method based on Bayes' theorem [10]. In the Naïve Bayes model, an example is handled with the different features and it can be classified as independent from each feature. All tweet text is performed with these three different classifiers and the algorithm steps are also shown in Fig. 1.

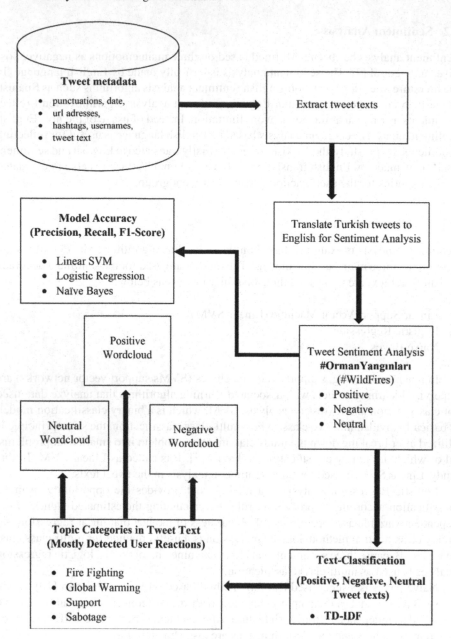

Fig. 1. Algorithm steps.

2.4 Classification

The pre-processed tweet text is evaluated with Term Frequency – Inverse Document Frequency (TD-IDF) algorithm. TD-IDF is defined as the calculation of how relevant a word in a series or corpus is to a text. TD-IDF is a calculated weight factor of a word that shows the importance in a text by using a statistical method [11]. TD-IDF weights are computed as Eq. 1 [12].

$$
weight_{w,t} = \begin{cases} \log(tf_{w,T} + 1) \log \frac{n}{x_w} \Rightarrow f_{w,T} \geq 1 \\ 0 \Rightarrow otherwise \end{cases} \tag{1}
$$

$tf_{w,T}$ is the frequency of word w in tweet. T and n is the number of tweets in "#OrmanYangınları" (#WildFires) Turkish hashtags and x_w is the number of tweets where word w includes. In each sentiment, the tweet texts have been examined by TD-IDF algorithm and the tweet text is categorized by the frequency of the word counts.

2.5 Model Accuracy

The accuracy of the proposed model has been evaluated with standard metrics that are called precision, recall and F1-Score [13]. The model accuracy is calculated by standard accuracy parameters. The accuracy parameters are TP (true positive), TN (true negative), FP (false positive), and FN (false negative).

Precision represents the model's ability to correctly predict the positives out of all the positive predictions it made. The precision score is a useful measure of the success of prediction when the classes are very imbalanced. The precision is shown as Eq. 2 [14].

$$
precision = \frac{TP}{TP + FP} \tag{2}
$$

Recall represents the model's ability to correctly predict the positives out of actual positives. This is unlike precision which measures how many predictions made by models are actually positive out of all positive predictions made. Recall is shown as Eq. 3 [15].

$$
recall = \frac{TP}{TP + FN} \tag{3}
$$

F1-Score represents the model score as a function of precision and recall score. F1-Score is a machine learning model performance metric that gives equal weight to both the Precision and Recall for measuring its performance in terms of accuracy, making it an alternative to Accuracy metrics. F1-Score is calculated as Eq. 4 [16].

$$
F_1 Score = \frac{2 \times (precision \times recall)}{(precison \pm recall)} \tag{4}
$$

Model accuracy is a machine learning model performance metric that is defined as the ratio of true positives and true negatives to all positive and negative observations. Model accuracy is calculated by Eq. 5 [17].

$$
accuracy = \frac{TP + TN}{TP + TN + FP + FN} \tag{5}
$$

2.6 Dataset

Twitter is a social media platform that provides scraping tweets to natural language processing researchers [18, 19]. In this study, 4647 Turkish tweet texts about wildfires between July and August 2021 have been used for sentiment analysis and classification. The tweets have been extracted by the Twitter developer account with scraping methods based on Python language [20]. Additionally, all process and evaluations have been applied by the same Python script and they have been completed in 3 h, 52 min, and 27 s.

2.7 Categorization

The tweets about on wildfires are examined among text and the mostly commented topics are divided into 4 categories.

The users have mostly discussed firefighting, global warming, support, and sabotage probability about wildfires during the active wildfires. While the categories are searched with the original words, they are also searched with the relational words and their prefix & suffix words. The searched Turkish words are also shown in Table 1.

Table 1. Categories.

No	Category name (Translation)	Searched words (Translation)
1	Yangınla Mücadele (Fire Fighting)	su (water), tanker (tanker), uçak (airplane), ucak (airplane), helicopter (helicopter), mücadele (fighting), ekip (team), itfaiye (fire service), yangın (fire), söndür (quenching), sondur (quenching), soğutma (cooling), tahliye (discharge), control (control), havadan (from air), çıkarma (landing), gemi (ship), yetersiz (insufficient), arama (research), kurtarma (save), acil (emergency)
2	Destek (Support)	Kızılay (Turkish Red Crescent), kizilay (Turkish Red Crescent), destek (support), yara (wound), ucak (airplane), uçak(airplane), helicopter (helicopter), mucadele (fighting), mücadele (fighting), yardım (aid), yardim (aid), kampanya (campaign), sahra (field), bagis (donation), bagış (donation), Azerbaycan (Azerbaijan), itfaiye (fire service), azeri (azeri), kardeş (brother), malzeme (equipment)
3	Küresel Isınma (Global Warming)	iklim (climate), değişikliği (change), küresel (global), kuresel (global), ısınma (warming), isinma (warming), dunya (world), dünya (world), nesil (generation), gelecek(future), doğa (nature), doga(nature), sera (greenhouse), ekosistem (ecosystem), çevre (environment), ekoloji (ecology), hayat (life)
4	Sabotaj (Sabotage)	sabotaj (sabotage), ateş (fire), ates(fire), tartışma(discussion), tartisma(discussion), idam(execution), asayiş (safety), asayis (safety), imar (zoning), kundak (arson), gozalti(custody), gözaltı(custody), algı(perception), çakmak (gaslighter), provokasyon (provakation), terror (terror), terör(terror), soruşturma (investigation), sorusturma (investigation), çocuk (child), cocuk(child), ceza (punishment)

A Turkish comment text is assumed for an example as follow:
Turkish Tweet:

"Bakan son durumu paylaştı: 7 bölgede yangınla mücadele devam ediyor. 4 helikopterle destek veriyoruz. Sabotaj ve terör olasılığını değerlendiriyoruz."

English Translation:

"The minister shared the latest situation: Firefighting is continuing in 7 regions. We give support with 4 helicopters. We are evaluating the sabotage and terrorism probability."

In this sample Turkish tweet, "Firefighting" word belongs to "firefighting" category, "support" and "helicopter" words belong to "support" category, "sabotage" and "terrorism" words belong to "sabotage" category. By this way, the root of the word is also evaluated for the categories.

3 Experimental Results

3.1 Statistical Analysis of User Reactions

The wildfires between July and August 2021 in Turkey became the most commented trend topic in Twitter. While most users made neutral comments about wildfires for wishes, some users supported firefighting in favor of the Turkish government. Some users complained about the lack of fire equipment. According to the sentiment analysis, because the users immediately wanted wildfires immediately to end, most users thought neutral and positive about wildfires. The sentiment analysis is shown as Fig. 2.

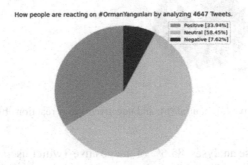

Fig. 2. Sentiment analysis of the twitter users on wildfires.

The tweet analysis has been performed by the most observed comment texts. The text-classification is made by using TD-IDF algorithm and the most used words are investigated. The categories are determined by the most used words as a result of the text-classification. The categories are listed below:

- Sabotage
- Support
- Fire Fighting
- Global Warming

According to the text-classification, the categories have been investigated for each sentiment class. The positive, neutral, and negative user reactions by the categories are also shown in Figs. 3(a), 3(b), and 3(c), respectively.

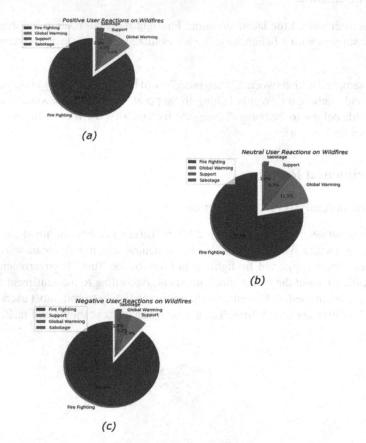

Fig. 3. The positive (a), neutral (b), and negative(c) user reactions by the categories.

According to these analyses, 85.6% of the positive Twitter users mostly wrote about wildfires for firefighting. 7% of them thought global warming, 4.5% of users support firefighting, and 2.9% have thought sabotage probability. Additionally, 77.9% of the neutral users have wished to be terminated the fires, 11.5% of neutral users have thought that fires consisted of global warming, 8.7% of neutral users thought that firefighting should be supported with more fire equipment. Moreover, 1.9% of neutral users emphasized the sabotage probability. Additionally, the number positive, negative, and neutral tweet text by the categories are also shown in Table 2.

Table 2. The number of tweets by the categories.

Category	Negative tweet text	Neutral tweet text	Positive tweet text
Sabotage	5	63	48
Support	16	282	74
Fire fighting	241	2528	1408
Global warming	9	374	115

On the other hand, when the negative comments are investigated by the analysis, 88.9% of the negative users complained of the firefighting. When the text-classification is analyzed, the most used words are also investigated. The most used words in comments have been drawn in the word clouds. A word cloud is a collection, or cluster, of words depicted in different sizes [21]. The most used words in positive, neutral, and negative sentiment are shown in Figs. 4(a), 4(b), and 4(c) separately. The users mostly shared their comments with the specified words in the word clouds. The text-classification is made by TD-IDF algorithm for the word cloud drawing.

Fig. 4. The positive (a), neutral (b), and negative (c) word clouds.

3.2 Model Evaluation

In the study, the sentiment analysis based on three different classification models are performed with standard metrics which are precision, recall, and F1-Score. The model evaluations are shown in Table 3. Due to the model evaluations; the highest accuracy model is firstly linear SVM, secondly Logistic Regression and thirdly Naïve Bayes classifier. The classifier models are measured by sklearn metrics in Python. The measured precision, recall, and F1-Score metrics are also shown in Table 3 for each sentiment group.

Table 3. Model evaluations.

Classifier	Metric	Negative	Neutral	Positive	Total accuracy
Naïve bayes	Precision	1,00	0,86	0,91	88%
	Recall	0,39	0,97	0,82	
	F1-Score	0,56	0,91	0,86	
	Support	31	260	174	
Logistic regression	Precision	1,00	0,85	0,97	89%
	Recall	0,42	1,00	0,82	
	F1-Score	0,59	0,92	0,89	
	Support	31	260	174	
Linear SVM	Precision	0,68	0,91	0,90	90%
	Recall	0,49	0,93	0,92	
	F1-Score	0,57	0,92	0,91	
	Support	35	271	158	

4   Conclusion and Results

In this study, the reactions of Twitter users on wildfires are investigated by using a free developer account. According to the Twitter policy, Twitter has a few limitations to the researchers for scraping the tweets such as date or count limitations. At the same time, some translation errors cause by the meaning slipping due to the allusive words and sentences, but the translation method gives more accuracy results than sentiment analysis of the original language due to the word limits. These situations make it difficult to detection of sentiment analysis.

Today, the protection of forest resources plays an important role in the industrialized world. The wildfire is a big problem for the protection of the ecological balance and forestry sources. Moreover, the global effect of the wildfires is another reason for the global warming. The user reactions on wildfires have been investigated and classified based on basic three sentiments in this study. The measures against forest fires can be carefully taken by considering the social media user reactions. Moreover, the latest situation of wildfires can be learned with real-time social media analysis. The measures in the future can be evaluated via user reactions in social media. The ideas of the society on forest sources can be considered by the sentiment analysis. It can be determined whether or not the sabotage and provocation probability by investigating doubtful social media accounts. All measures can be evaluated for the forest health by investigating of the specified comments in social media. Nowadays the virtual effect of society plays an important role for the authorities. While some authorities reply immediately to the user reactions as a whole, some can evaluate the measures that are expressed by the social media users. In the near future, social media will not only become importance for the protection of forest sources, but it will also become an indispensable element with the user opinions for the contributions of ecology protection.

References

1. İmamoğlu, S., Atik, C., Karademir, A.: Microbial problems in paper and paperboard mills using recovered paper as raw material. Kafkas Univ. J. Artvin Forest. Faculty **6**(1–2), 179–190 (2005)
2. Baysal, İ, Uçarlı, Y., Bilgili, E.: Forest fires and birds. Kastamonu Univ. J. Forest. Faculty **17**(4), 543–553 (2017)
3. Beşli, N., Tenekeci, M.E.: Prediction of wildfire using decision trees from satellite data. Dicle Univ. J. Eng. **11**(3), 899–906 (2020)
4. Çoşkuner, K.A.: Assessing forest fires in the North Eastern Anatolia with long term meteorological parameters. Artvin Çoruh Univ. J. Nat. Hazards Environ. **7**(2), 374–381 (2021)
5. Küçükosmanoğlu, A.: İstatistiklerle Türkiye'de Orman Yangınları. İstanbul Üniv. Orman Fakültesi **37**(3), 103–106 (1987)
6. Twitter: #OrmanYangınları, #ormanyanginlari [#WildFires]. Twitter International Company. Accessed July – August 2021
7. Prakruthi, V., Sindhu, D., Anupama Kumar, S.: Real time sentiment analysis of twitter posts. In: 2018 3rd International Conference on Computational Systems and Information Technology for Sustainable Solutions (CSITSS), pp. 29–34. IEEE, Bengaluru, India (2018)
8. Baker, O., Liu, J., Gosai, M., Sitoula, S.: Twitter sentiment analysis using machine learning algorithms for COVID-19 outbreak in New Zealand. In: 11th International Conference on System Engineering and Technology (ICSET), pp. 286–291. IEEE, Shah Alam, Malaysia (2021)
9. Diwakar, D., Kumar, R., Gour, B., Khan, A. U.: Proposed machine learning classifier algorithm for sentiment analysis. In: 2019 Sixteenth International Conference on Wireless and Optical Communication Networks (WOCN), pp. 1–6. IEEE, Bhopal, India (2019)
10. Ramanathan, V., Meyyappan, T.: Twitter text mining for sentiment analysis on people's feedback about Oman tourism. In: 2019 4th MEC International Conference on Big Data and Smart City (ICBDSC), pp. 1–5. IEEE, Muscat, Oman (2019)
11. El-Rahman, S.A., Al-Otaibi, F.A., Al-Shehri, W.A.: Sentiment analysis of twitter data. In: 2019 International Conference on Computer and Information Sciences (ICCIS), pp. 1–4. IEEE, Sakaka, Saudi Arabia (2019)
12. Hassan, R., Islam, M. R.: Impact of sentiment analysis in fake online review detection. In: 2021 International Conference on Information and Communication Technology for Sustainable Development (ICICT4SD), pp. 21–24. IEEE, Dhaka, Bangladesh (2021)
13. Jiang, L., Suzuki, Y.: Detecting hate speech from tweets for sentiment analysis. In: 2019 6th International Conference on Systems and Informatics (ICSAI), pp. 671–676. IEEE, Shanghai, China (2019)
14. Vanaja, S., Belwal, M.: Aspect-level sentiment analysis on e-commerce data. In: 2018 International Conference on Inventive Research in Computing Applications (ICIRCA), pp. 1275–1279. IEEE, Coimbatore, India (2018)
15. Woldemariam, Y.: Sentiment analysis in a cross-media analysis framework. In: 2016 IEEE International Conference on Big Data Analysis (ICBDA), pp. 1–5. IEEE, Hangzhou, China (2016)
16. Pholo, M.D., Hamam, Y., Khalaf, A., Du, C.: Combining TD-IDF with symptom features to differentiate between lymphoma and tuberculosis case reports. In: 2019 IEEE Global Conference on Signal and Information Processing (GlobalSIP), pp. 1–4. IEEE, Ottawa, ON, Canada (2019)

17. AlSalman, H.: An improved approach for sentiment analysis of Arabic tweets in twitter social media. In: 2020 3rd International Conference on Computer Applications and Information Security (ICCAIS), pp. 1–4. IEEE, Riyadh, Saudi Arabia (2020)
18. Wagh, R., Punde, P.: Survey on sentiment analysis using twitter dataset. In: 2018 Second International Conference on Electronics, Communication and Aerospace Technology (ICECA), pp. 208–211. IEEE, Coimbatore, India (2018)
19. Mandloi, L., Patel, R.: Twitter sentiments analysis using machine learning methods. In: 2020 International Conference for Emerging Technology (INCET), pp. 1–5. IEEE, Belgaum, India (2020)
20. Djatmiko, F., Ferdiana, R., Faris, M.: Review of sentiment analysis for Non-English language. In: 2019 International Conference of Artificial Intelligence and Information Technology (ICAIIT), pp. 448–451. IEEE, Yogyakarta, Indonesia (2019)
21. Dharaiya, S., Soneji, B., Kakkad, D., Tada, N.: Generating positive and negative sentiment word clouds from e-commerce product reviews. In: 2020 International Conference on Computational Performance Evaluation (ComPE), pp. 459–463. IEEE, Shillong, India (2020)

Green Energy-Based Efficient IoT Sensor Network for Small Farms

Amit Mishra[1][(✉)] [iD], Sandeep Singh[1] [iD], Karun Verma[1], Parteck Bhatia[1] [iD],
M. Ghosh[1], and Yosi Shacham-Diamand[2] [iD]

[1] Thapar Institute of Engineering and Technology, Patiala, Punjab, India
{amit_mishra,karun.verma,parteck.bhatia,mghosh}@thapar.edu
[2] School of Electrical Engineering, Tel Aviv, Israel
yosish@tauex.tau.ac.il

Abstract. The recent advancement in the Internet of Things (IoT) makes crop
management much smarter and helps optimize resource consumption in the agriculture industry. However, due to the high deployment and operational cost of
IoT-based infrastructure, it becomes pretty expansive to be afforded by small farm
holders. In this paper, an energy-efficient, low-cost, in-house wireless sensor network has been developed and established for collecting important field parameters
directly from small household farms. The sensor nodes equipped with in-situ sensors were placed in the test field. The parameters such as atmospheric temperature,
humidity, and soil moisture are measured through various sensors. Consequently,
the sensors' data is transferred from the sensor nodes to the Gateway via Long-
range (LoRA) communication. The Gateway is designed to push the sensor data
to the application server (ThingSpeak) through the Long-range wide-area network (LoRAWAN) protocol. The performance of the proposed LoRaWAN based
WSN was tested over the 868 MHz unlicensed ISM indoor network setup for an
entire season of rice crop and found satisfactory even in the harsh propagation
environment.

Keywords: Sensor network · Sensor node · Gateway · LoRAWAN

1 Introduction

According to one of the recent reports of the UN Food and Agriculture Organization, the
world will need to produce 70% more food in 2050 due to the exponential growth of the
world population. Moreover, slowing the yield trends and depletion of natural resources
such as fresh water and arable land have aggravated the problem. Several innovations
have been introduced to improve the agricultural yield with optimized resources and
workforce, such as Greenhouse farming [1], precision agriculture [2, 3], smart farming
[4, 5], etc. The concept of 'smart farming' enables farmers to reduce their agriculture
waste and enhance productivity with the help of IoT-based technologies [6]. These
solutions sense the vital parameters of soil and crop using sensors, monitor the crop
field, and automate the processes such as irrigation [7], spraying precise amounts of the

M. N. Seyman (Ed.): ICECENG 2022, LNICST 436, pp. 15–27, 2022.
https://doi.org/10.1007/978-3-031-01984-5_2

herbicide, pesticide, etc. The IoT-based technology in agriculture comprises specialized electronic equipment, wireless sensor network connectivity, firmware, and cloud services [8, 9].

IoT applications can be realized using various frameworks, such as sensor cloud, edge computing, and wireless sensor networks (WSNs) [10]. There are several competing LPWAN technologies commercially available, such as LoRa [11], Sigfox [12], RPMA [13], Telensa [14], and Weightless [15], each employing a different technique to achieve long-range low-power operation. These technologies are required to provide connectivity for many heterogeneous IoT devices scattered over a wide geographic area, where devices may communicate over distances exceeding 10 km [16].

Neumann et al. [17] conducted a measurement study of the performance of LoRa for indoor deployments using a single device and a single gateway with three channels at the EU ISM 868 MHz band. The measurement study on the coverage range of various LPWAN technologies for a single-cell LoRa deployment is conducted in Padova, Italy [18]. A sensor devices-based forecast mechanism for yield production and growth is proposed by Chen et al. [19] that also helps to stabilize the demand and supply chain of agronomic yields. Petäjäjärvi et al. [20] studied the performance degradation of LoRa under the Doppler effect in different mobility scenarios.

Petäjäjärvi et al. also developed a channel attenuation model for evaluating the communication range of LoRa based technology over the EU ISM 868 MHz band [21]. To measure the soil moisture, humidity, pH, and macronutrients NPK (Nitrogen, Phosphorus, Potassium), Goswami et al. [22] proposed an IoT-based monitoring system. Salam [23] motivated the industry farmer to adopt sustainable agro production practices through contemporary communication archetypes, primary sensor devices, and communication tools.

In our paper [6], 'on-the-ground' sensing is one of the essential building blocks required to complete the Holistic Integrated Precision Agriculture Network (HIPAN) for smallholder farms. There are low-cost mesh network-based U-sensor and M-sensor nodes available commercially for agriculture applications from the cold chain Logistics industry, such as CartaSense, Ltd [24]. However, these sensors are less expensive and affordable but have a low range of data transmission between nodes, nearly 200–250 m, and a short battery life of approximately 8 to 10 months. Moreover, there is no alternative power source backup for sensor nodes installed in the agriculture field. Unlike the CartaSense sensors, a LoRA-based wireless sensor network technology offers a robust solution to these agriculture applications and green power source backup with solar panels. Unfortunately, the commercial-grade LoRa-based systems use high-performance advanced concentrator chips that cost several hundred to several thousand dollars depending on their features, e.g., 8-channel or 64-channel.

It is critical to keep the cost low, especially in the scenarios of deploying commercial-grade LoRa-based solutions in smallholder farms. However, the commercial-grade 2G-3G technology-based sensor nodes such as Libelium [25] offer sensor data communication with solar-based power backup. But these are too costly to be affordable by small farmers. Fortunately, several low-cost microcontrollers such as Arduino (ATmega328P), Node-MCU (ESP8266), and ESP32 are available commercially, providing comparable performance along with cost-effectiveness. Therefore, this paper aims to design a cost-effective, efficient, green energy-operated LoRA-based single-channel communication system. The novelty of this work is to implement a generalized and robust LoRA based sensor node that can be interfaced with resistive, capacitive, volumetric, and other types of soil parameters sensors. This system uses low-cost microcontroller modules and can easily replace costly commercial-grade devices for small agriculture farms. The performance of the proposed sensor network system is analyzed in the test field powered with green energy for a complete rice crop season.

2 Network Topology

LoRa is the wireless platform of the Internet of Things (IoT) developed by Semtech. LoRa defines the lower physical layer, whereas LoRaWAN is a cloud-based medium access control (MAC) layer protocol. It acts mainly as a network layer protocol for managing communication between LPWAN gateways and routing protocol for sensor node devices, supported by the LoRa Alliance.

To keep the complexity of the network low, LoRa relies on a star topology in which sensor devices directly communicate with a gateway in a single-hop manner. The network topology of LoRAWAN is shown in Fig. 1. The mesh or multiple-hop network topology for LoRA technology is in the testing phase.

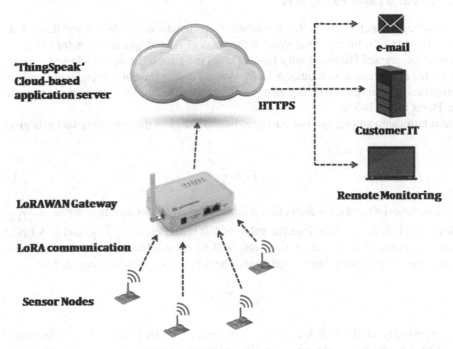

Fig. 1. LoRAWAN network topology.

2.1 LoRA Technology

LoRa is a proprietary communication technique based on the Chirp Spread Spectrum modulation (CSS) scheme. The CSS modulation is widely used in radar, military, and secure communications due to its relatively low transmission power requirements. It also offers robustness against channel degradation effects such as Doppler, in-band jamming interferers, and multipath fading.

LoRa operates in the unlicensed ISM (Industrial, Scientific, and Medical) radio frequency bands available worldwide. For example, IN865-867 (865–867 MHz) in India; EU433 (433.05–434.79 MHz) and EU863-870 (863–870/873 MHz) in Europe; AU915-928/AS923-1 (915–928 MHz) in Australia; US902-928 (902–928 MHz) in North America.

A typical LoRAWAN mote is classified into three categories. Class A supports bi-directional communication in which the devices use un-slotted random access during uplink transmission, whereas the receive window of dedicated time slot in downlink transmission. However, Class A consumes the lowest energy in a small load network scenario but provides long delays in the downlink. Class B offers bidirectional communication with scheduled downlink receive slots. The Gateway disseminates the schedule information via beacons. In Class C, the device continuously connected to the channel provides the lowest downlink latency but requires high power consumption.

2.2 Physical Layer Parameters

The basic parameters of LoRA modulation are bandwidth (BW), code Rate (CR), chirp Rate (C_hR), bit rate (R_b) symbol duration (T_s), and spreading factor (SF). The chirp (Compressed High-Intensity Radar Pulse) is a sinusoidal signal whose frequency increases or decreases with time. A LoRa symbol covers the entire frequency band and comprises 2^{SF} chirps. The chirp rate equals the bandwidth, i.e., one chirp per second per Hertz of bandwidth.

The relationship among symbol duration, bandwidth, and the spreading factor is given as:

$$T_s = \frac{2^{SF}}{BW} \tag{1}$$

The Lora uses forward error correction code, and the value of code rate is defined as $\frac{4}{(4+n)}$, with $n \in \{1, 2, 3, 4\}$. Therefore the value of CR is chosen as $\frac{4}{5}, \frac{4}{6}, \frac{4}{7}$, and $\frac{4}{8}$. A LoRA packet transmitted with a lower code rate will be more tolerant to interference than a signal transmitted with a higher code rate. The bit rate (R_b) can be computed as:

$$R_b = \frac{SF}{T_s}CR \tag{2}$$

The sensitivity of the LoRA receiver is influenced by its parameters and measured in dBm, i.e., the higher the negative dBm value, the better is the receiver sensitivity. In general, receiver sensitivity increases by decreasing the bandwidth, whereas it also decreases as the value of the spreading factor decreases.

3   Methodology

This section describes an overview of the proposed hardware of the single-channel LoRa-based system. The Lora-based network, including gateway and sensor nodes, is developed and deployed in the institute campus, having large buildings and open areas suitable for the testing of the system. One of the proposed LoRA nodes deployment sites is shown in Fig. 2. The respective Gateway is also mounted in one of the institutes' laboratories, approximately 800 m away from the nodes.

Fig. 2. Installation site of LoRA based sensor node.

3.1   Proposed Model

The proposed LoRAWAN Gateway is developed as a single channel, class A-type, and operated at 866.06 MHz frequency. The schematic diagram of Gateway is designed through the EasyEDA tool, and the respective gerber file is created. The customized

PCB is then fabricated from JLCPCB, Hong Kong, using the same gerber file prepared in the institutes' lab. Figure 3 shows the front view of the customized PCB with its layout. The bespoke PCB design makes the interfacing circuit simple and reduces the need for multiple external wire connections. It further reduces the need for frequent maintenance in remote areas, especially in agriculture applications.

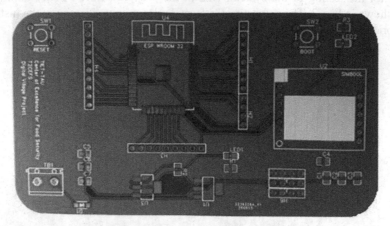

Fig. 3. The layout of customized PCB.

The cost of the proposed system is reasonably lower than the commercial devices due to the low-cost, open-source ESP32 microcontroller and RFM95W LoRA communication module. Moreover, we can use a similar customized PCB to implement both Gateway and sensor nodes with a few modifications. The proposed approach is flexible enough to control the transmission of sensor data because of the open-source nature of the programming language. When the high-quality commercial sensors are interfaced with the sensor nodes, the sensor node's cost may rise and depend on the type of sensor used.

3.2 Sensors Used

The sensor nodes are designed to measure three parameters of the field: air temperature, air humidity, and soil moisture of the target field using DHT22 and resistive soil moisture sensor. DHT22 sensor includes a high-precision temperature measurement device and capacitive sensor wet components, which provides air temperature in the range of 40–80 degrees centigrade and air relative humidity (RH) in 0–100%.

Similarly, a watermark soil moisture sensor (Irrometer 200SS) works by using electrical resistance and water content to gauge the soil's moisture levels. An electrical current is allowed to pass from one probe to the other, which makes the sensor measure the resistance of the soil between them. When the water content in the soil is high, it shows higher electrical conductivity, and therefore, a lower resistance reading is obtained, which indicates high soil moisture and vice versa. Regressive lab testing of Gateway and sensor node pair is done before deploying the complete system in the test field. Figure 4 shows the lab testing process of the resistive soil moisture sensor module and data transmission through the LoRAWAN communication.

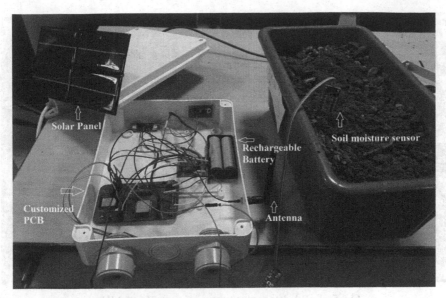

Fig. 4. Laboratory testing of LoRa-based sensor node.

3.3 Experimental Setup

The LoRA-Based end node and gateways are implemented using a dual-core module microcontroller ESP-32S. The microcontroller is also enabled with the features such as WiFi, Bluetooth, and Ultra-Low Power Consumption. To initiate the LoRA communication, RFM95W 868S2 LoRa Ultra-long Range Transceiver Module is interfaced with ESP32. The LoRA module supports 868 MHz SPI and can communicate data using GFSK, GMSK, LoRa OOK modulations.

An RTC module keeps the sensor node module in sleep mode for a fixed period, such as an hour, to make the system energy efficient. At the end of each hour, the sensor node becomes active and transmits the sensors reading in the form of a data packet towards the Gateway using LoRA protocol. This task is implemented with the help of I2C enabled, precise Real-Time Clock DS3231. The microcontroller (ESP32) circuit draws almost 58 mA in active mode in the sensor node module. However, in deep sleep mode, this current consumption is approximately 150 uA. Therefore, this low-power or sleep state mode achieves substantial energy savings, making the sensor node energy efficient.

Once the sensor node is paired with the Gateway, the LoRA signal communication is verified through a spectrum analyzer. Figure 5 shows the LoRa data packet transmission at 866.06 MHz. The data is then pushed from Gateway to the application cloud through LoRAWAN protocol.

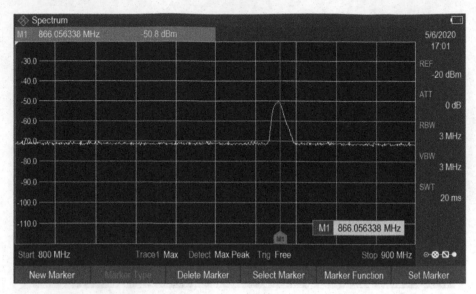

Fig. 5. LoRA data packet transmission at 866.06 MHz.

A solar-based power source is designed to charge the Li-Ion battery placed in the sensor node. The eHUB 2S 3A 7.4–8.4 V 18,650 BMS battery protection module protects the battery from overcharging. The complete interfacing circuit for the solar panel is shown in Fig. 6.

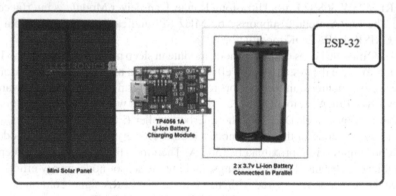

Fig. 6. Interfacing circuit for the solar panel.

In this work, the 'ThingSpeak' is used as a cloud-based application server, to where the sensors data is pushed and recorded with time stamps. It is a cloud-based IoT analytics platform that allows aggregating, visualizing, and analyzing live data streams of the sensors placed in the test field. The field sensor data, i.e., air temperature, humidity, and soil moisture, is integrated at the 'ThingSpeak' server and visualized in Fig. 7.

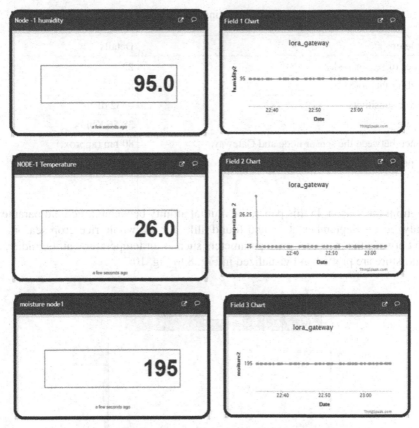

Fig. 7. Visualization of air humidity, temperature, and soil moisture sensor readings pushed on ThingSpeak server.

4   Result and Discussion

The LoRA-based LPWAN is implemented and tested using the parameters as shown in Table 1. The localized communication between the sensor node and Gateway is established using the WiFi protocol, i.e., IEEE 802.11n, available in the institute campus. The ESP32s use time-division multiplexing (TDM) to avoid collisions between gateway and sensor nodes during the data transmission. The Gateway transmits the data of each sensor node to the cloud server only for 10 min duration in every one hour of the entire day. A time difference of 30 min is maintained between the consecutive data transmission from the two sensor nodes. After completing the sensor data transmission for 10 min, each node goes back to sleep mode using the real-time clock (RTC) module. It saves the power requirement and makes the system energy efficient.

As mentioned in Sect. 3 earlier, the implemented LoRAWAN network system is installed and tested in the institute's fields. The sensor's data is pushed to the cloud for the entire season of the rice crop from July to November 2021. The various parameters of the testing field saved on the application server show dependency or relationship

Table 1 Testing parameters.

Parameter	Details
Number of sensor nodes	2
Spreading factor (SF)	8
Receiver sensitivity	−132 dBm
Data rate	38.56 Kbit/s
Distance between the sensor node and Gateway	800 m (approx.)
WiFi protocol	IEEE 802.11n

throughout the season. In this paper, the mutual affinity between three field parameters is analyzed for September 2021 and found alike for the whole rice crop season. The graph between the measured field parameters such as air temperature, air humidity, and soil moisture are plotted and visualized in Fig. 8 to Fig. 10.

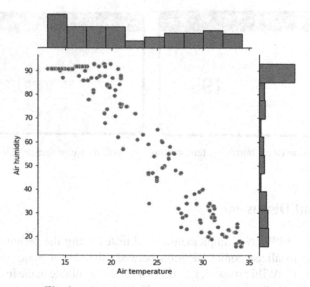

Fig. 8. Air temperature vs. Air humidity plot.

Figure 8 shows a plot between the targeted field's air temperature and relative humidity. As the air temperature of the field increases, the air relative humidity (%) tends to decrease, which is a natural phenomenon. The rise in air temperature also indicates the need for irrigation in the field.

Based on the irrigation requirement, the graph between soil moisture and air temperature is shown in Fig. 9. As the air temperature increases, the corresponding soil moisture value increases to indicate the low soil moisture contents, suggesting the need for irrigation required for the rice field. This phenomenon can be observed through frequent irrigation in the targeted area. Higher soil moisture values in the graph indicate less soil moisture contents in the field and vice versa.

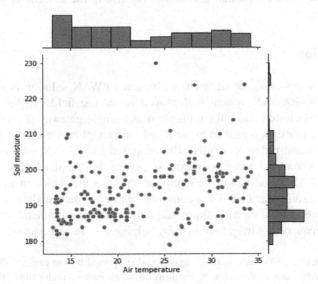

Fig. 9. Air temperature vs. Soil moisture plot.

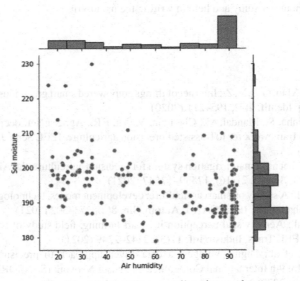

Fig. 10. Air humidity vs. soil moisture plot.

Similarly, the air relative humidity (%) and soil moisture vary approximately linearly, depicted in Fig. 10. The variations in these parameters are also observed under the influence of irrigation of the field. The low value of soil moisture indicates the time instances of the irrigation, which also shows the rise in the air relative humidity (%) values.

5 Conclusion

In this paper, a low-cost, robust, energy-efficient LPWAN solution is implemented. The proposed LoRAWAN system is deployed in the test fields of the institute, and its performance is tested under the multiple nodes-single gateway scenario in the star network. The sensor data is pushed to the cloud-based application server (ThingSpeak), recorded, and visualized successfully. The proposed LoRAWAN solution suits small farms due to its low cost and robustness. As part of the 'Digital Village' project, the developed LPWAN systems will be deployed in the actual fields in the village and collect the vital soil parameters for a complete season for data analytics. The analysis based on the yield of the farms will provide a few critical recommendations about the quantity and frequency of irrigation, thereby helping to save irrigated water.

Acknowledgements. This work is fully funded and supported by the project 'Digital Village: A Data-Driven Approach to Precision Agriculture in Small Farms,' under the TIET-TAU center of excellence for food security (T2CEFS) in Thapar Institute of Engineering and Technology (A central university), Patiala, Punjab, India. I thank all the co-authors for their expertise and assistance throughout our study and help in writing the manuscript.

References

1. Rayhana, R., Xiao, G., Liu, Z.: Internet of things empowered smart greenhouse farming. IEEE J. Radio Freq. Identif. **4**(3), 195–211 (2020)
2. Anand, T., Sinha, S., Mandal, M., Chamola, V., Yu, F.R.: AgriSegNet: deep aerial semantic segmentation framework for IoT-assisted precision agriculture. IEEE Sens. J. **21**(16), 17581–17590 (2021)
3. Boursianis, D., et al.: Smart irrigation system for precision agriculture-the AREThOU5A IoT platform. IEEE Sens. J. **21**(16), 17539–17547 (2021)
4. Yang, X., et al.: A survey on smart agriculture: development modes, technologies, and security and privacy challenges. IEEE/CAA J. Autom. Sin. **8**(2), 273–302 (2021)
5. Jinya, S., et al.: Aerial visual perception in smart farming: field study of wheat yellow rust monitoring. IEEE Trans. Industr. Inf. **17**(3), 2242–2249 (2021)
6. Fishman, R., et al.: Digital villages: a data-driven approach to precision agriculture in small farms. In: 9th International Conference on Sensor Network (SENSORNETS), pp. 1–6. Valletta, Malta (2020)
7. Jamroen, C., Komkum, P., Fongkerd, C., Krongpha, W.: An intelligent irrigation scheduling system using low-cost wireless sensor network toward sustainable and precision agriculture. IEEE Access **8**, 172756–172769 (2001)
8. Ojha, T., Misra, S., Raghuwanshi, N.S.: Internet of things for agricultural applications: the state of the art. IEEE Internet Things J. **8**(14), 10973–10997 (2021)

9. Kour, V.P., Arora, S.: Recent developments of the internet of things in agriculture: a survey. IEEE Internet Things J. **8**, 129924–129957 (2020)
10. Raza, U., Kulkarni, P., Sooriyabandara, M.: Low power wide area networks: an overview. IEEE Commun. Surv. Tutor. **19**(2), 855–873 (2017)
11. LoRa Alliance Homepage. https://www.lora-alliance.org. Accessed 2015
12. Sigfox Homepage. https://www.sigfox.com. Accessed 2010
13. Ingenue RPMA Homepage. https://www.ingenu.com/technology/rpma. Accessed 2008
14. Telensa Homepage. http://www.telensa.com. Accessed 2005
15. Weightless Homepage. http://www.weightless.org. Accessed 2016
16. Nokia: LTE M2M-optimizing LTE for the Internet of Things' Homepage. https://gsacom.com/paper/nokia-lte-m2m-optimizing-lte-for-the-internet-of-things/. Accessed 2017
17. Neumann, P., Montavont, J., Nol, T.: Indoor deployment of low-power wide-area networks (LPWAN): A LoRaWAN case study. In: 2016 IEEE 12th Wireless and Mobile Computing, Networking and Communications (WiMob), pp. 1–8. IEEE, New York, USA (2016)
18. Centenaro, M., Vangelista, L., Zanella, A., Zorzi, M.: Long-range communications in unlicensed bands: the rising stars in the IoT and smart city scenarios. IEEE Wirel. Commun. **23**(5), 60–67 (2016)
19. Wen-Liang, C., et al.: AgriTalk: IoT for precision soil farming of turmeric cultivation. IEEE Internet Things J. **6**(3), 5209–5223 (2019)
20. Petäjäjärvi, J., Mikhaylov, K., Pettissalo, M., Janhunen, J., Iinatti, J.: Performance of a low-power wide area network based on LoRa technology: doppler robustness, scalability, and coverage. J. Distrib. Sensor Netw. **13**(3), 1–16 (2017)
21. Petäjäjärvi, J., Mikhaylov, K., Roivainen, A., and Hanninen, T.: On the coverage of LPWANs: Range evaluation and channel attenuation model for LoRa technology. In Proc.14th International Conference on ITS Telecommunications, pp. 55–59, (2015)
22. Goswami, V., Singh, P., Dwivedi, P., Chauhan, S.: Soil health monitoring system. Int. J. Res. Appl. Sci. Eng. Technol. **8**(5), 1536–1540 (2020)
23. Salam, A.: Internet of things in agricultural innovation and security. In: Salam, A. (eds.) Internet of Things for Sustainable Community Development, pp. 71-112. Springer, Cham (2020).https://doi.org/10.1007/978-3-030-35291-2_3
24. CartaSense Ltd. Homepage. https://cartasense-coldchain.com/products/m-sensor-ms/. Accessed 2007
25. Libelium Homepage. https://www.libelium.com/iot-products/plug-sense/. Accessed 2006

Potential Benefits of Apps for Bike Sharing Systems in Cairo: The Bikeroons App Example

Lydia Youssef[1]([✉]) [iD], Mohamed Sherif[2], Mostafa ElHayani[2] [iD],
Abdulrahman Abdulrahman[2], and Hassan Soubra[2]

[1] German University, Cairo 11835, Egypt
[2] Al Tagmoa, Gamal Abdel Nasser, New Cairo 3, Cairo 11835, Egypt
lydiay711@gmail.com, Hassan.soubra@guc.edu.eg

Abstract. As new environmental challenges continue to rise, E-bikes have been gaining popularity due to their efficiency over cars in regard to fuel usage and especially when compared with their practicality over regular bikes when it comes to speed. A mobile application can help to get the most out of a transportation device such as an E-bike, which may, in turn, aid in lessening the traffic congestion problem in Cairo, the city in which this project is based. A smart bike app is meant to make life easier for those who own E-bikes as well as for those who need one temporarily for a ride. Most E-bike apps are made for personal usage; therefore, we've implemented a smart bike app that combines the features of both a bike sharing app and a personal bike app by creating an Android application that lets the user use either their own E-bike or a shared one, set a goal for the ride (destination or exercise), obtain their live location, and communicate with their personal E-bike.

Keywords: Mobile development · E-bike · Android · Sharing · Bike-sharing system · Autonomous vehicles · Raspberry Pi

1 Introduction

Infrastructure within the city, traffic congestion has become a pressing issue according to [1]. That is one reason why switching from an automobile to a bike as a form of transportation is an excellent idea. Furthermore, due to the recent COVID-19 pandemic, having a robust immune system is one of the most valuable assets a person can have to ensure his or her safety, according to Matheus Pelinski da Silveira et al. in their study [2]. Such immunity requires a decent amount of exercise which can easily be achieved through biking on a daily basis. A number of people, according to [3], argue that one of the reasons an ordinary bike, as compared to a car, is not the best option for them is due to its relatively slow speed and the time it takes for them to make their daily commutes. That is where E-bikes come into play. E-bikes allow their users to travel faster with less effort than they would on a regular bike due to the assistance of their electric motors, according to Sustrans [3]. An excellent way to encourage more people

M. N. Seyman (Ed.): ICECENG 2022, LNICST 436, pp. 28–39, 2022.
https://doi.org/10.1007/978-3-031-01984-5_3

to switch to E-bikes is to create a user-friendly mobile application for both those who own an E-bike as well as those who do not. Bikeroons, the Android mobile application created specifically for this purpose employs Open Street Maps as the tool to track both the user and their bike, to plot the desired ride destinations on, and to log the rider's tracks during a ride.

The rest of this paper is organized as follows. Section 2 explores the literature review on Bikes and E-bikes Apps. Section 3 introduces the proposed system in this paper and lists its features. Section 4 explains the details of the implementation of the proposed system. Section 5 shows results and graphs created from data collected from the app. Finally, conclusions and future work follow.

2 Literature Review

Extensive research on shared autonomous vehicle services has been conducted in recent years and therefore, a plethora of smart E-bike sharing and using apps have been published in prior years. Ouyang et al. [4] has conducted a study revolving around bike sharing apps and their popularity, which according to their research is related heavily to the features provided by the apps and further aspects.

Upon searching for specific bike sharing apps, we have discovered Inabike. InaBike is an Indonesian smart bike-sharing platform published in the Google Play Store by Warlina et al. in their paper [5]. It provides services for Yogyakarta, Denpasar, and other cities within Indonesia. It uses a QR-code system, a sign in/out system, an anti-theft system, a live location system, and a smart-lock. Likewise, BOSEH (Bike On Street Everybody Happy) is an Indonesian bike sharing app based in Bandung published by Rifiki et al. in their paper [6]. It features Google Maps, a sign in/out system, and other systems similar the ones utilized in InaBike.

Another app that was created for a similar purpose is Unicycle App, published by Azir et al. mentioned in their paper [7]. It is used for the purpose of roaming around campus on a bike. It is based in Malaysia and it uses Bluetooth as a means of communication between the bike and a user's phone, a sign in/out system, a QR-code-based system for security, and a payment system.

Similarly, GreenBikeNet is a mobile application published by Abu-Sharkh et al. in their paper [8] that provides cyclists with services that enhance and facilitate their riding experiences with their bikes. It uses ZigBee as a method of communication between the bike and a user's phone. It also features user- to-user multilingual voice communication via a translation system. It employs maps provided by Open Street Maps.

Pertaining to accident detection systems, which are useful in E-bike apps, Md. Motaharul *et al.* created an accident detection system based in Bangladesh. It uses a Raspberry Pi 3 and Arduino Uno. According to [9] in the event of an accident, the system contacts the nearest police stations, hospitals, and family members added by the user. The system does not contact them unless the user does not stop the alarm process after five seconds. In this paper we propose an Android smartphone application that offers a set of features that includes an amalgamation of those employed by the other apps in addition to enhanced/altered versions of them.

3 Proposed App: Bikeroons

The Bikeroons App proposed in this paper has many features.

3.1 General Features

The application's features are designed to be multifaceted to fit users' needs to the greatest extent. Bikeroons provides a number of features that are accessible for every ride. These features are:

- Sign in/Register: The user has to use the sign in/register feature before using Bikeroons.
- Password change: The user has the option to change their password. For the password change feature to alter the user's password successfully, the old password has to be entered correctly and the new password has to be between 8–20 characters long.
- Forgot password: The user has the option to reset their password by re- questing a random code to be sent to their email for the purpose of the user to access their email and type in the sent code. The code is then hashed and saved in the users' database. If the code matches the one saved in the database, the user gets the change to pick a new password.
- Remember me: The user has the option to save their login information in case of a successful login.
- Pause and resume ride: The user is able to pause the ride and resume it any time they wish.
- Ride log: The user can view their ride history. Every ride has the following information stored:

  1. The ride number.
  2. The route the user took during the ride.
  3. The duration of the ride in hours and minutes (HH:MM).
  4. The start time and date of the ride (DD/MM/YYYY HH:MM).
  5. The end time and date of the ride (DD/MM/YYYY HH:MM).

- Display ride information: throughout the ride, the following information which is constantly being updated will be displayed to the user:

  1. Speed, in kilometer per hour, of the bike.
  2. Distance, in kilometers, covered by the user.
  3. Total time, in minutes and seconds, elapsed during the ride.
  4. Power, in watts, of the user's pedaling.
  5. Revolutions per minute, which is obtained by the following Eq. (1), found in [10]:

$$rpm = \frac{\frac{meters}{miute}}{wheelCircumferences(inmeters)} \tag{1}$$

where the wheel circumference is set as 2.07, the circumference in meters of a 26-inch wheel-diameter, which is the wheel size of the bike we ran all of our tests on. According to [11], this is the most common wheel size for modern mountain bikes and is also common in hybrid bikes.

6. Live information of the temperature, in Celsius, and the humidity of Cairo
7. Battery percentage of the E-bike in use.

3.2 Charging Stations

Bikeroons offers the following set of features related to charging stations:

- View nearby charging stations: Upon clicking the button with the charging station icon, the locations of charging stations appear on the map.
- Display distance and route to station: when a user clicks on a charging station location, Bikeroons sends a brief notification showing the distance, in kilometers, between the user and the station. Bikeroons also simultaneously displays the route to the chosen station.
- Price of charging: The price of charging the bike will be displayed next to the charging station button at all times. The price depends upon both the E-bike's battery percentage and Cairo's electricity market prices.
- Hide stations: Upon the second click of the button with the charging station icon, all of the displayed stations and their routes become hidden on the map.

3.3 Emergency

The emergency feature is a simple function offered by Bikeroons to deal with accidents. The set of features of the emergency function includes:

- Emergency timer: A 5-s timer which will start once an accident is detected. If the user does not tap the screen to stop the alarm within a 5-s window, the app will sound an alarm in an attempt to attract the attention of passersby within the vicinity and send out an SMS, displayed in Fig. 1, to the user's emergency numbers with a message indicating that the user has been involved in an accident along with the exact location of the accident.
- Add emergency number: Enter an Egyptian phone number, it will be added to the user's emergency numbers list.
- Edit emergency number: Edit a previously added number, the number that was edited shall be replaced with the new one.
- Delete emergency number: Removes a previously added number.

3.4 Destination Mode

This application is designed for users who would like to ride a smart E-bike to their preferred destination. An example of a destination mode-based ride is shown in Fig. 2. Therefore, Bikeroons includes the following features:

– The user can choose their target location by pressing on the desired spot on the map. The selected location will be marked and the distance, in kilometers, between the user and the designated location will be displayed above the marker.

Fig. 1. The SMS sent from Bikeroons to the added emergency numbers

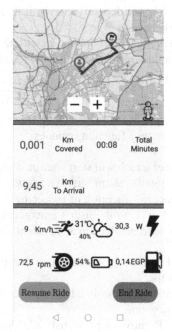

Fig. 2. A destination-based ride in Bikeroons, displaying various live information to the user

- The user will be prompted to either end or resume the ride when they reach their selected location. This is to inform the user that the destination has been reached.
- After choosing a target location, the user will have the option to display the travel route from the user's active location to their chosen destination.
- During the ride, the route between the user's active location and the destination will be displayed on the screen.

– During the ride, the distance, in kilometers, between the user and the destination will be displayed and updated regularly every five seconds.

3.5 Workout Mode

When a user chooses to workout using Bikeroons, they are given the option to choose from four possible workout goals which, upon completion, will prompt the user to either end the ride or to resume their workout.

The user can choose to set a goal based on how many calories they are aiming to burn. The user has to input their goal for how many calories they intend to burn. The number of calories burnt on a regular bike is computed by the following Eq. (2), which can be found on [12]:

$$c = \frac{(P * h)/4.18}{0.24} \tag{2}$$

where c is the number of calories burnt, P is the average power in watts, and h is the time elapsed in hours.

However, according to [12] people who use a pedal-assisted bicycle as opposed to a traditional bicycle burn around 25% less calories. Since Bikeroons is meant to function with E-bikes, the final number of calories burnt is calculated by the following Eq. (3):

$$Ec = c * 0.75 \tag{3}$$

where c is c from 2 and Ec is the approximate number of calories burnt on an E-bike.

The user can choose to set a goal based on how many hours, minutes, and seconds they want the ride to last. Once the designated time has elapsed, the user gets prompted to either end the ride or resume it.

The user can choose to set a goal based on the amount of distance, in kilo- meters, they want to cover. Similarly, once the chosen distance has been covered, the user will get prompted to either continue the ride or end it.

– If the user has no specific goal in mind, they can pick the "Freestyle" option. This option allows the user to log a ride on the E-bike with neither a workout goal nor a destination goal.

3.6 Rent My Own Bike

This feature lets a user, who owns a bike, share it and make a profit by allowing the user to set a price for the bike, track its location, and be informed as to whether or not it is in use. The renting fare is calculated as follows: The owner of the bike is asked to input the base, time based, and distance-based fares of their choice, as shown in Fig. 3. Any unchecked fare will be considered a zero. The total price is calculated by the formula 4.

$$Total\ Price = Base fare + (Distance fare * Kms) + (Time fare * H) \tag{4}$$

Where Kms stands for Kilometers traveled during the ride, while H stands for the length of the ride in hours.

Fig. 3. User setting the fare of their choice for others renting their bike.

4 Implementation Details

Bikeroons functions by connecting a user to a database of bikes so the user, in turn, can have access to the bikes available as well as their own personal bike, if applicable. This system is implemented at both the level of hardware and software.

4.1 Hardware

- To create a connection between Bikeroons and an E-bike, we attached a Raspberry Pi to our E-bike. A Raspberry Pi is a compact computer that is able to run Python scripts, according to [13]. These scripts are what will be used to run the software that handles the communication.
- To display QR codes, we used a 128 × 64 OLED GRAPHIC DISPLAY: ac- cording to [15], this is a small 0.96-inch Organic Light Emitting Diode (OLED) display screen with a size of 128 × 64 pixels. Each Raspberry Pi has an OLED display attached to it.
- E-bike model STV TX250: the E-bike used to test the functions of Bikeroons in Fig. 4.

Fig. 4. Project's prototype.

4.2 Software

To communicate with the Raspberry Pi attached to the bike, we use MongoDB, a database program according to [14]. We decided it is best to use a decentralized database plan which creates one main server connecting multiple sub-servers each with its own database, thus the sub-databases are separate and are able to function independently of one another. This arrangement is preferable for this project since if a database malfunctions with such a plan, the rest of the databases will not be affected, and it likewise adds room for horizontal scalability. There are four sub-databases and the main server responsible for running all of them. The sub-databases are: Users, Bikes, Cars, and Base Stations. Bikeroons deals with only the Users and Bikes sub-databases. The database plan is illustrated in Fig. 5. The way the communication works is by the E-bike's Raspberry Pi running a Python script continuously (every five seconds) to access the database to check for any new commands from the app. Such commands are essential to link a user to the available bike of their choice through the following method: as the user taps on a bike to choose it, Bikeroons generates a random code. This code then gets hashed and saved in the bike database. Meanwhile, since the bike is constantly listening for new commands, it will receive the randomly generated code, use it to create a QR code, and display it on the screen mentioned in 4.1. Bikeroons then checks if the scanned code is equal to the code it created. On one hand, if it is correct, the user database will be updated to include the newly linked bike name to the user, unlock the bike, and start the ride. On the other hand, If the code is incorrect the user will be asked to try again.

5 Results

The app was developed with Android Studio and tested on an Android phone (Huawei Y9 2019) version 9. In this part, we will analyze and assess the results to inspect the effectiveness of the framework. We used Heroku [16] to deploy our servers. Bikeroons depends on WiFi as its means of communication with the servers, therefore Bikeroons requires the user to have a stable connection to the internet. We will start by measuring

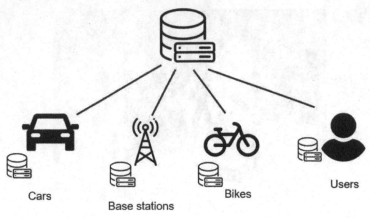

Fig. 5. The database plan of the project. Bikeroons deals only with the Users and the Bikes databases.

response times. Given the nature of our proposed device, we will be focusing on three following main aspects:

– General response times
– SMS send delay
– Live location refresh delay

When we tested Bikeroons for the response time of various requests through Heroku, we produced the following data in Figure 6 and found that the average time in seconds is 3.525. Furthermore, we tested the SMS sending feature and the time it took for the emergency numbers to receive the SMS through the app. We ran five tests and found that the values varied widely, displayed in Fig. 7. We concluded that the average time is 9.8 s. Moreover, to measure the time it takes, in seconds, to receive the E-mail containing the code for the password change feature, we ran five tests and concluded that the average amount of time is 2.436 s as shown in Fig. 9. Lastly, we measured the time it takes for the user's location to get updated. The results are displayed in Fig. 8. We found that, in average, the user's location gets updated every 5.75 s on the map.

5.1 Discussion

It is worth noting that since Bikeroons can access its user's location and communicate with their owned/rented bike in a reasonable amount of time, it also has the potential to call the bike to move to the user. This feature is developed from the app's end but not yet developed and tested on a smart E-bike. This proves that Bikeroons has the potential of carrying out such feature with a smart E-bike in the future.

In addition to possessing such potential, Bikeroons stands out from other similar bike sharing apps for several reasons. One being is its ability to allow the user to link their own smart E-bike to their account using a QR code. This lets the user track their bike as well as rent it to other users in addition to setting their own fares and in turn,

Response times

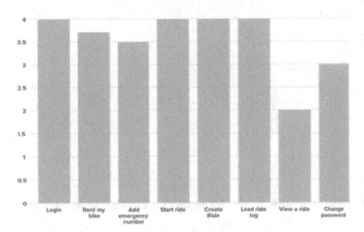

Fig. 6. Bikeroons' response times, in seconds, of various requests the app provides.

SMS Sending Delay

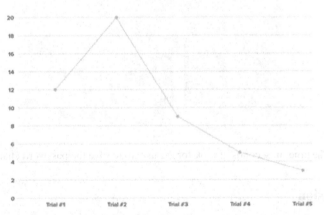

Fig. 7. The time, in seconds, it took for the emergency numbers to receive the SMS sent from Bikeroons.

earn money if desired. Another being its potential to show the user their bike's battery percentage, since it communicates with the bike, and calculate the price of a full charge according to the electricity market in Cairo. Bikeroons also stands out by having the optional alarm feature in case of an accident, for the chance of grabbing passersby's attention. Furthermore, we believe Bikeroons quite appeals to a wide range of people; such as those who own E-bikes, those who do not, athletes, and tourists. This is because Bikeroons supports features that would benefit such users.

User's Location Update

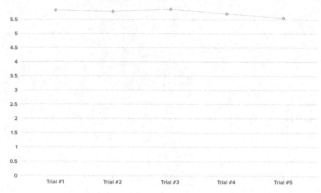

Fig. 8. The time, in seconds, it takes for the user's live location to get updated on the map.

Time taken for the E-mail to get sent

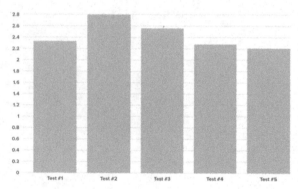

Fig. 9. The time, in seconds, it took for the user to receive the password change code.

6 Conclusion

E-bikes could play an important role in reducing the environmental challenges facing the world today, most notably in overpopulated cities such as Cairo. Apps for bike sharing systems could have a lot of potential benefits. In this paper, these aforementioned benefits are illustrated using the Bikeroons App as an example. Bikeroons' main objective is to enhance the riding experiences of the riders of both personal E-bikes and shared E-bikes. The user is then required to select the purpose of their ride, whether it's for the purpose of reaching a certain destination, exercising, or roaming freely. Bikeroons refines a user's experience with E-bike riding by displaying information to the rider such as the user's speed, the bike's revolutions per minute, the power output, the external temperature and humidity, the user's active location, the total duration of the ride, the battery percentage of the bike in-use, and the information about the location of charging stations. In the event that the user chooses a destination, the distance and the route to the destination will be displayed. If the user selected a workout mode with a set goal, their progress until they reach said goal will be displayed. In addition, the user will be prompted to end or resume the ride when their goal has been reached. Apart from rides, Bikeroons lets the user communicate with their smart E-bike if they possess one. Therefore, Bikeroons could prove to be useful for E-bike users as well as people who are interested in making a foray into the E-bike world!

References

1. The World Bank: Cairo Traffic Congestion study- Executive Note (2021). https://www.worldbank.org/en/country/egypt/publication/cairo-traffic-congestion-study-executive-note. Accessed 29 Dec 2021
2. da Pelinski, S.M., Fagundes, K.K.S., Bizuti, M.R., Starck, E., Rossi, R.C., Silva, D.T.R.: Physical exercise as a tool to help the immune system against COVID-19: an integrative review of the current literature. Clin. Exp. Med. **21**(7), 15–28 (2020)
3. Sustrans, 9 reasons to ride an electric bike. https://www.sustrans.org.uk/our-blog/get-active/2019/everyday-walking-and-cycling/9-reasons-to-ride-an-electric-bike. Accessed 9 Dec 2021
4. Ouyang, Y., Guo, B., Lu, X., Han, Q., Guo, T., Yu, Z.: Competitive analysis and popularity prediction of bike-sharing apps using multi-source data. IEEE Trans. Mob. Comput. **18**(8), 1760–1773 (2018)
5. Warlina, L., Hermawan, Y.A.: Smart bike sharing system as sustainable transportation. IOP Conf. Ser. Mater. Sci. Eng. **879**(1), 012153 (2020). (IOP Publishing, Hainan, China)
6. Rifki, R.M.A., Sultan, M.A.: The implementation of mobile commerce applications to order systems for bike-sharing programs in Bandung. In: Advances in Business, Management and Entrepreneurship, pp. 209–213. CRC Press (2020)
7. Ku Azir, K.N.F., et al.: UniCycle: an android application of bike sharing system in the digital campus. J. Phys. Conf. Ser. **1755**(1), 012010 (2021). (IOP Publishing, Diwaniyah, Iraq)
8. AbuSharkh, O.M.F., Dabain, Z.: GreenBikeNet: An intelligent mobile application with green wireless networking for cycling in smart cities. Mob. Netw. App. **21**(2), 352–366 (2016)
9. Islam, M.M., et al.: Design and implementation of a smart bike accident detection system. In: 2020 IEEE Region 10 Symposium (TENSYMP), pp. 386–389. IEEE (2020)
10. Markings, S.: How to Calculate Wheel Circumference (2018). https://sciencing.com/calculate-wheel-circumference-5959393.html. Accessed 9 Dec 2020
11. Western Bike Works: Tire Sizes (2021). https://sciencing.com/calculate-wheel-circumference-5959393.html. Accessed 9 Dec 2020
12. Wright, J.: (2020). https://pedalchile.com/blog/ebike-calories#:~:text=Calories%20burned%20per%20hour%3A%20294,lower%20than%20conventional%20bike%20riding). Accessed 9 Dec 2020
13. Raspberry Pi: What is a Raspberry Pi? (2020). https://www.raspberrypi.org/help/what-%20is-a-raspberry-pi/. Accessed 9 Dec 2020
14. Wikipedia contributors, MongoDB, Wikipedia, The Free Encyclopedia. https://en.wikipedia.org/w/index.php?title=MongoDB&oldid=1065102604. Accessed 9 Dec 2020
15. Industries: Monochrome 0.96" 128x64 OLED Graphic Display - STEMMA QT (2020). https://www.adafruit.com/product/326. Accessed 9 Dec 2020
16. Wikipedia contributors, Heroku, Wikipedia, The Free Encyclopedia. https://en.wikipedia.org/w/index.php?title=Heroku&oldid=1065407913. Accessed 9 Dec 2020

Preliminary Development of Virtual Try-On Platform for Batik Apparel Based on Mobile Augmented Intelligence Technology

Ardiman Firmanda(✉) [iD], Sritrusta Sukaridhoto [iD], Hestiasari Rante [iD], and Evianita Dewi Fajrianti [iD]

Politeknik Elektronika Negeri Surabaya, Jawa Timur 60111, Indonesia
ardimanfirmanda@live.com, {dhoto,hestiasari}@pens.ac.id

Abstract. During the COVID-19 pandemic, the government decided to suspend all arts cultural events to prevent the spread of the virus. This situation is a challenge for batik artisans to survive. This research aims to develop a virtual try-on platform that is an alternative medium for artisans to solve their problems. Development platforms based on augmented reality technology can be an option for the problems. Platform designed based on mobile devices has advantages in the practicality of use that is not limited by space and time. Implementation of human motion capture and hand gesture recognition provides an immersive experience for users. Motion capture is used for a virtual try-on scheme for batik apparel that can make users try batik apparel virtually and can automatically fit the user's body. In addition, the implementation of hand gesture recognition allows users to apply batik motifs to virtual apparel interactively combined with material fitting function, which can assist users in positioning batik motifs. Apart from technical matters, this platform also provides information about the history of batik motifs. Alpha testing is used in testing the platform and confusion matrix to validate the accuracy of implementing the functions that exist on the platform. The results of testing the accuracy of hand gesture recognition reached 97%, and human motion capture reached 93%, which means the system can run well. This paper describes the initial efforts made to develop a virtual try-on platform for batik apparel based on Augmented Intelligence Technology.

Keywords: Augmented reality · Batik · Body tracking · Cultural computing · Hand gesture · Virtual try-on

1 Introduction

Batik is one of the works of art that is the identity of Indonesia and one of Indonesia's unique cultural heritages. Batik has become a part of people's lives. The Covid-19 pandemic has recently become problematic in many aspects, one of which is batik exhibitions. Batik exhibition is one of the means to introduce and market what is used by batik businesses. However, to stop the spread of Covid-19, the authorities temporarily

M. N. Seyman (Ed.): ICECENG 2022, LNICST 436, pp. 40–54, 2022.
https://doi.org/10.1007/978-3-031-01984-5_4

suspended arts and cultural events [1]. Over the last decade, an increasing number of mobile applications have included augmented reality (AR) technologies that dynamically match virtual content and information with physical displays based on the user's environment. Mobile guides and instructional games are only a few examples of the types of apps available, which also include new media art and virtual exhibits [2]. AR is a technology that enables a user to better comprehend and interact with the area in which they are currently located via the application of artificial contextual information. Utilizing AR technology as a pedagogical [3] and didactic [4] tool may be very beneficial since it offers an engaging [5], attractive [6], and educational experience [7].

Augmented Intelligence is a new chapter in the history of augmented reality (AR) and artificial intelligence (AI), in which AI augments the functionality of AR and collaborates with humans to improve cognitive performance, learning, decision making, and provide new experiences in the world of technology [8, 9]. In this research, we implement the hand gesture recognition function and a virtual try-on system to apply the concept of Augmented Intelligence.

We started this research by collecting data, analyzing related research and similar existing platforms, as well as information and digital images of batik motifs, and then modelling the 3D platform objects used. Mobile Augmented Reality (MAR) was developed using the Unity 3D game engine which has rendering support features optimized for mobile known as the Universal Render Pipeline (URP). This is necessary to improve the realistic graphics, as it can potentially affect the level of immersion when using the platform. The realistic level of graphics can affect the level of virtual presence perceived by the user, as has been recognized in the relevant literature [10].

This study aims to develop an interactive virtual batik apparel trial platform using the concept of augmented intelligence. Furthermore, in Sect. 2, the materials and methods contain data collection needed for development, such as related work, reference technology such as mobile motion capture and hand gesture recognition, usage scenarios, and platform design. In Sect. 3, the results and discussion contain alpha testing on the platform. The confusion matrix method was used to determine the accuracy level of hand gesture reading and the human body on the platform. Finally, conclusions and future work are discussed.

2 Related Works

The reference in this research in the scope of mobile augmented reality (MAR) can be specifically classified into three categories: virtual try-on (VTO), hand tracking, and Gesture Recognition. The development of the VTO platform has been done a lot to support the fashion world. According to Hyunwoo et al. [11], virtual try-on technology can increase sales and reduce product return losses due to wrong purchases by consumers. Consumers are given the facility to try the product virtually to provide size and suitability guidelines in real-time [12].

Virtual Try-on (VTO) is a new technology concept used by some fashion apparel applications to help customers mix apparel without a dressing room [11]. Not only apparel but can make-up, accessories, jewelry, and others. The main techniques involved in 3D virtual dressing are modelling and fitting of users and apparel with body tracking technology. It is usual to model users by employing scanning devices, such as webcams, phone cameras, and depth cameras. In related previous works, the use of Microsoft Kinect to be a solution to this topic [12, 18].

The use of Microsoft Kinect is not in accordance with the research design, because this system is intended to run on a mobile platform and requires portability in its use. Since the motion capture feature was integrated into Apple's ARKit 3 Framework two years ago, it has allowed developers to implement body tracking on mobile platforms without the need for a Microsoft Kinect and a computer. Apple's ARKit framework enables the development of Augmented Reality applications on iOS devices by integrating camera and gesture features on the device [19–21]. As a result, in this study, researchers used Apple's ARKit Framework as a human motion capture framework. The application of virtual try-on technology is currently not only applied to clothing simulation trials [13] but has developed to virtual try-on watches [14] and virtual try-on of Footwear [15]. This technology works using a skeletal tracking algorithm to detect the human body using computer devices and human motion capture such as Kinect. Seeing on previous research, researchers want to bring this virtual try-on technology to the realm of mobile augmented reality.

In addition to virtual try-on, hand gesture recognition technology has also entered the realm of augmented reality, especially in the mobile field. Previous research [16, 17] proved the use of hand gesture recognition in an AR system to get a good response from the user's side. This technology works using a database of gestures and hand models and approach algorithms based on these 2D and 3D hand models. The system can detect a hand caught by the camera and know what gesture is being done. Research conducted by Shahrouz Yousefi [16] compared the touch screen technology that has been widely used in various MAR interactions, which is limited by more minor different touch gestures in 3D space. Therefore, the application of HT and GR in 3D physical space is exciting and is a technology update that can maximize 3D interaction.

3   Research Method

We present a new approach in cultural computing, especially batik, to provide a unique interactive experience in textured batik and try on batik apparel that have been textured virtually with augmented reality technology using ARKit SDK and Manomotion SDK to support human body tracking and hand gesture recognition. The contribution from this research is an implementation of hand gesture recognition for simulating giving batik textures to 3D apparel objects. Tracking a person's motion in the physical environment and then visualizing body motion using 3D apparel objects that have been set according to AR platform scenarios.

Platform development using Unity 3D Game Engine with Unity's ARFoundation Framework. ARFoundation allows working with augmented reality platforms in a multi-platform way within Unity 3D. So, if we want to develop the platform to run on other mobile operating systems like android, we can easily integrate it by updating the platform and rebuilding the app entirely from scratch. Figure 1 is the architecture of the Virtual Try-On Platform for Batik Apparel; the platform is divided into three parts.

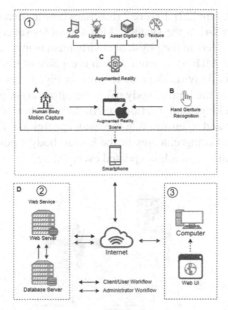

Fig. 1. Architecture design mobile vto platform.

First, a platform optimized for use on mobile devices equipped with augmented reality technology. There are Three SDK used on this platform according to the system design. The Augmented Reality SDK serves as the system's primary layer. Apple's ARKit is used as the augmented reality SDK on this. In ARKit, there are building augmented reality elements to make it look attractive and blend with the natural world, such as audio, lighting, digital assets, and texture. Motion capture and hand gestures SDKs are also integrated to provide an interactive and immersive platform experience.

The second is a web service that includes a web and database for managing online data. This scheme is used to avoid the rebuild process on the mobile platform, which takes time if the texture data and information from the batik used are changed. Mobile platform can communicate with the server and retrieve data from the database. The third is the development of a web UI that is used to simplify the process of adding, changing, and deleting existing data in the database. The data includes batik texture and batik texture information. Two types of users can use it, such as Admin and Batik Artisan, where Batik Artisan can manage batik data management and Admin can manage whom Batik Artisan can the development of a web UI that is used to simplify the process of adding, changing, and deleting existing data in the database. The data includes batik texture and batik texture information. Two types of users can use it, such as Admin and enter and use the system using the Web UI facility.

3.1 Human Body Motion Capture

For Apple's ARKit to function properly, it requires a supporting framework such as Apple's RealityKit. RealityKit developed by Apple is a framework for high-performance

3D simulation and rendering [22]. Figure 2 illustrates how human motion capture works with ARKit and RealityKit on the system. ARKit includes several Entity Classes that enable it to recognize objects in the physical environment using a camera called ARAnchor. This research used ARBodyAnchor, which is capable of tracking the position and movement of the human body on the rear camera. In Fig. 1 process 2, the system can recognize the structure of the human body using the information provided by ARKit by activating ARBodyTrackingConfiguration (). ARBodyAnchor is required to optimize body tracking accuracy and to ensure that the batik apparel 3D Virtual Object remains in place while accommodating changes in the human body's position from the initial position to the final position, which is updated every frame.

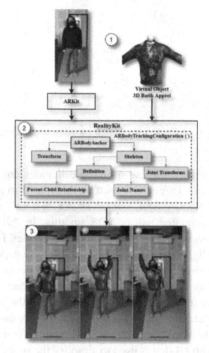

Fig. 2. Human motion capture process in ARKit and RealityKit.

ARKit's body-tracking functionality requires models to be in a specific format. Models that do not match the expected format may not work correctly [23]. Several essential things must be considered in the skeletal model format, such as joint names, rig structure, axis orientation and skeleton hierarchy for human motion capture. The model must use a scene coordinate system in which +Y represents up, +Z represents forward, and +X represents right. On the +Z axis, the model must also face forward.

Matching Model to 3D Batik Apparel. What makes it unique from the rest of the skeleton is that the spine must have seven joint and the neck must have four joint (Fig. 3). The skeleton structure cannot be changed unilaterally due to the possibility of affecting

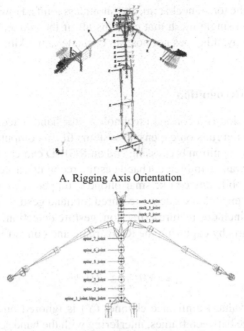

A. Rigging Axis Orientation

B. Spine and Neck Structure Required

Fig. 3. Requirements of the skeleton specification.

the human motion capture of the working function. However, importing 3D assets that are used as virtual objects can be used to modify the body mesh component. 3D assets are imported in a standard T or A pose and then manipulated by shifting the original position to match the ARKit skeleton model's orientation like on Fig. 4.

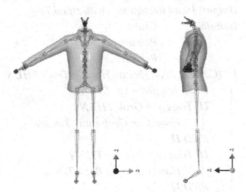

Fig. 4. Merging virtual assets and skeleton.

The skeleton does not have to bind the 3D object to every bone, even though it must contain all of the expected joints in the correct hierarchy. The example in this study, using human motion capture is intended for visualization using batik apparel, so the researcher only uses the torso, neck, arm, and shoulders joints. However, because virtual objects are bound in a single mesh that contains all of the connections required in the correct ARKit hierarchy, this does not pose an obstacle to tracking human bodies.

3.2 Hand Gesture Recognition

Hand gesture recognition is a common technology for hand detection. However, most hand gesture recognition runs on expensive systems like a computer with high specifications as a tool for recognition processing and an RGB-D camera for hand recognition sensors. Researchers want to implement hand gesture recognition technology into mobile device. A standard mobile device like smartphone equipped with an integrated camera is utilized to generate the video sequence required for hand gesture analysis. The gesture analysis step usually includes feature extraction, gesture detection, motion analysis and tracking. The step starts by capturing the RGB frame and converting it to YCbCr color space (see Eq. 1).

$$z_i = \alpha HCr_i - \beta HCb_i \tag{1}$$

In this case, the value Luminance channel (Y) is ignored on YCbCr color space since its values change between frames, interfering with the hand segmentation process. Parameter z on Eq. 1 indicates the weighted image of the hand and background samples respectively. HCr and HCb represent the Cr and Cb color information of the hand samples for the background. By adjusting the adjustable parameters α and β, it is possible to optimize hand segmentation [16].

ALGORITHM 1: HAND GESTURE RECOGNITION	
	Input: Read Human Hand
	Output: Hand Recognition with Hand Trigger
1	*Initialize:* Grab;
2	Pointer;
3	Release;
4	*IF (Camera Read Human Hand = True)* **THEN**
5	*Hand Trigger = On* **DO**
6	*IF Trigger = Grab* **THEN**
7	*Hand Can Grab Batik Texture;*
8	*END IF*
9	*IF Trigger = Pointer* **THEN**
10	*Hand Can Split Batik Texture;*
11	*END IF*
12	*ELSE*
13	*Trigger = Release;*
14	*END IF*

Manomotion SDK is a hand gesture recognition library that can work on mobile devices and cameras without needing a depth sensor [24]. This SDK supports the use of the Unity 3D integrated development environment (IDE) for system development as in this research. The hand gesture recognition database provided is quite complete and can be used. The current version of the database features data of four different gesture types: pinch (thumb and index finger), point (using the index finger), as well as grab normal (hand's back facing the user), and grab palm (hand's palm facing the user) [25]. In the platform created, researchers used 2 types of gestures such as grab and point. The following is the pseudocode Algorithm 1 scenario used.

Figure 5 illustrates a design scheme using pointer gestures. As can be seen, the point gesture function is used to trigger the batik texture object, which starts out as a single object and splits to four when the hand makes a pointing gesture and touches the batik object. This process aims to provide the user with a more varied and interactive experience when interacting with the system.

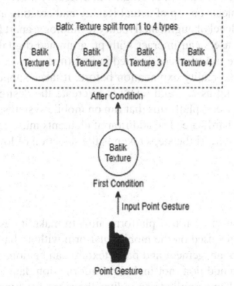

Fig. 5. Workflow from point gesture.

The use of grab gestures aims to apply batik texture to 3D apparel object interactively. Figure 6 illustrates a design scheme using grab gestures.

The platform will recognize hand gestures then the user grabs the 3D batik texture ball object. After touching the 3D object, the user can activate the grab gesture by holding hands in the second step. In the third process, users can bring texture objects such as holding a ball in the real world and then bring them closer to the 3D Shirt object. The last process the system will perform is a mesh renderer on the 3D shirt object after the texture hits it.

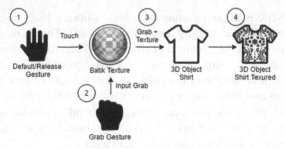

Fig. 6. Workflow from grab gesture.

3.3 Augmented Reality

Augmented Reality is a technology that combines the real world with digital objects generated by computers in real-time. Augmented Reality works by adding layers of programmed digital objects on top of actual Reality and creating a dynamic experience level. At the advanced level of augmented reality technology, apart from just viewing the information provided, users can interact with programmed digital objects and receive immediate feedback from Actions performed in real-time.

From the augmented reality explanation before, it takes supporting elements such as lighting, audio, digital assets, and textures to create the desired immersive reality. Unlike on computer devices, platforms that run on mobile systems, there are processing limitations on existing hardware. The addition of elements must be selective so that the platform can run well. One of the steps taken is the selection of low polygon 3D digital assets [26, 27].

3.4 Web Service

Implementing a web service on this platform aims to make it easier to manage information and batik textures used on the mobile platform without having to recompile the platform. Information management and batik texture can be done separately through a PHP-based website. In addition, not including information data and batik textures on the mobile platform when compiled can reduce the size of the installer for the mobile platform so that it can be distributed easily.

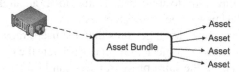

Fig. 7. Unity 3D AssetBundel workflow [28].

Researchers use AssetBundle from Unity 3D on this platform. AssetBundle is one of the asset management methods in Unity 3D, where non-coded assets such as models, textures, prefabs, and audio can remain connected to the platform even though the asset location is in cloud storage. The asset will be downloaded automatically if the mobile platform requires the asset. As described earlier, this method can reduce the initial install size of the mobile platform, load assets optimized for the end user's mobile platform, and reduce runtime memory pressure.

4 Experimental Result

Currently, the development has reached the stage of developing a mobile platform (Fig. 1). The system is usable, but all 3D asset data, textures, and information are accessed offline. For the platform development environment, researchers used tools such as Table 1.

Table 1. Development environment.

Development device	
Device	MacBook Pro mid 2014
OS	OS X 11.6 BigSur
Development software	
IDE	Unity 3D LTS 2020.3.x
Compiler	XCode 13
AR Library	ARFoundation 4.1 & ARKit 4
Hand Gesture Library	Manomotion SDK CE
Human Motion Capture Library	ARKit XR 4.2.1
Test device platform	
Device	Apple iPhone XS
Chipset	Apple 12 Bionic (7 nm)
CPU	Hexa-core (2 × 2.5 GHz Vortex + 4 × 1.6 GHz Tempest) + Neural Engine
GPU	Apple GPU (4-core graphics)
Main Camera	12 MP, f/1.8, 26 mm (wide), ½.55″, 1.4 μm, dual pixel PDAF, OIS

In addition to the development environment described in Table 1, the test also was conducted under standard lighting conditions of 275 lux (lx). Measurement of exposure using the AMS, Inc. TMD4906 sensor. This chapter discusses the results of the platform's development and implementation of human motion capture and hand gestures recognition. The researchers used alpha testing to determine and quantify the accuracy of reading hand gestures and body motions, which is the primary objective of this test. Researchers use confusion matrix to determine the level of accuracy. Confusion matrix is one method to compare the classification results of the system with the predicted classification results to determine how well the system is built [29].

Table 2. Confusion matrix.

	Predicted	
Actual	Positive	Negative
Positive	TP	FN
Negative	FP	TN

Confusion matrices represent counts from predicted and actual values. The term symbol letters in Table 2 can be represented as follows.

TP = True Positive
　　A test result that correctly indicates the presence of a condition or characteristic
TN = True Negative
　　A test result that correctly indicates the absence of a condition or characteristic
FP = False Positive
　　A test result that wrongly indicates that a particular condition or attribute is present
FN = False Negative
　　A test result that wrongly indicates that a particular condition or attribute is absent

The accuracy of the system is calculated Eq. 2. However, Eq. 2 used for a binary classification problem has only two classes to classify, preferably a positive and a negative class. Because there are more than two test classes in this study's confusion matrix, Eq. 3 is used to determine accuracy; this is a confusion matrix for multiple classes.

$$Accuracy = \frac{TP + TN}{TP + TN + FP + FN} \tag{2}$$

$$Accuracy = \frac{TP}{TP + TN + FP + FN} \tag{3}$$

In the confusion matrix for multiple classes, referring to Eq. 3 the value of True Positive (TP) is the result of the sum correct classified [30]. In Tables 3 and 4 the values of TP are marked with green boxes, and red boxes indicate True Negative (TN), False Positive (FP) and False Negative (FN). The value of TP + TN + FP + FN denotes the total number of experiments conducted. It is denoted in the Table by the Total of Trials.

Table 3. Confusion matrix hand gesture recognition.

	Predicted Condition			
Actual Condition	**Grab**	**Point**	**Release**	
Grab	20	1	0	**Total of Trial**
Point	0	18	0	
Release	0	1	20	
Total of Trial				60

$$Hand\ Gesture\ Accuracy = \frac{(20 + 18 + 20)}{60} = 0.97 = 97\% \tag{4}$$

Table 3 results from the alpha test data on the hand gesture recognition function, which is poured into the confusion matrix table. There are three hand gesture parameters used on the tested mobile platform: grab, point, and release. Testing is done by making a hand gesture and then directing the mobile camera that to capture the hand gesture. For each gesture, twenty tests were carried out, grab and release gestures there were no errors in recognition, while for point gestures there were two recognition errors. The recognition error occurs in the first second when the hand is within the camera's range, then a few moments later, the platform corrects the recognition error. However, we count this as inaccuracy of detection, because this data can be a record for improving detection accuracy performance in the future. The application of hand gestures on the platform like point gesture can be seen in Fig. 8 according to the workflow point gesture (Fig. 5).

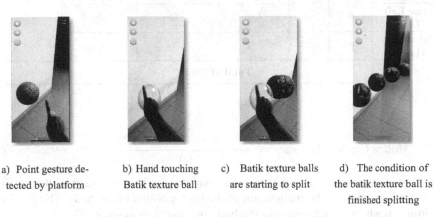

| a) Point gesture de-tected by platform | b) Hand touching Batik texture ball | c) Batik texture balls are starting to split | d) The condition of the batik texture ball is finished splitting |

Fig. 8. Point gesture simulation on the platform.

The application for grab gestures can be seen in Fig. 9. This is following the Grab Gesture workflow in Fig. 6.

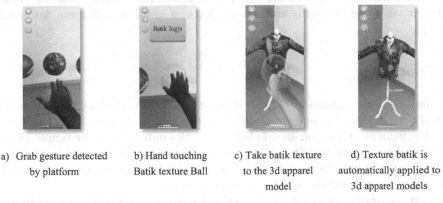

| a) Grab gesture detected by platform | b) Hand touching Batik texture Ball | c) Take batik texture to the 3d apparel model | d) Texture batik is automatically applied to 3d apparel models |

Fig. 9. Grab gesture simulation on the platform.

Accuracy testing is also carried out on the human motion capture function. In Table 4, we can see the results of the tests carried out.

Table 4. Confusion matrix human body motion capture.

Actual Condition	Predicted Condition					
	Front	Back	Raise Right Hand	Raise Left Hand	Raise Two Hand	
Front	12	3	0	0	0	
Back	0	9	0	0	0	
Raise Right Hand	0	0	12	0	0	Total of Trials
Raise Left Hand	0	0	0	11	0	
Raise Two Hand	0	0	0	1	12	
Total of Trial						60

$$Motion\ Capture\ Accuracy = \frac{(12 + 9 + 12 + 11 + 12)}{60} = 0.93 = 93\% \quad (5)$$

Of the five parameters tested, there is one parameter whose accuracy level is smaller than the others, namely the recognition of the back position of the body. The platform sometimes reads the rear position of the body into the front position. This is because in 2D, the front and back of the human body look almost the exact (Fig. 2). The platform must read other parameters such as the face of the human to be able to detect the front or back view of the body.

According to the results of tests conducted using the alpha testing method, as well as calculating the accuracy of hand gesture recognition and human motion capture using a confusion matrix, a value of more than 90% was obtained, indicating that the mobile platform can operate normally and that development of the next platform design can continue.

5 Conclusion

We aim to provide alternative solutions to issues facing batik artisans impacted by the COVID-19 pandemic and introduce technology that benefits the community's interests. The development of a mobile-based platform enables distribution to be simplified and used anywhere and anytime. The addition of hand gesture recognition and human motion tracking capabilities to the virtual try-on experience for batik apparel creates an entirely new interactive and immersive experience for users.

From the current stage of the result, the implementation of hand gesture recognition and human motion tracking can run well. The results of the accuracy calculation using the confusion matrix, which gets an average value of above 90%, indicate that the mobile platform can read hands and humans as desired.

Other future work will include integrating web services on the mobile platform, according to the architectural design of the platform in Fig. 1. Web service integration can make it easier to update existing batik data on the mobile platform without rebuilding the platform, which tends to take a long time longer.

References

1. Nabi, S., Mishra, V.P.: Analysis and Impact of COVID-19 on economy and organization. In: International Conference on Computational Intelligence and Knowledge Economy (ICCIKE), pp. 219–224. IEEE, Dubai, United Arab Emirates (2021)
2. Miranto, C., Rante, H., Sukaridhoto, S., Pasila, F., Aliwarga, H.: Preliminary Development of virtual reality for batik exhibition. Psychol. Educ. J. **57**(9), (2020)
3. Behzadan, A.H., Kamat, V.R.: Enabling discovery-based learning in construction using telepresent augmented reality. Autom. Constr. **33**, 3–10 (2013)
4. Puyuelo, M., Higón, J.L., Merino, L., Contero, M.: Experiencing augmented reality as an accessibility resource in the UNESCO heritage site called "La Lonja." Procedia Comput. Sci. **25**, 171–178 (2013)
5. Wojciechowski, R., Cellary, W.: Evaluation of learners' attitude toward learning in ARIES augmented reality environments. Comput. Educ. **68**, 570–585 (2013)
6. Kysela, J., ŠTorková, P.: Using augmented reality as a medium for teaching history and tourism. Procedia Soc. Behav. Sci. **174**, 926–931 (2015)
7. Fajrianti, E.D., et al.: Design and development of human anatomy learning platform for medical students based on augmented intelligence technology. In: International Electronics Symposium (IES), pp. 195–202. IEEE, Surabaya, Indonesia (2021).
8. Hebbar, A.: Augmented intelligence: enhancing human capabilities. In: 2017 Third International Conference on Research in Computational Intelligence and Communication Networks (ICRCICN), pp. 251–254. IEEE, Kolkata, India (2017)
9. Wójcik, M.: Augmented intelligence technology. The ethical and practical problems of its implementation in libraries. Libr. Hi Tech. **39**(2), 435–447 (2020)
10. He, Z., Wu, L., Li, X.R.: When art meets tech: the role of augmented reality in enhancing museum experiences and purchase intentions. Tour. Manage. **68**, 127–139 (2018)
11. Hwangbo, H., Kim, E.H., Lee, S.H., Jang, Y.J.: Effects of 3D Virtual "try-on" on online sales and customers' purchasing experiences. IEEE Access **8**, 189479–189489 (2020)
12. Liu, T., Li, L., Zhang, X.: Real-time 3D virtual dressing based on users' skeletons. In: 4th International Conference on Systems and Informatics (ICSAI), pp. 1378–1382. IEEE, Hangzhou, China (2017)
13. Yuan, M., Khan, I.R., Farbiz, F., Yao, S., Niswar, A., Foo, M.H.: A mixed reality virtual clothes try-on system. IEEE Trans. Multim. **15**(8), 1958–1968 (2013)
14. Gunes, S., Sanli, O., Ergun, O.O.: Augmented reality tool for markerless virtual try-on around human arm. In: IEEE International Symposium on Mixed and Augmented Reality - Media, Art, Social Science, Humanities and Design, pp. 59–60. IEEE, Fukuoka, Japan (2015)
15. Chu, C.H., Cheng, C.H., Wu, H.S., Kuo, C.C.: A cloud service framework for virtual try-on of footwear in augmented reality. J. Comput. Inf. Sci. Eng. **19**(2), (2019)
16. Yousefi, S., Kidane, M., Delgado, Y., Chana, J., Reski, N.: 3D gesture-based interaction for immersive experience in mobile VR. In: 2016 23rd International Conference on Pattern Recognition (ICPR), pp. 2121–2126. IEEE, Cancun, Mexico (2016)

17. Ekneling, S., Sonestedt, T., Georgiadis, A., Yousefi, S., Chana, J.: Magestro: Gamification of the data collection process for development of the hand gesture recognition technology. In: IEEE International Symposium on Mixed and Augmented Reality Adjunct (ISMAR-Adjunct), pp. 417–418. IEEE, Munich, Germany (2018)
18. Kusumaningsih, A., Kurniawati, A., Angkoso, C.V., Yuniarno, E.M., Hariadi, M.: User experience measurement on virtual dressing room of Madura batik clothes. In: 2017 International Conference on Sustainable Information Engineering and Technology (SIET), pp. 203–208. IEEE, Malang, Indonesia (2017)
19. ARKit. https://developer.apple.com/documentation/arkit. Accessed 8 Sept 2021
20. Capturing Body Motion in 3D. https://developer.apple.com/documentation/arkit/content_a nchors/capturing_body_motion_in_3d. Accessed 8 Sept 2021
21. ARBodyAnchor. https://developer.apple.com/documentation/arkit/arbodyanchor. Accessed 8 Sept 2021
22. RealityKit. https://developer.apple.com/documentation/realitykit/. Accessed 8 Sept 2021
23. Validating a Model for Motion Capture. https://developer.apple.com/documentation/arkit/con tent_anchors/validating_a_model_for_motion_capture. Accessed 8 Sept 2021
24. ManoMotion hand tracking SDK. https://www.manomotion.com/mobile-ar/. Accessed 8 Sept 2021
25. ManoMotion Gesture Documentation. https://sdk.manomotion.com/SDK_Pro_v1.4.8/. Accessed 8 Sept 2021
26. Caradonna, G., Lionetti, S., Tarantino, E., Verdoscia, C.: A Comparison of low-poly algorithms for sharing 3D models on the web. In: Cefalo, R., Zieliński, J., Barbarella, M. (eds.) New Advanced GNSS and 3D Spatial Techniques. Lecture Notes in Geoinformation and Cartography, pp. 237–244. Springer, Cham (2017). https://doi.org/10.1007/978-3-319-56218-6_19
27. Bullinger, H.J., Behlau, L.: Technology Guide: Principles – Applications – Trends. Springer, Heidelberg (2009)
28. AssetBundle. https://docs.unity3d.com/AssetBundlesIntro.html. Accessed 8 Sept 2021
29. Visa, S., Ramsay, B., Ralescu, A.L., Knaap, E.V.D.: Confusion matrix-based feature selection. In: Proceedings of the 22nd Midwest Artificial Intelligence and Cognitive Science Conference (MAICS), vol. 710, pp. 120–127 (2011)
30. Makhtar, M., Neagu, D.C., Ridley, M.J.: Comparing multi-class classifiers: on the similarity of confusion matrices for predictive toxicology applications. In: Yin, H., Wang, W., Rayward-Smith V. (eds.) Intelligent Data Engineering and Automated Learning - IDEAL 2011, LNCS, vol. 6936, pp. 252–261. Springer, Berlin (2011). https://doi.org/10.1007/978-3-642-23878-9_31

Artificial Intelligence

Low Light Image Enhancement on Mobile Devices by Using Dehazing

Yücel Çimtay$^{(\boxtimes)}$ (iD) and Gokce Nur Yilmaz (iD)

Ted University, Cankaya 06420, Ankara, Turkey
{yucel.cimtay,gokce.yilmaz}@tedu.edu.tr

Abstract. The images which are captured in indoors and/or outdoors may be badly impacted when sufficient light does not exist. The pictures' low dynamic range and high noise levels may have an impact on the overall success of computer vision systems. Computer vision applications become more powerful in low light situations when low light picture augmentation approaches are used to boost image visibility. Low light photos have a histogram that is very similar to hazy photographs. As a result, haze reduction techniques can be utilized to increase low light photo contrast. An image improvement approach based on inverting low lighting images and applying picture dehazing with an atmospheric light scattering model is suggested in this paper. The suggested technique has been implemented on the Android operating system. The proposed method delivers about 3 frames per second for 360p video on the Android operating system. It is extremely feasible to increase this real-time performance by employing more powerful hardware.

Keywords: Dynamic range · Poor vision · Clear image · Light

1 Introduction

In online and offline computer vision applications in transportation, security, military and video surveillance, low light image and video improvement is critical. As a result, the number of image enhancement research has significantly grown in recent years [1]. Due to inescapable environmental and/or technical restrictions, many photographs are taken in inadequate lighting settings. Insufficient and unbalanced light source in the region, poor item placement against excessive back light, and capturing an image with an under-exposure are just a few examples. The obtained quality of such low light images are harmed, and the information transfer is inadequate. The dynamic range of a picture is expanded using histogram- enhancement based technologies. There are both global [2, 3] and local [4, 5] improvement techniques. Histogram Equalization improves the contrast and brightness of a picture by stretching its dynamic range by uniformly distributing pixel values. However, because the correction is made globally, it causes unanticipated local overexposure and noise amplification. A variety of techniques based on the Retinex theory [6], which decomposes a picture into two components: reflectance and illumination, are also available. Naturalness preserved enhancement (NPE) [7] was presented for

© ICST Institute for Computer Sciences, Social Informatics and Telecommunications Engineering 2022
Published by Springer Nature Switzerland AG 2022. All Rights Reserved
M. N. Seyman (Ed.): ICECENG 2022, LNICST 436, pp. 57–67, 2022.
https://doi.org/10.1007/978-3-031-01984-5_5

the improvement of non-uniform illumination image, and Multilayer Fusion (MF) [8] advocated using multi-layer fusion to improve image quality under various lighting situations. Dehazing-based methods [9, 10] consider the inverted low light image to be hazy, and use dehazing to enhance visibility. Gamma correction adjusts the gamma characteristic of a picture to perform nonlinear color editing, identifying the obscure and bright sections of the image signal and boosting the contrast ratio between them. [11] proposes a dynamically defined adaptive gamma correction technique based on the image's statistical features. The research has been dominated by learning-based methodologies in terms of low light photo improvement. The study in [12] introduces the first convolutional deep network (LL-Net) for low light image enhancement, which perform image contrast augmentation and denoising techniques based on deep auto-encoders. Kindling the darkness (KinD) which is introduced in [13] demonstrated a novel decomposition system, a reflection image improvement network, and an illumination map enrichment network that excelled in low light picture augmentation. Image-to-image translation is now an essential approach to accomplish image augmentation, which is performed by transforming distorted images to crisp images, thanks to General Adversarial Networks (GAN)'s excellent generative capabilities. Cycle-Consistent Adversarial Networks (CylceGAN) is suggested in [14], and it shows remarkable capability in the field of picture domain transfer. Unsupervised Image-to-Image Translation (UNIT) is suggested by [15], and it learnt shared-latent representation for heterogeneous picture translation. Figure 1 is an example to low light imagery enhancement. There can be seen the ground truth, the degraded image and the enhanced image.

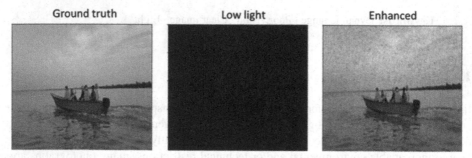

Fig. 1. Ground truth, low light and enhanced images.

This study presents a method based on low light image enhancement by using dehazing. For applying dehazing, the light scattering atmosphere model which is shown in Fig. 2 is used in this study.

The atmospheric scattering model is introduced in Eq. 1–3, where H (x, λ) stands for the hazy picture, T (x, λ) is reflected illumination from scenery and transmitted through haze and AL (x, λ) is the reflected air light from haze. The sensor accumulates the incoming lights and the output is the hazy imagery. In Eq. 2, t (x, λ) is transmission of haze, RL (x, λ) is the reflected light from the scenery and atmospheric light is L_∞. Transmission component is introduced as $e^{-\alpha(\lambda)d(x)}$ RL (x, λ) where d (x) is the scene depth map and α (λ) is coefficient of scattering term related to capturing wavelength. Equation 3

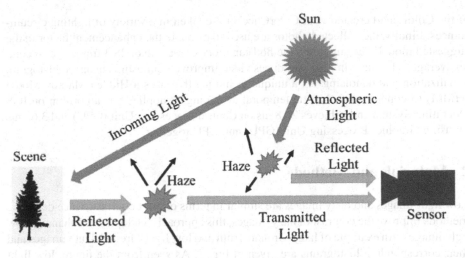

Fig. 2. Model of atmospheric scattering.

shows that when the distance between the sensor and the ground increases, transmission decreases and when the distance between the sensor and the ground decreases, transmission increases.

$$H(x, \lambda) = T(x, \lambda) + AL(x, \lambda) \tag{1}$$

$$= t(x, \lambda)RL(x, \lambda) + L_\infty(1 - t(x, \lambda)) \tag{2}$$

$$= e^{-\alpha(\lambda)d(x)}RL(x, \lambda) + L_\infty\left(1 - e^{-\alpha(\lambda)d(x)}\right) \tag{3}$$

The precise computation of the term of transmission and atmospheric light is the crucial issue here. One of the most often utilized strategies is the Dark Channel Prior (DCP) Method [16]. The per-pixel dark channel prior is utilized for haze estimation in basic DCP.

There are several research on low light picture enhancing in the literature. When it comes to real-time or near-real-time applications, however, there are always bottlenecks such as algorithm complexity, hardware limits, and high financial expenditures. Nonetheless, some successful investigations are now underway.

The study in [17] proposes a real time low light video enhancement method based on Dark channel subtraction, illumination map estimation, gain estimation and finally tone mapping to the input image. This method is implemented on Texas Instruments' TDA3x processor [18] and achieves 18 ms per frame processing time. In [19], an Field Programmable Gate Array (FPGA) is used to create a real-time low light image enhancing technique. This approach aims to increase picture accuracy while simultaneously minimizing image noise. The study in [20], proposes a real-time low light improvement approach for insightful analysis. To begin, an improvement model for Red-Green-Blue (RGB) tone space is created. Then, in order to assess the impact of light intensity, photos

of the Color chart created with ColorChecker are taken in a variety of lighting circum-
stances. Finally, the collected photos are used to evaluate the enhancement factor in the
suggested model. The suggested method can process at a rate of 28.3 frames per second
on average. The study in [21] introduces video improvement using enhanced histogram
equalization and denoising via a unique technique that uses a Hidden Markov Model
(HMM) to conduct probabilistic temporal averaging. It applies this algorithm on IOS
Operating System and achieves 24.8 ms on Central processing Unit (CPU) and 3.66 ms
by using Graphics Processing Unit (GPU) and CPU together.

2   Materials and Method

Low light images and hazy images are similar in terms of poor contrast. Since dehazing
methods improve the contrast of hazy images, this approach is adopted to enhancing low
light images. An example of hazy-Ground Truth and low light-Ground Truth images and
their corresponding histograms are given in Fig. 3. As seen from the figure, low light
image and hazy image exhibits the similar poorness of contrast comparing with Ground
Truth (GT) images. Therefore, enhancing the contrast and brightness is aimed by low
light image enhancing methods.

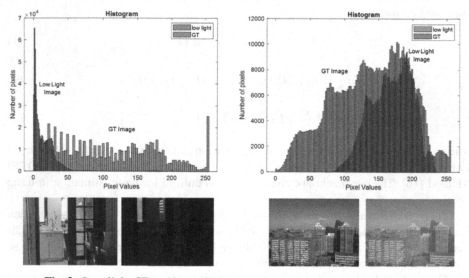

Fig. 3. Low light-GT and Hazy-GT image pairs and corresponding histograms.

In this work, we develop a method based on the study implemented in [10] with addi-
tional steps of, applying the dehazing method in [22] and filtering the result with guided
filter. The work in [22] estimates atmospheric light and map transmission using the DCP
technique, information fidelity, and picture entropy. Prior estimate of the dark channel
picture, atmospheric light estimation, transmission estimation, transmission refinement
using guided filter, and reconstructing the haze free picture are the steps. Reconstruction

is done using Eq. 2. To improve the visual quality of the resulting recovered image of [10], a guided filter is applied as well.

Two examples of ground truth image, low light image, recovered images by using [10] and proposed approach are given in Figs. 4, 5 and 6. The image pairs are selected from the low light image dataset called 'LOL' [23].

Fig. 4. Low light image enhancement [10] for Sample 1. First row, left to right: Low light image, Ground Truth Image. Second row, left to right: Result of [10], Result of proposed approach.

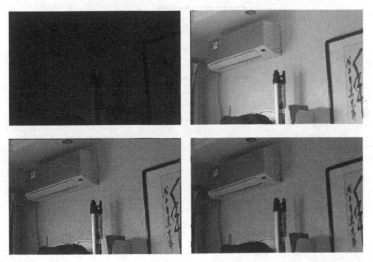

Fig. 5. Low light image enhancement [10] for Sample 2. First row, left to right: Low light image, Ground Truth Image. Second row, left to right: Result of [10], Result of proposed approach.

Fig. 6. Low light image enhancement [10] for Sample 3. First row, left to right: Low light image, Ground Truth Image. Second row, left to right: Result of [10], Result of proposed approach.

In the literature, as far as we are studying, there is no complete study on enhancement of low light image on the Android systems in near real time. In this work, we used MAT-LAB SIMULINK for implementing the proposed method. For building and distributing MATLAB programs and MATLAB SIMULINK models, MATLAB SIMULINK supports Android devices [24]. The SIMULINK model we developed is given in Fig. 7.

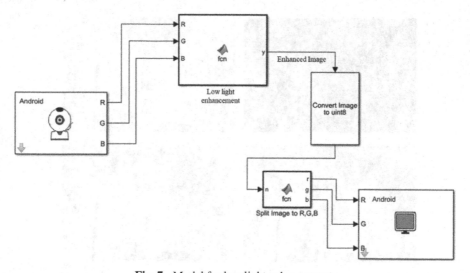

Fig. 7. Model for low light enhancement.

The live imagery which is captured by the device camera is read by the 'Android Camera' block. One can set and change the camera resolution by also using this block. The 'Low light enhancement' function uses real-time video input to execute the proposed low light image enhancement algorithm. The image type conversion block is the next block in Simulink, and it transforms the type of its input to double. The 'Split Image' block divides a RGB image into its R, G, and B color components. Then, using the 'Android Video Display' block, these color elements are presented on the device's screen.

'Android Studio' [25] was used to deploy the project on an Android smartphone. In addition, the MATLAB routines are converted to C++ code, and java code is generated for user modifications and new function declarations. The Qualcomm® SnapdragonTM 665 Octa-core CPU in the Android device we utilized has a frequency of up to 2 GHz. It comes with 3 GB of Random Access Memory (RAM). The camera's video resolution can be increased to 4 K at 30 frames per second.

Figure 8 shows the overall system diagram for real time implementation. Low light enhancement module produces the recovered image by using camera data and resulted image is displayed on the screen.

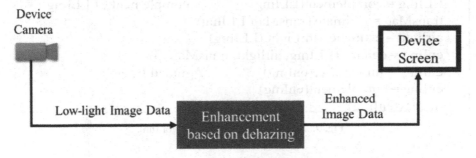

Fig. 8. Overall system diagram.

The pseudocode of proposed method with its implementation on Android OS is given in Fig. 9.

```
def dehaze (LLImg, airlight, transMap, β)
    enImg=(LLImg-airlight*(1-e^(-β*transMap)))/ e^(-β*transMap)
    return enImg

def estimateAtmLight(LLImg)
    //estimation of atmospheric light
    return airlight

def estimateTransMap(LLImg)
    //estimation of transmission map
    return transMap

β = 0.25 //scattering coefficient

While True
    LLImg = readImage ()
    LLImg = complement(LLImg)        // complement of LLImg
    transMap = estimateTransMap(LLImg)
    airlight = estimateAtmLight (LLImg)
    enImg = dehaze (LLImg, airlight, transMap, β)
    enImg = guidedfilter(enImg)        //guided filter
    enImg = complement(enImg)
    display(enImg)
```

Fig. 9. Pseudocode of proposed algorithm.

3   Results

Table 1 compares different good low light image enhancement methods using structural similarity index measure (SSIM), Feature similarity index measure (FSIM) and Peak Signal to Noise ratio (PSNR) on the LOL dataset. As can be seen from the table, our strategy outperforms [22] and is one of the best methods available. GLAD [27] is the most successful method in terms of SSIM, FSIM and PSNR scores. DIE [26] and Dong [22] are the worst ones in terms of PSNR and SSIM respectively. Proposed method's PSNR is above 5 methods, SSIM and FSIM are above 4 and 2 methods shown in the table. The other advantage of proposed method is that it is very basic to implement whereas most others present very complex algorithms.

Table 1. Average PSNR, SSIM and FSIM results[a] for LOL dataset.

Methods	Year	PSNR	SSIM	FSIM
Dong [22]	2014	16.71	0.47	0.88
MF [8]	2016	16.96	0.50	0.92
DIE [26]	2019	14.01	0.51	0.91
GLAD [27]	2018	19.71	0.68	0.93
LIME [28]	2016	16.75	0.44	0.85
EnlightenGan [29]	2021	17.48	0.65	0.92
Zero-DCE [30]	2020	14.86	0.56	0.92
Proposed	2022	16.97	0.56	0.91

[a] The Higher the better

This study is implemented on Android operating system. We tested it for different camera resolutions and handle promising frame processing speed. The results for different image resolutions are shown in Table 2.

Table 2. Low light imagery processing time.

Image resolution	Per frame processing time (in sec.)
360p (480 × 360)	0.37
480p (864 × 480)	0.91
720p (1280 × 720)	1.97
1080p (1920 × 1080)	4.41

From Table 2, we can say that the mean processing time for High Definition (HD) imagery is 1.97 s per frame. In addition, proposed approach achieves 3 fps for 360p video resolution. Figure 10 shows the android application with (a) low light image (b) enhanced image.

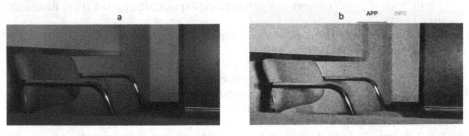

Fig. 10. Android application (a) camera image (b) enhanced image.

4   Conclusion

This study presents a dehazing based low light picture enhancement method. This method is implemented on Android Operating system and promising visual quality and frame processing time scores have been achieved. One of the contributions of the proposed method is that it brings a new view point by presenting a way of applying dehazing techniques to low light image enhancing area. The second contribution is that it applies low light image enhancing on live video and on Android operating system. It can work in near real time. The next step for this approach will be based on reducing the frame processing time and increasing the PSNR, SSIM and FSIM scores.

References

1. Wang, W., Yuan, X.: Recent advances in image dehazing. IEEE/CAA J. Auto. Sin. **4**(3), 410–436 (2017)
2. Pandey, A.K., et al.: Investigating the role of global histogram equalization technique for 99m technetium-methylene diphosphonate bone scan image enhancement. Ind. J. Nucl. Med. **32**(4), 283–288 (2017)
3. Chien, S., Chang, F., Hua, K., Chen, I., Chen, Y.: Contrast enhancement by using global and local histogram information jointly. In: International Conference on Advanced Robotics and Intelligent Systems (ARIS), pp. 75–75. IEEE, Taipei, Taiwan (2017)
4. Hussain, K., Rahman, S., Rahman, M.M., et al: A histogram specification technique for dark image enhancement using a local transformation method. IPSJ T Comput. Vision Appl. **10**(3), (2018)
5. Min, Y., Changming, Z.: Study and comparison on histogram-based local image enhancement methods. In: 2nd International Conference on Image, Vision and Computing (ICIVC), pp. 309–314. IEEE, Chengdu, China (2017)
6. Yoon, J., Choe, Y.: Retinex based image enhancement via general dictionary convolutional sparse coding. Appl. Sci. **10**(12), 439 (2020)
7. Wang, S., Zheng, J., Hu, H.-M., Li, B.: Naturalness preserved enhancement algorithm for non-uniform illumination images. IEEE Trans. Image Process. **22**(9), 3538–3548 (2013)
8. Fu, X., Zeng, D., Huang, Y., Liao, X., Ding, X., Paisley J.: A fusion-based enhancing method for weakly illuminated images. Signal Process. **129**, 82–96 (2016)
9. Zijun, G., Chao, W.: Low light image enhancement algorithm based on retinex and dehazing model. In: 6th International Conference on Robotics and Artificial Intelligence (ICRAI), pp. 84–90. Association for Computing Machinery, New York, USA (2020)
10. Dong, X., et al.: Fast efficient algorithm for enhancement of low lighting video. In: Proceedings of IEEE International Conference on Multimedia and Expo (ICME), pp. 1–6. IEEE, Barcelona, Spain (2011)
11. Rahman, S., et al.: An adaptive gamma correction for image enhancement. EURASIP J. Image Video Process. **2016**, 35 (2016)
12. Lore, K.G., Akintayo, A., Sarkar, S.: Llnet: a deep autoencoder approach to natural low light image enhancement. Pattern Recogn. **61**, 650–662 (2017)
13. Zhang, Y., Zhang, J., Guo, X.: Kindling the darkness: a practical low light image enhancer. In: Proceedings of the 27th ACM International Conference on Multimedia, pp. 1632–1640. ACM, Nice, France (2019)
14. Zhu, J.Y., Park, T., Isola, P., Efros, A.A.: Unpaired image-to-image translation using cycle-consistent adversarial networks. In: IEEE International Conference on Computer Vision (ICCV). IEEE, Venice, Italy (2017)

15. Liu, M.Y., Breuel, T., Kautz, J.: Unsupervised image-to-image translation networks. In: 31st Conference on Neural Information Processing Systems (NIPS), pp. 700–708. ACM, Long Beach, CA, USA (2018)
16. Kaiming, H., Jian, S., Xiaoou, T.: Single image haze removal using dark channel prior. IEEE Trans. Pattern Anal. Mach. Intell. 33(12), 2341–2353 (2011)
17. Navinprashath, R.: Real time enhancement of low light images for low cost embedded platforms. Image Sens. Image. Syst. 4(4), 361–1–361 (2019).
18. Datasheet. https://www.ti.com/lit/ds/symlink/tda3la.pdf?ts=1640100257206. Accessed 22 Dec 2022
19. Tian, S., Tian, Y., Jue, J.: Real-time low light-level image enhancement algorithm applies to FPGA. In: Proceedings of SPIE - The International Society for Optical Engineering, (2011)
20. Hu, X., Zhuo, L., Zhang, J., Jiang, L.: A real-time low light enhancement algorithm for intelligent analysis. In: International Conference on Progress in Informatics and Computing, pp. 273–278. IEEE, Shanghai, China (2016)
21. Patrick, M., Nobie, R., Imran, T.: Low light mobile video processing. Stanford University (2013)
22. Park, D., Park, H., Han, D.K., Ko, H: Single image dehazing with image entropy and information fidelity. In: IEEE International Conference on Image Processing (ICIP), pp.4037–4041. IEEE, Paris, France (2014)
23. Wei, C., Wang, W., Yang, W., Liu, J.: Deep Retinex decomposition for low light enhancement, arXiv (2018).
24. Simulink Android Support. https://www.mathworks.com/hardwaresupport/android-programming-simulink.html. Accessed 21 Dec 2022
25. Android Studio. https://developer.android.com/studio. Accessed 21 Dec 2021
26. Zhang, Q., Nie, Y., Zheng, W.S.: Dual illumination estimation for robust exposure correction. In Comput. Graph. Forum 38(7), 243–252 (2019)
27. Wang, W., Wei, C., Yang, W., Liu, J.: Low light enhancement network with global awareness. In: 13th IEEE International Conference on Automatic Face & Gesture Recognition, pp. 751–755. IEEE, Xi'an, China (2018)
28. Guo, X., Li, Y., Ling, H.: Low light image enhancement via illumination map estimation. IEEE Trans. Image Process. 26(2), 982–993 (2016)
29. Jiang, Y., et al.: Enlightengan: deep light enhancement without paired supervision. IEEE Trans. Image Process. 30, 2340–2349 (2021)
30. Guo, C, et al: Zero reference deep curve estimation for low light image enhancement. In: Proceedings of the IEEE/CVF Conference on Computer Vision and Pattern Recognition, pp. 1780–1789. IEEE, Seattle, WA, USA (2020)

Document Image Classification with Vision Transformers

Semih Sevim[1]([⊠]) [iD], Sevinç İlhan Omurca[2] [iD], and Ekin Ekinci[3] [iD]

[1] Bandırma Onyedi Eylul University, 10200 Bandırma, Turkey
`ssevim@bandirma.edu.tr`
[2] Kocaeli University, 41001 Kocaeli, Turkey
`silhan@kocaeli.edu.tr`
[3] Sakarya University of Applied Sciences, 54050 Sakarya, Turkey
`ekinekinci@subu.edu.tr`

Abstract. Document image classification has received huge interest in business automation processes. Therefore, document image classification plays an important role in the document image processing (DIP) systems. And it is necessary to develop an effective framework for this task. Many methods have been proposed for the classification of document images in literature. In this paper we propose an efficient document image classification task that uses vision transformers (ViTs) and benefits from visual information of the document. Transformers are models developed for natural language processing tasks. Due to its high performances, their structures have been modified and they have started to be applied on different problems. ViT is one of these models. ViTs have demonstrated imposing performance in computer vision tasks compared with baselines. Since, scans the image and models the relation between the image patches using multi-head self-attention Experiments are conducted on a real-world dataset. Despite the limited size of training data available, our method achieves acceptable performance while performing document image classification.

Keywords: Document image classification · Deep learning · Transformers · Vision transformers

1 Introduction

In recent years, with the automation of business processes, digitized documents called as document images have started to quickly replace physical documents. Many physical documents, from scientific papers to bank receipts, application forms to transcripts, agreements to resumes, technical reports to magazines, are now in the form of document images and, it has become necessary to propose methods for DIP. Because such documents are an important and rich source of information and knowledge both visually and textually. At the heart of the DIP there is document image classification, which is a crucial task in supervised learning [1, 2].

© ICST Institute for Computer Sciences, Social Informatics and Telecommunications Engineering 2022
Published by Springer Nature Switzerland AG 2022. All Rights Reserved
M. N. Seyman (Ed.): ICECENG 2022, LNICST 436, pp. 68–81, 2022.
https://doi.org/10.1007/978-3-031-01984-5_6

Document image classification is a sub-task of image classification which aims to assign a given document image to one of the predefined classes. Also, document image classification has a wide research interest in artificial intelligence applications [3]. This task can be handled under three headings, namely textual-based methods, structural-based methods and hybrid methods [4, 5]. Textual-based methods are relied on the textual content of the document image extracted by using Optical Character Recognition (OCR) [6]. Thus, the document image classification problem turns into a text classification problem. Such a problem has been studied a lot in the literature and successful results have been obtained [7, 8]. However, the biggest disadvantage here is due to OCR. Because, poor quality of document images and incapacity of text recognition methods cause errors in OCR results [9]. To enhance the capability of textual-based methods structural-based methods have been preferred in the literature [10]. By learning the layout features of the document images, classification is made according to the structural similarity over these layouts [11]. In structural-based methods, Convolutional Neural Networks (CNNs) has gained great attention due to its remarkable success for document image classification task [12]. Hybrid models are used to combine textual and structural features to take advantage of the unique strengths of each of features and also to eliminate the error caused by OCR. Due to these, hybrid methods show state-of-the-art classification accuracy in document image classification task [2].

In this study, to achieve document image classification by using structural based features we evaluate the ViTs which have recently gained attention and begin to replace CNN in computer vision tasks [13, 14]. The document images for experiments were pull from Kocaeli University digital document management system. To these system students upload twelve different type of document images. The reason why such a system is needed is to prevent students from uploading documents under wrong classes. Because this error is frequently encountered and it is difficult and time consuming to manually assign existing documents to the correct classes. The major contributions of our papers are as follows:

- We answer the question of whether ViTs are successful in document image classification.
- It is to automate the process of document image classification.
- We achieve 62.73% F1-Score for the proposed task.

The rest of the paper is organized as follows. Section 2 covers the related work about document image classification. Section 3 presents the ViTs in detail. Section 4 summarizes datasets used for evaluation as well as evaluation metrics and all the relevant experimental details along with the corresponding results. Finally, we conclude the paper with conclusion in Sect. 5.

2 Related Works

In the literature, various studies for document image classification have started to gain momentum. As many of the early studies for this task depend on OCR to extract textual content from document images [15]. However, document image classification has been evolved according to take account layout features and fusion of textual and layout features. In this section, we briefly review the document image classification approaches which are based on the used features.

There are limited number of studies which use only textual features for classification task. One of them was made by Baumann et al. [16]. In their study, OfficeMAID system was developed to classify scanned mails into pre-defined classes by using context information extracted with two different OCR tools. Eken et al. [17] extracted textual content by using OCR and applied classical machine learning algorithms for classification task. To classify Turkish document images Şahin et al. [18] proposed a keyword-based approach. For each class class-specific keywords were extracted from OCRed documents and documents were assigned to the class with which the maximum number of keywords matches.

The ancestor of the work using visual features can be considered as the Kang et al.'s study [11]. They benefited from hierarchical nature of document layout and assumption that documents belonging to the same class showed similar structure and applied CNN for classification task. Kumar et al. [19] trained random forest classifier with Support Vector Machines (SVM) with a codebook of SURF descriptors and obtained state-of-the-art results on structurally similar document images. Handcrafted features and CNN extracted features were compared in [20] and it was seen that with CNN based features more accurate classification results were achieved. In [21], AlexNet in which the weights learned on ImageNet dataset were used as the initial weights were trained for classification task. Roy et al. [22] trained ensemble of six Deep CNN (DCNN) for a whole document and their specific-regions and combined the results of each DCNNs with SVM. Csurka [23] calculated Run-Length Histogram (RLH) and Fisher Vector (FV) descriptors for document images. Then, applied classical machine learning algorithms to these descriptors for classification task. In another study of Csurka et al. [24] shallow features, deep features based on CNN, and combination of these were used and best results were obtained with CNN based visual features. Yaman et al. [25] applied AlexNet, GoogLeNet, VGG-16 and achieved best results with VGG-16. Zavalishin et al. [26] devised MSER-based approach which used three type of descriptors to obtain layout of the documents, Spatial Local Binary Pattern (SLBP), Grayscale Runlength Histogram (GRLH) and BRISK descriptors combined with FVs based on Bernoulli Mixture Model (BMMFV). Then, the output of these descriptors were given to SVM to make prediction. Tensmeyer and Martinez [27] examined the factors affecting performance of the CNN for document image classification tasks and claimed that shear transformers, multi-scale training and testing, batch normalization instead of Dropout improved the performance of the model. In [28], a real-time document image classification architecture was proposed. In this architecture features extracted with AlexNet were fed into Extreme Learning Machine for prediction. In the another study of the Afzal et al. [29] used both pre-trained and not pre-trained CNN models. In [30], multiple transfer learning model were proposed to make region based classifiers and then to combine these algorithms into one for better classification. Hassanpour and Malek [31] used SqueezeNet trained both with weights from ImageNet and random weights. They observed that with weights from ImageNet more accurate classification results were obtained. Mohsenzadegan et al. [32] realized document image classification with six channel CNN. To extract visual features from dataset Jadli et al. [33] applied well known pre-trained CNN models namely, VGG-19, InceptionV3, DenseNet121 and MobileNetV2. Then, the classical feature selection algorithms were applied to determine most representative feature subset among extracted ones to improve classification performance. In [34], Deep Convolutional Generative Adversarial Networks (DCGAN) based data augmention was realized to create fake and hybrid datasets in addition to the original document image dataset. Then, CNN were applied to compare classification performance. Sevim et al. [4] proposed a soft-voting architecture of NASNet-Large, InceptionV3 and EfficientNetB3 to take advantage of the all three models.

Noce et al. [35] combined visual and textual features by embedding textual content to improve classification accuracy of visually indistinguishable document images. With the help of OCR and Natural Language Processing (NLP) keywords in the documents were associated with pre-defined classes then each class was assigned a unique color. Thus, performance improvement was achieved by visualizing textual information. In [36], a multimodal network was designed which was trained with OCR learnt textual features and MobileNetv2 learnt visual features were. Jain and Wigington [37] proposed multimodal fusion mechanism which combines spatial word embeddings and image features from VGG-16. In [38], EfficientNet models and CNN models were compared in terms of document image classification. In [39], the authors introduced Layout LM which modeled textual information and layout information jointly. Bakkali et al. [40] proposed a fusion mechanism which hybridized token embeddings and image structural information. In their another study [12] cross-modal deep networks for document image classification were applied to train NASNet-Large extracted image features and Bert extracted textual features jointly. In the third study by the same authors [41] a self-attention based mutual learning strategy were proposed which aimed to learn positive knowledge between image and text modalities. Mandivarapu et al. [42] used Graph CNN to model textual, visual and layout information. Another study using Graph CNN was done by Xiong et al. [43]. Siddiqui et al. [44] investigated the effect of zero shot learning on document image classification tasks. So, the authors learnt image and textual embedding features and calculated their matchings. The experiments on the benchmarks showed that zero shot learning achieved better performance compared to the past studies. Sellami and Tabbone [45] applied Multi-view Encoder-Decoder Neural Networks to learn shared representation between deep visual and textual features and model them jointly. In [46] few-shot meta-learning based on domain-shift were proposed by modelling visual and textual features together.

3 Vision Transformers

Transformer models which are based on self-attention mechanism performs outstanding success in NLP tasks [47, 48]. This success also attracted the attention of researchers working with computer vision. Therefore, it has become necessary to develop a transformer model to be applied to computer vision problems and ViTs have been developed [49]. The architecture of the ViTs is depicted with Fig. 1.

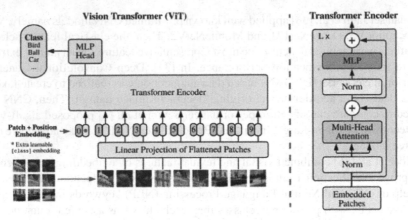

Fig. 1. Architecture of ViT [49].

The working logic of the ViTs is as follows: for a 2D-image $x \in \mathbb{R}^{H \times W \times C}$, where (H, W) represents the resolution of the original image, C represents the number of channels, to transform this image into a sequence of flattened 2D patches $x_p \in \mathbb{R}^{N \times (P^2 \cdot C)} (1 \leq p \leq N)$. While (P, P) represents the resolution of each image patch, N represents the number of patches. N is calculated according to $N = HW/P^2$ and also refers to the effective input sequence length for the Transformer. The Transformer uses fixed hidden vector with size D across all its layers, so the patches are flattened and mapped into to the D dimensions with a trainable linear projection by using Eq. 1. The output of the Eq. 1 is called as patch embeddings.

$$z_0 = \left[x_{class}; x_P^1 E; x_P^2 E; \ldots ; x_P^N E \right] + E_{pos}, E \in \mathbb{R}^{(P^2 \cdot C) \times D}, E_{pos} \in \mathbb{R}^{(N+1) \times D} \quad (1)$$

$$z'_\ell = MSA(LN(z_{\ell-1})) + z_{\ell-1}, \ell = 1 \ldots L \quad (2)$$

$$z_\ell = MLP\left(LN\left(z'_\ell\right)\right) + z'_\ell, \ell = 1 \ldots L \quad (3)$$

$$y = LN\left(z_L^0\right) \quad (4)$$

In the equations above LN is Layernorm layer, MSA is a Multi-head Self Attention block. Like BERT's [class] token, the y-state (Eq. 4) at the output of the Transformer encoder (z_L^0) prepares a learnable addition to the array of embedded patches ($z_0^0 = x_{class}$) that serves as the image representation. A classification header z_L^0 is added to the during both pre-training and tuning. The classification header is implemented by a Multi-Layer Perceptron (MLP) with a hidden layer at pre-training time and a single linear layer at fine-tuning time. MLP contains two linear layers with a Gaussian Error Linear Units (GELU) non-linearity. Position embeddings are added to patch overlays to preserve position information. The resulting array of embedding vectors serves as input to the encoder.

4 Experiments

In this study, we use ViT as an alternative to structural-based methods. The architecture of transformers is developed to apply to natural languages tasks. Therefore, some modifications should be made to these models to use on computer vision problems. We perform the necessary operations for the model setup. We also make the data suitable for the classification process with preprocessing steps. In order to evaluate the experiment results, we use precision, recall and F1-Score metrics. In addition, the receiver operating characteristic (ROC) curve is used to visualize the results.

4.1 Dataset

The dataset is composed of the official documents that are used by students in their application to Kocaeli University. There are 1044 documents in the dataset. These are grouped under 12 predefined classes. Each of the documents contains one or more pages of colorful images. The first page of the all documents is chosen to be used as a sample of documents. The samples in the dataset are not evenly distributed and there are fewer samples compared to similar studies. The dataset is divided into two as 90% training and 10% test data. The information about the dataset given in Table 1.

Table 1. Summary of dataset.

Document class	Number of samples
ALES	100
CV	100
Equivalence Certificate	71
Course Content	100
Course List	100
Diploma	100
Prep Class Status Certificate	100
Student Certificate	100
OSYM Result Documents	49
OSYM Placement Certificate	58
Transcript	99
Foreign Language Certificate	98

4.2 Image Preprocessing

The used dataset contains documents in pdf file format, but image files are required for the structural classification methods. That's why all documents are converted to image files as the first step of preprocessing. In the conversion process, 100 dots per inch (dpi) resolution is used and 3-channel 1170×827 sized images are obtained.

The size of images is too much for operations and not suitable for the usage of the model. Each image should be divided into smaller patches to use in the ViT. Therefore, the images are resized to $144 \times 144 \times 3$. This size has been chosen to minimize information loss and to perform operations easily. As a final step, the images are divided into small $12 \times 12 \times 3$ patches. Each image is represented by 144 patches. Patches for a sample image from dataset is given with Fig. 2.

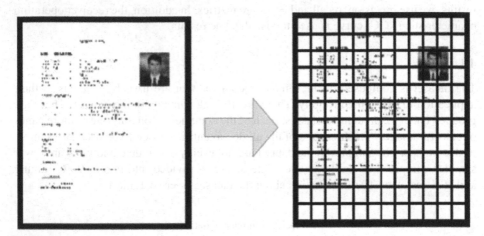

Fig. 2. Patches for a sample image.

4.3 Evaluation Metrics

Precision indicates the proportion of positive predictions which are made correctly. Recall gives the proportion of correctly predicted samples in the positive class. The harmonic average of the precision and recall values gives the F1-Score. In order to calculate these metrics, values such as true positive (TP), false positive (FP) and false negative (FN) must be known. TP is the number of correct positive predictions. Conversely, FP is the number of false positive predictions. FN indicates the number of incorrectly predicted positive samples.

$$Precision = TP/(TP + FP) \qquad (2)$$

$$Recall = TP/(TF + FN) \qquad (3)$$

$$F1 - Score = 2 * (Precision * Recall)/(Precision + Recall) \qquad (4)$$

4.4 Model

The ViT model used in the experiments is created from scratch based on the basic transformer model. Unlike general transformer models, a projection layer is added to the model as the first layer. The embedding operation is performed on the patches using the projection layer and this layer projects the flattened patches into a lower-dimensional space. This layer contains 256 nodes. The position embedding layer used in the model takes the order of patches as input and produces a 256-dimensional output vector. The outputs of projection and position embedding layers are added linearly, the result is sent to the attention mechanism. There are 4 parallel attention mechanisms in the transformer layer. The key and query sizes in the attention mechanism are also set to 256. 4 transformer blocks were added to the model sequentially. Dense layers consist of 1024 and 512 nodes and they have been added to the end of the model for classification. GELU is chosen as the activation function in model layers.

Cross-entropy is used as a loss function for training the ViT model. Adam is chosen as the optimizer. The learning rate is assigned as 10^{-4} for training and mini-batch value is set to 32. Model training takes approximately 50–60 epochs. When the number of epochs is increased, overfitting occurs. The architecture of the model is given with Fig. 3.

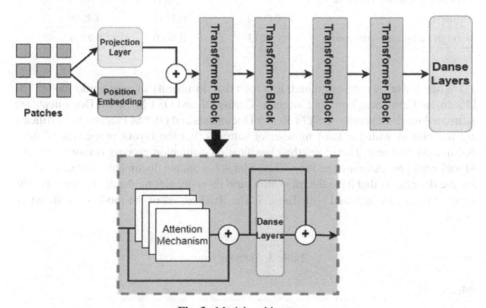

Fig. 3. Model architecture.

4.5   Experimental Results

The test results are evaluated according to the precision, recall and F1-Score metrics and the values in the Table 2 are obtained.

Table 2. Experimental result.

Class	Precision	Recall	F1-score
ALES	0.5833	0.7000	0.6364
CV	0.6364	0.7000	0.6667
Equivalence Certificate	1.0000	0.5714	0.7273
Course Content	0.6000	0.6000	0.6000
Course List	0.4000	0.8000	0.5333
Diploma	1.0000	0.8000	0.8889
Prep Class Status Certificate	0.0000	0.0000	0.0000
Student Certificate	0.5714	0.8000	0.6667
OSYM Result Documents	1.0000	0.6000	0.7500
OSYM Placement Certificate	0.8333	0.8333	0.8333
Transcript	0.6000	0.3333	0.4286
Foreign Language Certificate	0.7273	0.8000	0.7619

When the results are examined, it is seen that documents such as Diploma, OSYM Placement Certificate, Foreign Language Certificate and OSYM Result Documents are estimated more accurately. OSYM Result Documents and OSYM Placement Certificate are the classes with the least number of samples, but the layout properties of these documents vary less. Therefore, the classification estimation process is more accurate. Model could not estimate the Prep Class Status Certificate documents correctly. These are the documents that have the most structural diversity among the all documents. The average scores are depicted with Table 3. The ROC curves of the models are shown in Fig. 4.

Table 3. Average scores.

Metric	Average score
Accuracy	0.6442
Average precision	0.6498
Average recall	0.6442
Average F1-score	0.6273

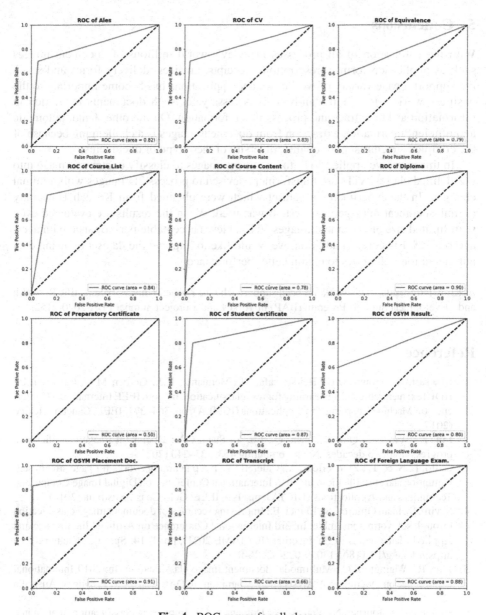

Fig. 4. ROC curves for all classes.

5 Conclusions

With the automation of all processes in today's world millions of document images such as application forms, prescriptions, receipts, invoices, delivery forms and so on are support a wide variety of workflows and applications has become important to the business world. More importantly, it is necessary for such documents to be rich in information and to extract and process this information. On the other hand, automatic and efficient information extraction from document images is a challenging because of the complex structures, poor quality, diversity of these type of documents.

In this paper we applied ViTs to document images to classify document image into pre-defined classes. ViTs are transformers devised to process 2D images with minimal changes. In the experiments a dataset which were obtained from Kocaeli University digital document management system was used. When the results are evaluated even with limited size of document images ViT achieves acceptable performance with average 62.73% F1-score. In addition, we would like to improve the dataset by using data augmentation techniques to obtain better performance.

Acknowledgments. This work has been supported by the Kocaeli University Scientific Research and Development Support Program (BAP) in Turkey under project number FBA-2020-2152.

References

1. Kowsari, K., Brown, D.E., Heidarysafa, M., Meimandi, K.J., Gerber, M.S., Barnes, L.E.: HDLTex: hierarchical deep learning for text classification. In: 16th IEEE International Conference on Machine Learning and Applications (ICMLA), pp. 364–371. IEEE, Cancun, Mexico (2017).
2. Liu, L., Wang, Z., Qiu, T., Chen, Q., Lu, Y., Suen, C.Y.: Document image classification: progress over two decades. Neurocomputing **453**, 223–240 (2021)
3. Gallo, I., Noce, L., Zamberletti, A., Calefeti, A.: Deep neural networks for page stream segmentation and classification. In: 2016 International Conference on Digital Image Computing: Techniques and Applications (DICTA), pp. 1–6. IEEE, Gold Coast, Australia (2016)
4. Sevim, S., İlhan Omurca, S., Ekinci, E.: Improving accuracy of document image classification through soft voting ensemble. In: 3rd International Conference on Artificial Intelligence and Applied Mathematics in Engineering (ICAIAME 2021), pp. 1–14. Springer, Cham (2021). https://doi.org/10.1186/s13059-022-02636-8
5. Jain, R., Wigington, C.: Multimodal document image classification. In: 2019 International Conference on Document Analysis and Recognition (ICDAR), pp. 71–77. Sydney, Australia (2019)
6. Augereau, O., Journet, N., Vialard, A., Domenger, J.P.: Improving classification of an industrial document image database by combining visual and textual features. In: 2014 11th IAPR International Workshop on Document Analysis Systems, pp. 314–318. IEEE, Tours, France (2014)
7. Kowsari, K., Meimandi, K.J., Heidarysafa, M., Mendu, S., Barnes, L., Brown, D.: Text classification algorithms: a survey. Information **10**(150), 1–68 (2019)
8. Srinivasulu, K.: Health-related tweets classification: a survey. In: Gunjan, V.K., Zurada, J.M. (eds.) International Conference on Recent Trends in Machine Learning, IoT, Smart Cities and Applications Advances in Intelligent Systems and Computing, vol. 1245, pp. 259–268, Springer, Singapore (2021). https://doi.org/10.1007/978-981-15-7234-0

9. Nguyen, Q.D., Le, D.A., Phan, N.M., Zelinka, I.: OCR error correction using correction patterns and self-organizing migrating algorithm. Pattern Anal. Appl. **24**, 701–721 (2021)

10. Kumar, J., Ye, P., Doermann, D.: Learning document structure for retrieval and classification. In: 21st International Conference on Pattern Recognition (ICPR), pp. 1558–1561. IEEE (2012).

11. Kang, L., Kumar, J., Ye, P., Li, Y., Doermann, D.: Convolutional neural networks for document image classification. In: 2014 22nd International Conference on Pattern Recognition, pp. 3168–3172. IEEE, Tsukuba, Japan (2014)

12. Bakkali, S., Ming, Z., Coustaty, M., Rusinol, M.: Cross-modal deep networks for document image classification. In: 2020 IEEE International Conference on Image Processing (ICIP). pp. 2556–2560. IEEE (2020)

13. Hatamizadeh, A., et al.: UNETR: Transformers for 3D medical image segmentation. CoRR abs/2103.10504 (2021). http://arxiv.org/abs/2103.10504

14. Liu, Y., Sangineto, E., Bi, W., Sebe, N., Lepri, B., Nadai, M.: Efficient training of visual transformers with small datasets. Adv. Neural. Inf. Process. Syst. **34**, 1–13 (2021)

15. Mandivarapu, J.K., Bunch, E., You, Q., Fung, G.: Efficient document image classification using region-based graph neural network. CoRR abs/2106.13802 (2021). http://arxiv.org/abs/2106.13802

16. Baumann, S., et al.: Message extraction from printed documents—a complete solution—. In: Fourth International Conference on Document Analysis and Recognition, pp. 1055–1059. IEEE, Ulm, Germany (1997)

17. Eken, S., Menhour, H., Köksal, K.: DoCA: a content-based automatic classification system over digital documents. IEEE Access **7**, 97996–98004 (2019)

18. Şahin, S. et al.: Dijital dokümanların anahtar kelime tabanlı doğrulanması. In: 6. Ulusal Yüksek Başarımlı Hesaplama Konferansı. Ankara, Turkey (2020)

19. Kumar, J., Ye, P., Doermann, D.: Structural similarity for document image classification and retrieval. Pattern Recogn. Lett. **43**, 119–126 (2014)

20. Harley, A.W., Ufkes, A., Derpanis, K.G.: Evaluation of deep convolutional nets for document image classification and retrieval. CoRR abs/1502.07058 (2015). http://arxiv.org/abs/1502.07058

21. Afzal, M.Z., et al.: Deepdocclassifier: document classification with deep convolutional neural network. In: 2015 13th International Conference on Document Analysis and Recognition (ICDAR), pp. 1111–1115. Tunis, Tunisia (2015)

22. Roy, S., Das, A., Bhattacharya, U.: Generalized stacking of layerwise-trained deep convolutional neural networks for document image classification. In: 2016 23rd International Conference on Pattern Recognition (ICPR), pp. 1273–1278 (2016)

23. Csurka, G.: Document image classification, with a specific view on applications of patent images. CoRR abs/1601.03295 (2016). http://arxiv.org/abs/1601.03295

24. Csurka, G., Larlus, D., Gordo, A., Almaz´an, J.: What is the right way to represent document images?. CoRR abs/1603.01076 (2016). http://arxiv.org/abs/1603.01076

25. Yaman, D., Eyiokur, F.I., Ekenel, H.K.: Comparison of convolutional neural network models for document image classification. In: 2017 25th Signal Processing and Communications Applications Conference (SIU), pp. 1–4. IEEE, Antalya, Turkey (2017)

26. Zavalishin, S., Bout, A., Kurilin, I., Rychagov, M.: Document image classification on the basis of layout information. Electr. Imaging **2017**, 78–86 (2017)

27. Tensmeyer, C., Martinez, T.R.: Analysis of convolutional neural networks for document image classification. CoRR abs/1708.03273 (2017). http://arxiv.org/abs/1708.03273

28. Kölsch, A., Afzal, M.Z., Ebbecke, M., Liwicki, M.: Real-time document image classification using deep CNN and extreme learning machines. In: 2017 14th IAPR International Conference on Document Analysis and Recognition (ICDAR), pp. 1318–1323. Kyoto, Japan (2017)

29. Afzal, M.Z., Kölsch, A., Ahmed, S., Liwicki, M.: Cutting the error by half: Investigation of very deep CNN and advanced training strategies for document image classification. CoRR abs/1704.03557 (2017). http://arxiv.org/abs/1704.03557

30. Das, A., Roy, S., Bhattacharya, U.: Document image classification with intra-domain transfer learning and stacked generalization of deep convolutional neural networks. CoRR abs/1801.09321 (2018). http://arxiv.org/abs/1801.09321

31. Hassanpour, M., Malek, H.: Document image classification using squeezenet convolutional neural network. In: 2019 5th Iranian Conference on Signal Processing and Intelligent Systems (ICSPIS), pp. 1–4. IEEE, Shahrood, Iran (2019)

32. Mohsenzadegan, K., et al.: A convolutional neural network model for robust classification of document-images under real-world hard conditions. In: Developments of Artificial Intelligence Technologies in Computation and Robotics: Proceedings of the 14th International FLINS Conference (FLINS), pp. 1023– 1030. World Scientific (2020)

33. Jadli, A., Hain, M., Hasbaoui, A.: An improved document image classification using deep transfer learning and feature reduction. Int. Adv. Trends Comput. Sci. Eng. **10**, 549–557 (2021)

34. Jadli, A., Hain, M., Jaize, A.: A novel approach to data augmentation for document image classification using deep convolutional generative adversarial networks. In: Motahhir, S., Bossoufi, B. (eds.) Digital Technologies and Applications, ICDTA 2021, LNNS, vol. 211, pp. 135–144. Springer, Cham (2021). https://doi.org/10.1007/978-3-030-73882-2

35. Noce, L., Gallo, I., Zamberletti, A., Calefati, A.: Embedded textual content for document image classification with convolutional neural networks. In: Proceedings of the 2016 ACM Symposium on Document Engineering, pp. 165–173. ACM, Vienna, Austria (2016)

36. Audebert, N., Herold, C., Slimani, K., Vidal, C.: Multimodal deep networks for text and image-based document classification. CoRR abs/1907.06370 (2019). http://arxiv.org/abs/1907.06370

37. Jain, R., Wigington, C.: Multimodal document image classification. In: 2019 International Conference on Document Analysis and Recognition (ICDAR), pp. 71–77. IEEE, Sydney, Australia (2019)

38. Ferrando, J., et al.: Improving accuracy and speeding up document image classification through parallel systems. In: Krzhizhanovskaya, V., et al. (eds.) Computational Science – ICCS 2020. ICCS 2020. LNCS, vol. 12138, pp. 387–400. Springer, Cham (2020). https://doi.org/10.1007/978-3-030-50417-5_29

39. Xu, Y., Li, M., Cui, L., Huang, S., Wei, F., Zhou, M.: Layoutlm: pre-training of text and layout for document image understanding. In: Proceedings of the 26th ACM SIGKDD International Conference on Knowledge Discovery & Data Mining, pp. 1192–1200. ACM (2020)

40. Bakkali, S., Ming, Z., Coustaty, M., Rusinol, M.: Visual and textual deep feature fusion for document image classification. In: Proceedings of the IEEE/CVF Conference on Computer Vision and Pattern Recognition Workshops, pp. 562–563. IEEE (2020)

41. Bakkali, S., Ming, Z., Coustaty, M., Rusinol, M.: EAML: ensemble self-attention based mutual learning network for document image classification. Int. J. Doc. Anal. Recogn. (IJDAR) **24**, 1–18 (2021)

42. Mandivarapu, J.K., Bunch, E., You, Q., Fung, G.: Efficient document image classification using region-based graph neural network. CoRR abs/2106.13802 (2021). https://arxiv.org/abs/2106.13802

43. Xiong, Y., Dai, Z., Liu, Y., Ding, X.: Document image classification method based on graph convolutional network. In: Mantoro, T., Lee, M., Ayu, M.A., Wong, K.W., Hidayanto, A. N. (eds.) Neural Information Processing. ICONIP 2021, LNCS, vol. 13108, pp. 317–329. Springer, Cham (2021). https://doi.org/10.1007/978-3-030-92185-9_26

44. Siddiqui, S.A., Dengel, A., Ahmed, S.: Analyzing the potential of zero-shot recognition for document image classification. In: Lladós, J., Lopresti, D., Uchida, S. (eds.) Document Analysis and Recognition – ICDAR. LNCS, vol. 12824, pp. 293–304. Springer, Cham (2021). https://doi.org/10.1007/978-3-030-86337-1_20

45. Sellami, A., Tabbone, S.: EDNets: deep feature learning for document image classification based on multi-view encoder-decoder neural networks. In: Lladós, J., Lopresti, D., Uchida, S. (eds.) Document Analysis and Recognition – ICDAR. LNCS, vol. 12824, pp. 318–332. Springer, Cham (2021). https://doi.org/10.1007/978-3-030-86337-1_22

46. Mandivarapu, J.K., Bunch, E., Fung, G.: Domain agnostic few-shot learning for document intelligence. CoRR abs/2111.00007 (2021). https://arxiv.org/abs/2111.00007

47. Vaswani, A., et al.: Attention is all you need. CoRR abs/1706.03762 (2017). https://arxiv.org/abs/1706.03762

48. Devlin, J., Chang, M.W., Lee, K., Toutanova, K.: Bert: pre-training of deep bidirectional transformers for language understanding. CoRR abs/1810.04805 (2018). https://arxiv.org/abs/1810.04805

49. Dosovitskiy, A., et al.: An image is worth 16x16 words: transformers for image recognition at scale. CoRR abs/2010.11929 (2020). https://arxiv.org/abs/2010.11929

Rice Plant Disease Detection Using Image Processing and Probabilistic Neural Network

İrfan Ökten[1]([✉]) [iD] and Uğur Yüzgeç[2] [iD]

[1] Tatvan Vocational School, Bitlis Eren University, Bitlis 13200, Turkey
iokten@beu.edu.tr
[2] Bilecik Seyh Edebali University, Bilecik 11210, Turkey
ugur.yuzgec@bilecik.edu.tr

Abstract. Considering the worldwide rice consumption, it is seen that rice has an important place. The rice plant is the most cultivated plant after corn and wheat from the grass family. One of the latest research topics in agriculture is the identification or classification of diseases from images of a plant's leaves. In this study, a computer-aided classification system has been developed to detect whether the rice plant is diseased or not. This developed system consists of four different stages. These are image pre-processing, segmentation, feature extraction, and classification. First, the images were pre-processed with the median filtering method, then OTSU method was used for segmentation. The GLCM (Gray Level Co-occurrence Matrix) method was used to extract the features of the segmented images. Then, it was determined whether the rice plant is diseased from the image by using the Probabilistic Neural Network (PNN), one of the Artificial Neural Networks (ANN) models. An interface has been developed to do all these stages from one place. The accuracy rate of this system, which detects the disease of the rice plants, was determined as 76.8%.

Keywords: Artificial Neural Network · Classification · Probabilistic Neural Network · Image processing · Rice crop

1 Introduction

The total crop in agricultural products has gained importance with the increase in the world population. For this reason, the detection of plant diseases affecting the total crop has also become one of the important research topics. Plant diseases are one of the reasons that reduce the yield and quality of agricultural products [1]. If these diseases which cause both yield and quality decline are not prevented, the total crop will be directly affected. The main problem regarding the plant diseases is that the plants cannot be monitored at regular intervals. It is important to constantly monitor the diseases that may occur in the plant, as they vary annually depending on the weather conditions. It is a bit more difficult to monitor plants growing in wetlands, such as rice plant, which is the subject of this study, compared to other plant species. This study is about detecting the diseases of rice plant, which is consumed in almost every country in the world, using

M. N. Seyman (Ed.): ICECENG 2022, LNICST 436, pp. 82–94, 2022.
https://doi.org/10.1007/978-3-031-01984-5_7

image processing and artificial neural networks. Generally, diseases in plants are caused by various fungi, bacteria or viruses. The most common diseases found in rice plants are Bacterial Leaf Blight, Brown Spot, Leaf Smut, Leaf Blast and Sheath [2]. These diseases show differences according to the growing region. Some of these diseases are not seen at all in certain regions. Therefore, it is difficult to obtain the data necessary for the classification of all diseases. In this study, two classifications were made according to the data set obtained. The first class includes images of Brown Spot, Hispa and Leaf Blast, and the second class includes images of healthy rice plants.

Artificial neural networks show great promise in the detection of diseases in agricultural areas today. Some of the studies on disease detection in agricultural products with Artificial Neural Network in the literature are as follows. In recent years, artificial neural networks and deep learning methods have been used to analyze diseases of tea [3], apple [4], tomato [5], grapevine, peach and pear [6], wheat [7]. Malvika et al. used image preprocessing, feature extraction and Artificial Neural Network to detect cotton leaf disease early [8]. Detection of plant diseases is limited by the visual abilities of the person. Therefore, computer visualization methods have started to be used more for the detection of plant diseases. V. Ramya and M. Anthuvan Lydia used Backpropagation Neural Network after various pre-processing processes to find the health status of the plant [9].

Gunawan et al. used an artificial neural network to extract features with image preprocessing to classify two diseases of the rice plant (Brown Spot, Leaf Smut). They obtained a 66.3% accuracy rate of rice plant disease using a 1-output ANN with 4 inputs (area, red, green and blue) [10].

Sahith et al. detected rice crop disease using RandomForest, REPTree and J48 decision tree algorithms used in machine learning. They extracted the features of the plant images using the ColorLayoutFilter function supported by WEKA. In the study, the performance results of RandomForest, REPTree and J48 decision tree algorithms were obtained as 76.19%, 57.14% and 64.28%, respectively [11].

Harshadkumar et al. removed the background of the images and extracted their features with K-means clustering to detect 3 diseases of the rice plant. They made classification with the Support Vector Machine (SVM) with the features they extracted. They achieved an accuracy rate of 73.33% in their classification test [12].

First of all, for this study, the data set of the diseased and healthy leaves of the rice plant was obtained from the Kaggle web page [13]. GLCM (gray level co-occurrence matrix) was used to extract the features of the leaves of the rice plant and to create a quantitative leaf feature system. Diagnosis and classification of the disease were made using healthy and diseased rice plant images and Probabilistic Neural Network (PNN) model. PNN has a simple structure and fast learning ability and is widely used in pattern recognition [14]. The neural network model was trained with the images of healthy and diseased rice plant leaves found on the Kaggle website. In order to test the accuracy of the trained network, the images of diseased and healthy rice plants, which were not used in the training phase, were given to the network and the results were observed. An accuracy rate of 76.8% was obtained as a result of the test.

2 Materials and Methods

This study consists of four stages in order to find out the health status of the rice plant. In the first stage, image preprocessing is carried out to improve plant images, that is, to repair noise and defects. In the second part, the diseased part of the image was found by the Otsu segmentation method. In the third step, the features of the segmented image are extracted with GLCM (Gray Level Co-occurence Matrix). Then, in the classification part, which is the last step, a model that detects whether the rice plant is diseased or healthy has been developed using the Probabilistic Neural Network (PNN), by making use of these features. The block diagram of the proposed system is shown in Fig. 1.

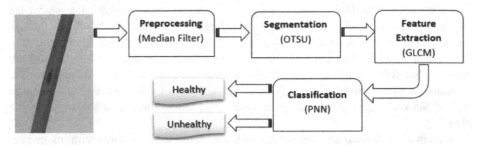

Fig. 1. Diagnostic stages of rice plant disease.

2.1 Data Set

PNN, one of the artificial neural networks, was used for the detection of plant disease. The rice plant leaf images required for training the network were obtained from the Kaggle web page. From a total of 534 images obtained, 400 images of rice were used for training, and 134 images of rice were used for testing. The images of three diseased (Brown Spot, Hispa, Leaf Blast) and healthy rice plants from Kaggle dataset are given in Fig. 2.

2.2 Image Pre-processing

It is difficult to interpret the images taken from the camera with the software. In the images taken with the camera, image distortions occur in conditions such as weather conditions, handshaking, sun angle, etc. [15]. Various image filtering methods are used to improve or reduce the distortions in these images. Among these filtering methods, median, unsharp, imnoise, average, or Gaussian filters are generally used.

Filtering operations represent new pixel values obtained as a result of changing pixel values. With the help of filters applied to clear the noise in the images, operations such as sharpening the images, making sense of the color levels, blurring, and increasing the brightness are performed. It was observed that the software developed after the noises were removed detected the disease more clearly.

In this study, median filtering was used to detect plant disease. Median filtering is the process of replacing the median value with the middle value when the selected pixels

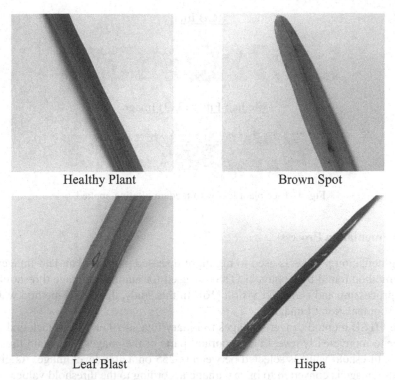

Healthy Plant   Brown Spot

Leaf Blast   Hispa

Fig. 2. Diseased and healthy leaf images of rice plant from Kaggle dataset.

are ordered from smallest to largest. In Fig. 3, an application of the Median filtering with 3×3 pixels is shown. There are 9 pixels in total in the 3×3 matrix. When these pixels are ordered, the Median value is 160. In the 3×3 matrix, the Median value 160 is written instead of 143, which is the middle value.

120	150	178	201	141
183	140	123	175	101
215	180	143	160	134
210	201	170	104	133
113	109	103	120	197

| 104 |
| 123 |
| 140 |
| 143 |
| 160 |
| 170 |
| 175 |
| 180 |
| 201 |

120	150	178	201	141
183	140	123	175	101
215	180	160	160	134
210	201	170	104	133
113	109	103	120	197

Fig. 3. 3×3 Median filter application.

A 3×3 Median filter was applied to all images of the rice plant. Figure 4 shows the image of rice and the image after applying the median filter together.

RGB Image

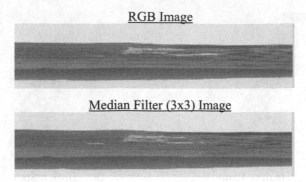

Median Filter (3x3) Image

Fig. 4. Rice plant leaf with median filtering applied.

2.3 Segmentation Process

The segmentation process is used to highlight diseased parts in plant leaf images. The OTSU method found by Nobuyuki OTSU is used for automatic image thresholding in image processing and computer vision [16]. In this study, the OTSU method was used for the segmentation of images.

The OTSU method converts images to binary images (0 or 255) (black and white) in order to more clearly reveal the important parts of the images. To obtain the binary image, a threshold value is selected between 0–255 on a gray level image. As given in Eq. 1, the image is converted to binary image according to the threshold value.

$$binary\_image(x, y) = \begin{cases} if\ image(x, y) < threshold \rightarrow 0 \\ if\ image(x, y) > threshold \rightarrow 1 \end{cases} \tag{1}$$

Here x and y are the image pixel coordinate values. The OTSU method finds this threshold by minimizing the variance of within-class density or maximizing variance between classes [17]. The images in the rice plant dataset were converted to gray level while pre-processing. After applying the median filter, which is one of the image pre-processing methods, to the rice plant images, OTSU segmentation process was applied. Figure 5 shows the OTSU segmentation process for the rice plant images.

2.4 Feature Extraction

After pre-processing of rice plant images, OTSU was subjected to segmentation process. At this stage, feature extraction of the images of the rice plant leaf was made with GLCM.

GLCM is a feature extraction method introduced by M. Haralick, and it is used to extract the feature of a grayscale image [18]. GLCM defines the relationship between two neighboring pixels. The first of these pixels is known as the reference pixel and the second as the neighboring pixel. The distribution in the matrix is adjusted according to the distance and angle between pixels [19].

Besides the distance between pixels, it is also necessary to know the orientation of the pixel pairs. The most common known directions are $\theta = 0, 45, 90, 135$ and their symmetrical counterparts. An example of co-occurrence matrix is given in Fig. 6, with

RGB Image

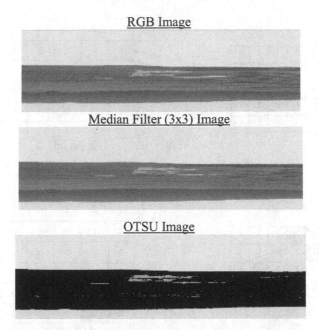

Median Filter (3x3) Image

OTSU Image

Fig. 5. Application of OTSU method to the rice plant image.

the number of gray levels calculated as 5, the inter-pixel distance $d = 1$, and the direction angle $\theta = 0°$, $45°$. Here, the pixel pair numbers (1,1) and (1,3) in the image are written as 2 and 1, respectively in the GLCM matrix when the direction angle is selected as $0°$. When the number of pixel pairs in the image (5,2) is selected as $45°$, 2 is written sequentially in the GLCM matrix. GLCM matrix is created by doing these operations in other pixel pairs.

Texture analysis methods are used to analyze the leaf tissue of the plant. These methods generate a set of statistical attributes of pixel density. The gray level differences between two different pixels in separate places are compared. Different textures can be found by revealing texture properties. Texture features in this study were extracted using GLCM. For each image, 20 texture properties such as Correlation, Homogeneity, Energy, Contrast, Entropy have been extracted. These features extracted from each image are given in Table 1.

Below are the formulas of 5 (correlation, homogeneity, energy, contrast and entropy) commonly used features out of 20 extracted.

$$\text{Correlation,} \qquad \frac{\sum_{i,j}(ij)P_{ij} - \mu_x\mu_y}{\sigma_x\sigma_y} \qquad (2)$$

$$\text{Homogeneity,} \qquad \sum_{i,j}\frac{P_{ij}}{1+|i-j|} \qquad (3)$$

$$\text{Energy,} \qquad \sum_{i,j}P_{ij}^2 \qquad (4)$$

$$\text{Contrast,} \qquad \sum_{i,j}|i-j|^2 P_{ij} \qquad (5)$$

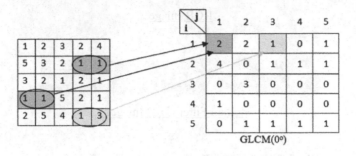

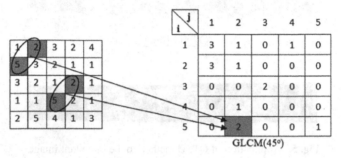

Fig. 6. Example of constructing GLCM matrix.

Table 1. 20 feature names extracted from each image.

1. Energy	6. Homogeneity	11. Sum average	16. Sum of squares
2. Entropy	7. Correlation	12. Sum variance	17. Maximum probability
3. Dissimilarity	8. Autocorrelation	13. Sum Entropy	18. Maximal correlation coefficient
4. Contrast	9. Cluster shade	14. Difference variance	19. Inverse difference normalized
5. Inverse difference	10. Cluster prominence	15. Difference entropy	20. Inverse difference moment normalized

$$\text{Entropy,} \qquad -\sum_{i,j} P_{ij} \log P_{ij} \qquad (6)$$

Here, the values μ_x, μ_y, σ_x and σ_y are the mean and standard deviation of the rows and columns of the probability density function P_{ij}. Pij are probabilities calculated with GLCM. i and j are the spatial coordinates of the function P_{ij}. 20 features extracted using GLCM are then used in classification processes, and an output indicating whether the plant is healthy or not is obtained.

2.5 Classification with PNN

PNN is a network formulation of probability density estimation (PDF) developed by Donald Specht [20]. In addition, PNN is also an ANN model and basically uses the Bayesian method and performs a probabilistic classification. Parzen Approach is generally preferred for density calculation of classes. In the formula given in Eq. 7, n indicates the number of data for training, m indicates the size of the input space, and i indicates which pattern. σ is the correction factor that controls the precision of the Gaussian function. The x value is the features extracted with GLCM.

$$F(x) = \frac{1}{2(\pi)^{\frac{m}{2}}\sigma^{m_n}} \sum_{i=1}^{n} exp\left[-\frac{(x - x_i)^T(x - x_i)}{2\sigma^2}\right] \tag{7}$$

PNN model consists of input layer, pattern layer, summation layer and output layer [21]. The general structure of the network presented in this study is shown in Fig. 7.

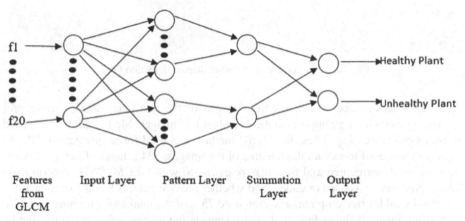

Fig. 7. Probabilistic neural network model.

In this study, the rice plant images, which were extracted with GLCM, were trained with the PNN classification method. Then, two outputs were taken to determine whether the rice plant images are healthy or unhealthy.

3 Discussion and Results

Matlab program which is a package program developed specifically for use in the field of mathematics was used to detect the disease of rice plant. It is thought that the system to be developed should first detect the disease and then present this detection to the user through an interface. For this purpose, the graphical user interface (GUI - Graphical user interfaces) in the Matlab program was used. In order to realize the proposed application in this study, a personal computer with a graphics card NDIVIA GeForce MX150, a Processor Intel(R) Core(TM) i7-8550U and installed memory (RAM) 20 GB was used.

It is planned to apply the disease detection software primarily on RGB image datasets. For this purpose, an interface design has been made in the Matlab GUI environment that will enable disease detection. The interface of the program that detects the disease is shown in Fig. 8.

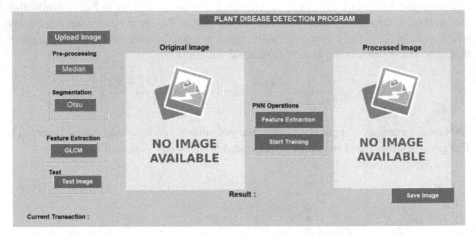

Fig. 8. The interface of the plant disease detection GUI.

In the interface that will detect the diseases of the rice plant, firstly, image pre-processing methods were applied to the rice plant leaf images. Median filters were used in image pre-processing. Then, the OTSU method was used for segmentation. GLCM algorithm was used to extract the features of the images. 534 images of rice plant were pre-processed, segmented and then feature extracted with GLCM. PNN (Probabilistic Neural Network) was used to understand whether the rice plant is healthy or unhealthy. The PNN used for rice crop classification used 75% of the images for training and 25% for testing. Figure 9 shows how to do these steps in the user interface program step by step.

The confusion matrix is summarized in Fig. 10. A total of 134 rice plant leaf images (67 diseased images, 67 healthy images) were used to obtain the confusion matrix. The confusion matrix consists of the True Positive (TP), False Positive (FP), True Negative (TN), and False Negative (FN) values. In the test process, TN, FN, FP and TP values were found to be 55, 19, 12, 48, respectively. The confusion matrix results show that the proposed model has an accuracy rate of 82.09% for the diseased rice plant and 71.64% for the healthy rice plant.

Table 2 shows the accuracy, specificity, recall, sensitivity, sensitivity and f1-score of the study test results performed with PNN according to the values in the confusion matrix.

Comparison of the proposed model with ANN, SVM, RandomForest, REPTree, J48 and Deep Learning is given in Table 3.

Sethy et al. used a combination of deep learning methods and support vector machine for the detection of rice plant disease [22]. They obtained high accuracy rates after the training procedures. In deep learning methods, feature extraction is done in convolutional

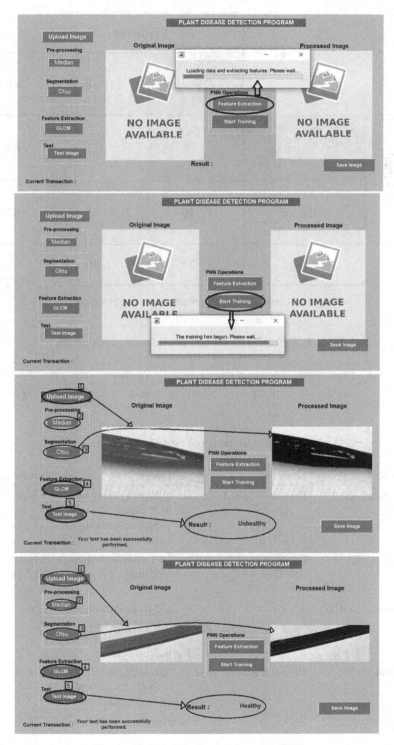

Fig. 9. Use of plant disease detection GUI.

	Predicted		
	Unhealthy	**Healthy**	**Total**
Unhealthy	**55**	12	67
Healthy	19	**48**	67
Total	74	60	

(Actual)

Fig. 10. Confusion matrix obtained for the PNN model.

Table 2. Performance measures of confusion matrix results.

Data set size	Specificity	Accuracy rate	Recall	Precision	f1-score	Sensitivity
134	82%	76,8%	71,6%	80%	75,5%	71,6%

Table 3. Comparison of the proposed model with other related studies.

Researchers	Methods	Dataset	Performance
Harshadkumar et al. (2017)	K-means + SVM	NIKON D90 digital SLR camera (Gandhinagar, Gujarat, India)	%73,33
Sahith et al. (2019)	RandomForest REPTree J48	UCI machine learning repository	%76,19 %57,14 %64,28
Gunawan et al. (2021)	ANN	UC Irvine Machine learning repository, AgWiki, GitHub and internet sources	%66,3
Sethy et al. (2020)	Deep Learning + SVM	Nikon DSLR-D5600 with 18–55 mm lens (Western Odisha)	%98.38
Proposed model	PNN	Kaggle	%76,8

layers. When the network is trained with images with large file size, it takes days or weeks to train the deep learning network. For example, Sethy et al.'s deep learning training took 28 h. The accuracy rate of this proposed method was lower than the studies conducted with deep learning methods. However, the training time of the proposed method takes approximately 5 min. Considering the training time, the proposed model takes a shorter time than deep learning models.

In this study, rice producers will be able to use this interface program developed. Thanks to this interface, farmers will be able to learn the health status of the plant quickly.

4 Conclusions

Within the scope of this study, the disease of rice plant was detected with PNN model, which is one of the Artificial Neural Networks. For the detection of the disease, leaf images of 534 rice plants were obtained and PNN was trained with these images. In order to obtain more successful results in PNN training, image features were extracted after preprocessing and segmentation on the image. An accuracy rate of 76.8% was obtained when the rice plant leaf images that it had never seen were given to the PNN, which was trained with the features extracted with GLCM. A user interface has been developed to perform all these operations. Thanks to this developed interface, the health status of rice plant images obtained from different sources has been determined quickly.

Within the scope of this study, it can be used in the detection of diseases in different plant species as well as the detection of rice plant disease. In this study, internet pages with a data set were used, considering the geographical conditions, to obtain images of rice plants. When the detection of the disease in the rice plant is compared with the deep learning studies, it has been seen that the training period is much shorter. However, the accuracy rate was lower than deep learning methods. Considering the time and accuracy rates in the detection of the disease, it was concluded that the accuracy rate should be increased a little more.

In future studies, it is thought to increase the accuracy rate with the proposed model. Different image preprocessing, different ANN, different feature extraction methods or different segmentation algorithms can be used in future studies on the user interface program. It is considered to detect rice plant disease by using deep learning methods and different camera technologies.

References

1. Weizheng, S., Yachun, W., Zhanliang, C., Hongda, W.: Grading method of leaf spot disease based on image processing. In: Computer Science and Software Engineering, 2008 International Conference on IEEE, vol. 6, pp. 491–494. IEEE, Wuhan, China (2008)
2. Rice Production (Peace Corps), Chapter 14 – Diseases of rice. http://www.nzdl. Accessed 19 Oct 2021
3. ChandraKarmokar, B., Ullah, M.S., Kibria Siddiquee, M., Kazi, M., Alam, R.: Tea leaf diseases recognition using neural network ensemble. Int. J. Comput. Appl. **114**(17), 27–30 (2015)
4. Wang, G., Sun, Y., Wang, J.: Automatic image-based plant disease severity estimation using deep learning. Comput. Intell. Neurosci. (2017)

5. Fuentes, A., Yoon, S., Kim, S.C., Park, D.S.: A robust deep-learning-based detector for real-time tomato plant diseases and pests recognition. Sensors **17**(9), 2022 (2017)
6. Sladojevic, S., Arsenovic, M., Anderla, A., Culibrk, D., Stefanovic, D.: Deep neural networks based recognition of plant diseases by leaf image classification. Comput. Intell. Neurosci. (2016)
7. Lu, J., Hu, J., Zhao, G., Mei, F., Zhang, C.: An in-field automatic wheat disease diagnosis system. Comput. Electr. Agri. Part A **142**, 369–379 (2017)
8. Ranjan, M., Weginwar, M.R., Joshi, N., Ingole, A.B.: Detection and classification of leaf disease using artificial neural network. Int. J. Tech. Res. Appl. **3**(3), 331–333 (2015)
9. Ramya, V., Lydia, M.A.: Leaf disease detection and classification using neural networks. Int. J. Adv. Res. Comput. Commun. Eng. **5**(11), 207–210 (2016)
10. Gunawan, P.K., Kencana, E.N., Sari, K.: Classification of rice leaf diseases using artificial neural network. J. Phys. Conf. Series **1722**(1), 012013 (2021)
11. Sahith, R., Reddy, P.V.P., Nimmala, S.: Decision tree-based machine learning algorithms to classify rice plant diseases. Int. J. Innov. Technol. Explor. Eng. (IJITEE) **9**(1), 5365–5368 (2019)
12. Harshadkumar, B.P., Jitesh, P.S., Vipul, K.D.: Detection an classification of rice plant diseases. Intell. Decis. Technol., IOS Press **11**(3), 357–373 (2017)
13. Kaggle Homepage. https://www.kaggle.com/vbookshelf/rice-leaf-diseases. Accessed 12 Dec 2021
14. Tang, Z.: Leaf image recognition and classification based on GBDT-probabilistic neural network. J. Phys. Conf. Series **1592**, 012061 (2020)
15. Tan, L., Jiang, J.: Chapter 13 - Image Processing Basics, Digital Signal Processing. (Third Edition), pp. 649–726 (2019)
16. Sezgin, M., Sankur, B.: Survey over image thresholding techniques and quantitative performance evaluation. J. Electron. Imaging **13**(1), 146–165 (2004)
17. Otsu, N.: A threshold selection method from gray-level histograms. IEEE Trans. Sys. Man. Cyber **9**(1), 62–66 (1979)
18. Haralick, R.M., Shanmugam, K., Dinstein, I.: Textural features for image classification. IEEE Trans. Syst. Man Cyber. **3**(6), 610–621 (1973)
19. Demirhan, A., Güler, İ: Özörgütlemeli harita ağları ve gri düzey eş oluşum matrisleri ile görüntü bölütleme. J. Gazi Univ. Faculty Eng. Arch. **25**(2), 258–291 (2010)
20. Specht, D.F.: Probabilistic neural networks. Neural Netw. **3**, 109–118 (1990)
21. Başçıl, M.S., Çetin, O., Er, O., Temurtaş, F.: A study on Parkinson's disease diagnosis using probabilistic neural network. Electr. Lett. Sci. Eng. **8**(1), 1–10 (2012)
22. Sethy, P.K., Barpanda, N.K., Rath, A.K., Behera, S.K.: Deep feature based rice leaf disease identification using support vector machine. Comput. Electr. Agri. **175**, 105527 (2020)

Sentiment Analysis Covid-19 Spread Tracing on Google Play Store Application

Usman Wijaya(✉) ⓘ, Yogi Yulianto, Meita D. Anggraeni, Setia B. J. A. Prabowo,
M. Izul Ula, and Ema Utami ⓘ

Universitas Amikom Yogyakarta, Yogyakarta 55281, Indonesia
usman.wijaya@ukrida.ac.id

Abstract. Sentiment analysis of users of tracing the spread of Covid-19 using Google Playstore application review in Southeast Asia, especially the *"Peduli Lindungi"* application in Indonesia, the *"Trace Together"* application in Singapore, *"My Sejahtera"* in Malaysia. The dataset used is a total of 6000 reviews from each application of 2000 reviews during the period June to December 2021. Sentiment analysis classification uses random forest algorithm and logistic regression resulted negative sentiment dominant. Sentiment positive vs negative for the *"Peduli Lindungi"* was 29% vs 71%, the *"Trace Together"* was 25% vs 75%, and *"My Sejahtera"* was 32% vs 68%. Classification performance checked by confusion matrix, logistic regression and random forest resulted in almost the same accuracy, but logistic regression was better with details of accuracy 87%, 84%, and 85%, precision 89%, 85%, 85%, F1 score and recall 86%, 84%, 85% respectively for the *"Peduli Lindungi"*, the *"Trace Together"*, and *"My Sejahtera"* applications, respectively.

Keywords: Sentiment analysis · Covid-19 · Google play store

1 Introduction

Covid-19 has become a global disaster. WHO has declared Covid-19 a global pandemic [1]. Since its discovery at the end of 2019 until now, scientists have worked hard to carry out research from finding a vaccine to preventing the spread of Covid-19. Specifically for methods of preventing the spread of Covid-19, the government in various countries, especially Southeast Asia, has made various attempt, including the implementation of a lockdown and delimitation on people's movements. One of the delimitations on people's movement is tracking position using an Android-based application that is widely used by most people in Southeast Asia, namely the Google Play Store [2].

Several position tracking applications in several Southeast Asian countries include the *"Peduli Lindungi"* application in Indonesia, the *"My Sejahtera"* application in Malaysia, the *"Trace Together"* application in Singapore, the *"Morchana"* application in Thailand, and the *"PC-Covid"* application in Vietnamese. Each of these applications has the same function to suppress the spread of Covid-19.

M. N. Seyman (Ed.): ICECENG 2022, LNICST 436, pp. 95–108, 2022.
https://doi.org/10.1007/978-3-031-01984-5_8

Since being discovered at the end of 2019 in Wuhan, China, Covid-19 has always been a trending topic in various media, both print and electronic [3]. Several researchers have conducted sentiment analysis studies on Twitter social media regarding the Covid-19 case, such as sentiment analysis on the increase in the spread of Covid-19 [4], sentiment analysis on the impact of Covid-19 lockdown policy [5], and sentiment analysis on the Covid-19 vaccine [6].

On this occasion the researcher intends to analyze the p ublic sentiment given to several applications related to Covid-19 from several countries in Southeast Asia. The application that will be studied is the application tracing the spread of Covid-19 from the Google Play Store, namely the "*Peduli Lindungi*" application, the "*Trace Together*" application, and the "*My Sejahtera*" application. From the three applications, the sentiment of acceptance and public response to the use of the application is sought. As known, every application has advantages and gets positive feedback from users, but many users also give negative feedback. The sentiments studied at this time have an impact on the wider community and application developers.

2   Related Works

Covid-19 is a new disease which is scientifically and medically not fully understood by scientists. Between the discrepancy in research on the Covid-19 epidemic, there is a lack of adequate information on data dissemination. The research completed by Boon and Skunkan (2020) is to study the public's understanding about the trend of the virus spreading during the Covid-19 pandemic posted by Twitter social media users. Between December 13th and March 9th, 2020, data mining was conducted on Twitter to collect a total of 107,990 tweets linked to Covid-19. To detect and analyze the spread of Covid-19 through time, the researchers used the frequency of most searched terms, sentiment analysis, and topic modeling. The most prevalent tweet subjects, as well as clustering and identifying themes based on keyword analysis, were identified using a natural language processing (NLP) technique and the latent Dirichlet allocation algorithm. The study's findings reveal three major aspects of public sentiment: first, public awareness and concern about the Covid-19 pandemic; second, people's perspectives on Covid-19; and third, based on modeling of topics and themes related to Covid-19, such as the pandemic emergency, how to control Covid-19, and reporting on Covid-19. Sentiment analysis can provide important information on Covid-19 pandemic as well as people's perspectives on Covid-19. This study demonstrates that Twitter is an effective communication platform for understanding public attitude around Covid-19 concern and awareness [7].

The increase in the number of Covid-19 cases is increasing exponentially and causing global concern and panic. The fact that tweets containing news related to Covid-19 filled the Twitter page almost every day throughout 2020. This study analyzed two types of tweets collected during the pandemic. In one case, around twenty-three thousand most-retweeted tweets in the time span from January 1st, 2019 to March 23rd, 2020, the maximum number of tweets represented neutral or negative sentiment. On the other hand, a dataset containing 226,668 tweets collected in the time span between December 2019 and May 2020 shows that there are several positive sentiment tweets and neutral tweets tweeted by netizens. The results of the classification of positive and negative sentiments have been validated using deep learning with an accuracy of up to 81%. The implementation of fuzzy logic correctly identifies sentiments from Twitter. The accuracy for this model is 79%. [8].

The impact of the pandemic on people's social lives is reflected in the digital ecosystem of social life. The case study researched by Pedrosa et al. (2020) took place in Spain. Fear and anxiety about the Covid-19 pandemic causes strong emotions and sentiments both positive and negative. Public sentiment on social media about the Covid-19 pandemic during March to April 2020 obtained 106,261 communication data taken through API analysis and Web Scraping techniques. The study of how social media has affected risk communication in an uncertain context and its impact on emotions and sentiments stems from a semantic analysis of Spanish society during the Covid-19 pandemic. The data that has been taken is labeled with a scale of 1 and 0 with IBM Watson Analytics service, where 0 represents the complete absence of this emotion and 1 represents an absolute. Then the model was built using the Super Vector Machine (SVM) classification algorithm with an accuracy of 91% [9].

Sentiment analysis of comments on tweets from users of the social media platform Twitter based on keyword trends, most of which are Covid-19 and coronavirus themes. Application of data analysis and concepts of classified NLP text analysis techniques for sentiment analysis. Data mining is used to extract relevant attributes from the conversational content database on Twitter, a machine learning algorithm for sentiment classification using Recurrent Neural Network (RNN). The training model works much more accurately, with a smaller margin of error in determining emotional polarity. Positive sentiment regarding Covid-19 from Twitter users in Spain was obtained by 71%, and negative sentiment by 29% [10].

People's sentiments on the Covid-19 vaccine were analyzed using deep learning techniques. The dataset is taken from tweets expressing feelings of Twitter users from July 2021 to December 2021. The sentiments analyzed are comments on vaccine types that are already available worldwide using the Valence Aware Dictionary for Sentiment Reasoner (VADER) tools. Sentiment polarity is divided into sentiment 33.96% positive, 17.55% negative, and 48.49% neutral. The deep learning model Recurrent Neural Network (RNN), Long Short-term Memory (LSTM), and Bidirectional LSTM (Bi-LSTM), were used to classify, the results were that Bi-LSTM and LSTM produced almost the same accuracy, namely 90.83% and 90.59% respectively. Confusion matrices such as precision and F1-score are used to measure model performance [11].

Research conducted by Cherish (2020) examines sentiment analysis of the impact of online learning due to the implementation of the Covid-19 quarantine at universities in the Philippines. The dataset was obtained from 2000 respondents from all students. The result is that 66.6% is negative sentiment, 4.1 is positive sentiment, and the remaining 29.4% is neutral. Most of the students stated that they were not ready with the online learning system because they were worried about internet signal interference [12].

3   Methods

This study looks for sentiment analysis of the use application of the Covid-19 spread tracing on Playstore in Southeast Asian countries, especially the *"Peduli Lindungi"* application in Indonesia, *"Trace Together"* in Singapore, and *"My Sejahtera"* in Malaysia. The dataset was taken as many as 6000 random user review, each 2000 reviews from *"Peduli Lindungi"*, *"Trace Together"*, and *"My Sejahtera"*. Furthermore, the dataset is text preprocessed using the NLP technique, namely remove emoji, remove punctuation, stop words and case folding. After the text preprocessing process, the next step is to carry out exploratory data by labeling positive and negative sentiments manually with the help of linguistic experts. Then the data that has been labeled is analyzed using the random forest classifier and Logistic Regression models. The performance of the built model is checked for accuracy with a confusion matrix. For more details, the stages of the model development method can be seen in Fig. 1.

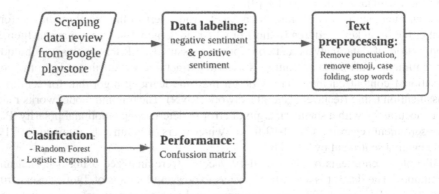

Fig. 1. Flow chart google play store sentiment analysis.

3.1   Random Forest

Random Forest is an algorithm that mixes forecasts from several decision trees to provide a more accurate final prediction. This approach is used to construct a decision tree with root nodes, internal nodes, and leaf nodes by selecting attributes and data at random in accordance with relevant standards. The root node, also known as the root of the decision tree, is the node at the very top. A branching node with at least two outputs and only one input is called an internal root. The leaf node, also known as the terminal node, is the final node in the chain, with just one input and no output. The entropy value and the value of information acquisition are calculated first in the decision tree. The formula in Eq. 1 is used to determine the entropy value, whereas the gain value is calculated using the method in Eq. 2. [13].

$$Entropy(Y) = \Sigma_1 p(c|Y)log_2 p(c|Y)p \tag{1}$$

where Y is a collection of cases/trees and p(c|Y) is the proportion of Y values to class c in Eq. (2) [13].

$$Information\ Gain\ (Y, a) = Entropy(Y) - \Sigma|Yv|Ya|ve\ Values\ Entropy(Yv) \tag{2}$$

where Value (a) is all possible values in the case set a, Yv is a subclass of Y with class v associated with class a [13].

3.2 Logistic Regression

Logistic regression classifier can be solved by Eq. (3) [14].

$$log\text{P\_i}/(1 - \text{P\_i}) = \beta^{tx\_i} \qquad (3)$$

3.3 Confusion Matrix

Classification performance is checked based on the accuracy obtained from the number of correct predictions generated by the model, to calculate accuracy using Eq. (4) [14].

$$A = \frac{(TP + TN)}{(TP + FN + TN + FN)} \times 100\% \qquad (4)$$

Precision is how relevant the results are to what we are looking for, to calculate precision using Eq. (5) [14]:

$$P = \frac{TP}{(TP + FP)} \times 100\% \qquad (5)$$

Recall is how relevant the data collection generated by the system is, to calculate recall using Eq. (6) [14].

$$R = \frac{TP}{(TP + FN)} \times 100\% \qquad (6)$$

4 Results and Discussion

This study uses the google-play-scraper library which is provided open source on the pypi.org website. The google-play-scraper library itself allows researchers to extract data in the form of information related to applications, review times, application reviews, ratings, response times from developers, replies from application version developers, images from users, and usernames who gave reviews. After scraping using the google-play-scraper library, we will get a return in the form of JSON (JavaScript Object Notation) which will then be converted to excel format using the pandas library to make data processing and analysis easier.

Commands and scripts for scraping google play store data in python can be seen in Fig. 2.

```
[ ]  from google_play_scraper import Sort, reviews
     import json
     import pandas as pd

     result, continuation_token = reviews(
         'com.telkom.tracencare',
         lang='en', # defaults to 'en'
         country='sg', # defaults to 'us'
         sort=Sort.MOST_RELEVANT, # defaults to Sort.MOST_RELEVANT
         count=5, # defaults to 100
     )

     result, _ = reviews(
         'com.telkom.tracencare',
         continuation_token=continuation_token # defaults (load from the beginning)
     )
     # merapihkan json
     jsonResult = json.dumps(result, indent=4, sort_keys=True, default=str)
     print(jsonResult)

     with open('data.json', 'w') as outfile:
         json.dump(jsonResult, outfile)
```

Fig. 2. Script of scraping google play store.

4.1 Scraping data

Scraping examples of user review datasets for "*Peduli Lindungi*", "*Trace Together*", and "*My Sejahtera*" applications can be seen in Table 1.

Table 1. Application user review table.

Username	Time review	Review	Apps
Edyh Widiyanto	2021-12-26 11:27:32	It's a bold move to make this app mandatory while it's far from user-friendly. The certificates won't appear although I have entered the right data (and to think about it, why can't they make it easier by only inputting the data once on the profile and it will integrate to the certificates and vaccines data). Not to mention the check-in issues. Please take everyone's review here as a constructive feedback and fix the app	"*Peduli Lindungi*"
Alex Loo	2021-12-26 02:43:43	Love the Otter.. Give 5 stars for him. So cute hahaha. For the app itself.. Hmmm speed can be improved as it's quite slow. Also sometimes need to disable/enable Bluetooth for TTT to work	"*Trace Together*"

(*continued*)

Table 1. (*continued*)

Username	Time review	Review	Apps
Sheridan Chen	2021-11-11 08:08:58	The app asks me to run an update on it. However, after running the update and even rebooting my mobile phone, the app continues to show a pop-up screen asking me to either update or remind me later. The only way I could get rid of the pop-up screen was to select either of the 2 option. Since I have already done the update, I chose "remind me later" which removes the pop-up screen but the app no longer shows my covid health status. Has the update been sufficiently tested before rollout??!!	*"My Sejahtera"*

4.2 Text Preprocessing

The data preprocessing stage is divided into four processes, namely Case Folding, Tokenizing, Stopwords Removal and Stemming. Case Folding is the stage to equalize the cases of all characters which are generally changed to lowercase. Then the text that has been used as lowercase is separated for each word through the tokenizing process. Then, stopwords removal is carried out from these words, namely the removal of words that can be ignored or do not fit the context. The last is the stemming stage, which is changing the words that have affixes into the basic words. After each news content has been processed, it is followed by the data filtering stage with two criteria, namely the content has more than one word and the word has a vector representation. Each word is then searched for its vector representation using a pretrained Word2Vec model. The example of several text preprocessing in this research can be seen in the Table 2.

Table 2. Text preprocessing.

Original	Text preprocessing	Type of text preprocessing
One of the worst apps I ever experienced. Crashes all the time. Goes haywire with location settings. When relogging just removes prior actions. Get this sorted out! This app is too crucial to deliver poor UI/UX!	One of the worst apps i ever experienced. Crashes all the time. Goes haywire with location settings. When relogging just removes prior actions. Get this sorted out! this app is too crucial to deliver poor ui/ux!	Case folding

(continued)

Table 2. (*continued*)

Original	Text preprocessing	Type of text preprocessing
One of the worst apps I ever experienced. Crashes all the time. Goes haywire with location settings. When relogging just removes prior actions. Get this sorted out! This app is too crucial to deliver poor UI/UX!	One of the worst apps i ever experienced crashes all the time goes haywire with location settings when relogging just removes prior actions get this sorted out this app is too crucial to deliver poor uiux	Remove punctuation
One of the worst apps I ever experienced. Crashes all the time. Goes haywire with location settings. When relogging just removes prior actions. Get this sorted out! This app is too crucial to deliver poor UI/UX!	One worst apps ever experienced. Crashes time. Goes haywire location settings. relogging removes prior actions. Get sorted! app crucial deliver poor ui/ux!	Stop words

4.3 Train Split Label

From a dataset of 2000 reviews for each application, the dataset is divided into 80% for training data and 20% for test data. The data is labeled with positive and negative sentiments manually by linguistic experts. The labeling process by linguistic experts is carried out after the review sentence is done by text preprocessing, it is intended that all labeled sentences are final and ready for the labeling process. An example of the results of labeling several reviews from the *"Peduli Lindungi"*, *"Trace Together"*, and *"My Sejahtera"* applications can be seen in Table 3.

Table 3. Sentiment labelling.

Username	Time review	Review text (after preprocessing)	Apps	Sentiment
Alex Loo	2021-12-26 02:43:43	love the otter give 5 stars for him so cute hahaha for the app itself hmmm speed can be improved as its quite slow also sometimes need to disable enable bluetooth for ttt to work	*"Trace Together"*	Negative

(*continued*)

Table 3. (*continued*)

Username	Time review	Review text (after preprocessing)	Apps	Sentiment
Chuu Chuu train	2021-12-04 04:39:55	After the otter update my phone cannot be scanned on the trace together scanner in the malls anymore it says it cannot detect so i can only use qr code hard to enter places with gantry like systems the one that opens and closes which only allows scanning of trace together token or phone qr code must go through the staff personally which is very troublesome pretty sure i'm not the only one based on the other reviews please fix this	*"Trace Together"*	Negative
Edyh Widiyanto	2021-12-26 11:27:32	It's a bold move to make this app mandatory while it's far from user-friendly. The certificates won't appear although I have entered the right data (and to think about it, why can't they make it easier by only inputting the data once on the profile and it will integrate to the certificates and vaccines data). not to mention the check-in issues. Please take everyones review here as a constructive feedback and fix the app	*"Peduli Lindungi"*	Negative
Fathur Firmansyah	2021-12-20 15:04:25	We all know the devs won't ever give us the option to disable location permission that turns on all the time. Its getting worse even, can't get inside the app without turning it on. Guess I'll just avoid any place where checking in is mandatory. Update i am glad now the app is only mandating location access for scanning, and can be turned off afterwards. no other issues otherwise	*"Peduli Lindungi"*	Positive
Sheridan Chen	2021-11-11 08:08:58	The app asks me to run an update on it however after running the update and even rebooting my mobile phone the app continues to show a popup screen asking me to either update or remind me later the only way i could get rid of the popup screen was to select either of the 2 option since i have already done the update i chose remind me later which removes the popup screen but the app no longer shows my covid health status has the update been sufficiently tested before rollout	*"My Sejahtera"*	Positive

(*continued*)

Table 3. (*continued*)

Username	Time review	Review text (after preprocessing)	Apps	Sentiment
Sean	2021-11-26 10:30:33	ever since new moving otter update app doesnt register nfc bluetooth tapping on safe entry anymore even after clearing data uninstalling and rebooting the phone and then reinstalling the app only works for the next day then it goes haywire and doesn't tap scan instead throws up yellow error on the receiving ipad safe entry app on the business end not been able to rectify it phone bluetooth works normally otherwise pretty sure I'm not alone devs please help tq	"*My Sejahtera*"	Negative

4.4 Cloud Words

From cloud words, you can find out the positive and negative sentiments of each application, it can be seen through the words unable for negative sentiment and the word good for positive sentiment. Figure 3 shows the word representation for positive and negative sentiment in each application.

a. *Peduli Lindungi* apps   b. "*Trace Together*" apps   c. "*My Sejahtera*" apps

Fig. 3. Cloud words tracing Covid-19 application in google playstore.

4.5 Sentiment Analysis

By using the random forest classifier algorithm according to Eq. 1 and the logistic regression algorithm according to Eq. 2 classifications of positive and negative sentiments were carried out. As a result, both the random forest and logistic regression algorithms classify dominantly as negative sentiment for the "*Peduli Lindungi*", "*Trace Together*", and "*My Sejahtera*" applications. The details are that the "*Peduli Lindungi*" application generates 71% negative sentiment, the "*Trace Together*" application generates 68% negative sentiment, and "*My Sejahtera*" generates 75% negative sentiment.

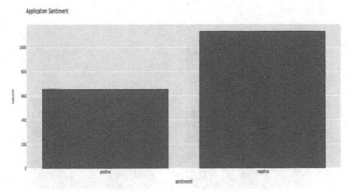

Fig. 4. Sentiment analysis *"Peduli Lindungi"*.

For more details, the depiction of sentiment analysis for the *"Peduli Lindungi"* application can be seen in the bar chart in Fig. 4.

The sentiment analysis bar chart of the *"Trace Together"* application can be seen in Fig. 5.

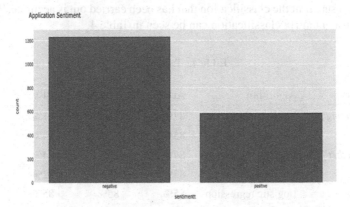

Fig. 5. Sentiment analysis *"Trace Together"*.

The sentiment analysis bar chart of *"My Sejahtera"* application can be seen in Fig. 6.

Reviews of users of tracing the spread of Covid-19 in Indonesia, Singapore, and Malaysia who gave negative responses due to technical issues using the application itself. Not from the benefits of the application the benefits of that application. Greater benefits are obtained with this application. With this application for tracing the spread of Covid-19, tracing people in crowds, traveling from abroad, and vaccine information can be obtained with this application.

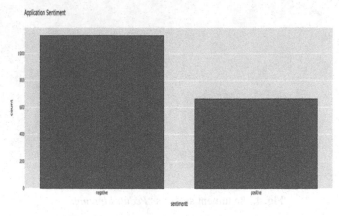

Fig. 6. Sentiment analysis *"My Sejahtera"*.

4.6 Performance

To measure the results of the classification of the random forest algorithm and logistic regression, the confusion matrix method with accuracy, F1 score, precision, and recall are used to ensure that the classification that has been carried out is accurate. The results of the confusion matrix classification can be seen in Table 4.

Table 4. Test results.

Application	Algorithm	Accuracy	Precision	F1 score	Recall
"Peduli Lindungi"	Logistic regression	87%	89%	87%	87%
	Random forest	85%	86%	84%	85%
"Trace Together"	Logistic regression	84%	85%	84%	84%
	Random forest	83%	85%	82%	83%
"My Sejahtera"	Logistic regression	85%	85%	85%	85%
	Random forest	85%	85%	84%	85%

Table 4 shows that the classification results for the three applications can be stated to be accurate and can be used to provide recommendations to those in need.

5   Conclusion

This study conducted a sentiment analysis study of users of the Covid-19 tracing application on Google Playstore in the Southeast Asia Region, especially Indonesia, Singapore, and Malaysia. From the application user review dataset, the review results lead to negative sentiments. With details of the *"Peduli Lindungi"* application from Indonesia generating 71% negative sentiment, *"Trace Together"* from Singapore generating 68%

negative sentiment, and *"My Sejahtera"* from Malaysia generating 75%. Of these three Covid-19 tracing applications, all of them produce negative sentiment, it does not mean that each government's program in suppressing the spread of Covid-19 has failed, the negative sentiment given from application reviews mostly comes from technical reviews of application use, not from the tracing method.

Sentiment analysis classification uses the random forest classifier and logistic regression algorithms with accuracy above 85% for both algorithms so that the results of the sentiment analysis classification of *"Peduli Lindungi"*, *"Trace Together"*, and *"My Sejahtera"* applications are confirmed to be accurate.

This research still has many shortcomings, in the future this research can be developed by comparing the sentiment analysis of user ratings with the results of user reviews. It could be that the user rating gives a bad rating, but the comment review gives good comments with the two contradicting review results of course this can potentially be sarcastic.

Acknowledgements. The author thanks all parties that provide support for this research study. Special thanks to linguist Mr. David Sutjipto for his help in labeling review of the tracing Covid-19 application in google playstore and department of Information Technology, Universitas Amikom, Yogyakarta.

References

1. Kompas.com (2021). https://www.kompas.com/sains/read/2020/03/12/083129823/who-res misebut-virus-corona-covid-19-sebagai-pandemi-global?page=all. Accessed 21 Dec 2021
2. Setiadi, D., Rahayuningsih, N., Surianti, S., Anwar, S.: Android smartphone among young people. Int. J. Educ. Vocation. Stud. **1**(5), 514–518 (2019)
3. Kumar, A., Singh, R., Kaur, J., Pandey, S., Sharma, V., Thakur, L., Kumar, N.: Wuhan to world: The COVID-19 pandemic. Front. Cell. Infect. Microbiol. **11**, 242 (2021)
4. Simanjuntak, T.N., Pramana, S.: Sentiment analysis on overseas tweets on the impact of COVID-19 in Indonesia. Indonesian J. Stat. Appl. **5**(2), 304–313 (2021)
5. Barkur, G., Vibha, G.B.K.: Sentiment analysis of nationwide lockdown due to COVID 19 outbreak: evidence from India. Asian J. Psych. **51**, 102089 (2020)
6. Shamrat, M.F.M.J., Chakraborty, S., Imran, M.M., Muna, J.N., Billah, M.M., Das, P., Rahman, O.M.: Sentiment analysis on twitter tweets about Covid-19 vaccines using NLP and supervised KNN classification algorithm. Indonesian J. Electr. Eng. Comput. Sci. **23**(1), 463–470 (2021)
7. Boon-Itt, S., Skunkan, Y.: Public perception of the covid-19 pandemic on twitter: sentiment analysis and topic modelling study. JMIR Public Health Surv. **6**(4), 1–17 (2020)
8. Chakraborty, K., Bhatia, S., Bhattacharyya, S., Platos, J., Bag, R., Hassanien, A.E.: Sentiment analysis of COVID-19 tweets by deep learning classifiers—a study to show how popularity is affecting accuracy in social media. Appl. Soft Comput. **97**, 106754 (2020)
9. Pedrosa, C.H., Nunez, P.S., Pelaez, J.I.: Sentiment Analysis and emotion understanding during the covid-19 pandemic in Spain and Its impact on digital ecosystems. Int. J. Environ. Res. Public Health **17**(15), 1–22 (2020)
10. Nemes, L., Kiss, A.: Social media sentiment analysis based on COVID-19. J. Inf. Telecommun. **5**(1), 1–15 (2021)
11. Alam, K.N., et al.: Deep learning-based sentiment analysis of covid-19 vaccination responses from twitter data. In: Computational and Mathematical Methods in Medicine, pp. 1–15. Hindawi (2021)

12. Pastor, C.K.L.: Sentiment analysis on synchronous online delivery of instruction due to extreme community quarantine in the Philippines caused by COVID-19 pandemic. Asian J. Multi. Stud. **3**(1), 1–6 (2020)
13. Truong, Q., Nguyen, M., Dang, H., Mei, B.: Housing price prediction via improved machine learning techniques. Proc. Comput. Sci. **174**, 433–442 (2020)
14. Harshvardhan, G., Venkateswaran, N., Padmapriya, N.: Assessment of Glaucoma with ocular thermal images using GLCM techniques and Logistic Regression classifier. In: 2016 International Conference on Wireless Communications, Signal Processing and Networking (WiSPNET), pp. 1534–1537. IEEE, Chennai, India (2016)

Parameter Selection of Contrast Limited Adaptive Histogram Equalization Using Multi-Objective Flower Pollination Algorithm

Umut Kuran[1]([✉]) [iD], Emre Can Kuran[2] [iD], and Mehmet Bilal Er[1] [iD]

[1] Harran University, Şanlıurfa 63000, Turkey
{ukuran,bilal.er}@harran.edu.tr
[2] Bandırma Onyedi Eylül University, Balıkesir 10200, Turkey
ekuran@bandirma.edu.tr

Abstract. Contrast enhancement is one of the major fields of image processing. It is a technique that is employed in devices in order to enhance the visual quality. Contrast enhancement usually deals with low contrast and bad illumination of the scenery. There are many different methods, which are devised to overcome the problems of enhancing image quality, exist in the literature. Histogram equalization (HE) is one of these techniques. To handle the drawbacks of HE, a local contrast limited adaptive histogram equalization (CLAHE) method, which is a variant of adaptive histogram equalization (AHE), is exploited. CLAHE differs from AHE in the sense that it accepts two parameters, namely, number of tiles (NT) and clip limit (CL). Good selection of CLAHE parameters is significant for the images gained in the end. In this study, multi-objective flower pollination algorithm (MOFPA) enhanced CLAHE (MOFPAE-CLAHE) is proposed to select the most appropriate parameters for CLAHE. MOFPA evaluates the fitness of the resulting images by employing a multi-objective fitness function which uses entropy and fast noise variance estimation (FNVE). For evaluation, 3 different datasets are used. The results are compared with the other state-of-the-art methods using entropy, absolute mean brightness error (AMBE), peak signal-to-noise ratio (PSNR), structural similarity index (SSI) and computational time (CT). The experimental results show that the proposed MOFPAE-CLAHE method could be used for contrast enhancement, since it outperforms most of the cutting-edge algorithms.

Keywords: Contrast enhancement · Histogram equalization · Parameter optimization

1 Introduction

In the recent decades, video cameras are not only used for recording but also employed for surveillance and tracking systems. However, images obtained from the cameras are subject to distortion, noise and poor (very low) contrast. Thus, studies in image enhancement gained attraction and therefore image enhancement has become an active area [1].

© ICST Institute for Computer Sciences, Social Informatics and Telecommunications Engineering 2022
Published by Springer Nature Switzerland AG 2022. All Rights Reserved
M. N. Seyman (Ed.): ICECENG 2022, LNICST 436, pp. 109–123, 2022.
https://doi.org/10.1007/978-3-031-01984-5_9

The term contrast expresses the difference between the brightest and darkest portions of an image [2]. Low contrast and uneven illumination cause low quality [3]. Images with low contrast may cause decline in the performance of image processing systems such as consumer electronics [4]. There are other factors that have an impact on the image quality, such as noise. Noise is an addition to image such that it can distort or make the image loss its details [5]. A high quality image can be defined as an image that has appropriate contrast and little distortion [6]. The contrast enhancement method is a widely used preprocessing technique for image enhancement in the field of computer vision to eliminate problems mentioned above. Contrast enhancement algorithms can be divided into two categories as follows: (i) transform domain contrast enhancement algorithms and (ii) spatial domain contrast enhancement algorithms [7]. Transform domain based algorithms are employed to decompose an image into different sub-bands and manipulate them separately. There are several studies that make use of transform domain techniques [8–10]. Transform domain based algorithms have two main drawbacks. First, they could increase the artifacts in the image. Second, different parts of the image may not be improved in terms of contrast quality equally [11]. Spatial approaches are commonly used and they directly manipulate intensity values of images in the spatial domain. Some proposed methods in the literature employ spatial approaches [12–14]. As a contrast enhancement method, histogram equalization (HE) is a widely employed spatial domain method because of its simple implementation and ease of use. HE, as a global approach [15], computes the cumulative distribution function (CDF) from the image histogram and tries to match this histogram with a uniform distribution. HE carries out this process by using a mapping function, hence, large pixels are mapped to large range gray levels whereas other gray levels with smaller pixels are mapped to smaller ranges. This situation causes saturation, noise and loss in data [16]. With the purpose of overcoming issues revealed by HE, many methods are proposed. The proposed HE algorithms could be divided into five sub-groups: (i) global HE algorithms, (ii) sub-image histogram based HE algorithms, (iii) recursive sub-image histogram based HE algorithms, (iv) exposure based HE algorithms and (v) local HE algorithms. Global HE methods are the most simple HE algorithms. Sub-image histogram based methods like brightness preserving bi-histogram equalization (BBHE) [17] and equal area dualistic sub-image histogram equalization (DSIHE) [18] are proposed in order to both preserve entropy and brightness. These two methods separate image into two distinct histograms. BBHE divides image histogram according to the mean value of the image whereas DSIHE employs the median value of the image for this procedure. Then, the sub-histograms are equalized separately by considering their upper bounds and lower bounds. Recursive sub-image histogram based HE algorithms such as recursive sub-image histogram equalization (RSIHE) [19] and recursive mean-separate histogram equalization (RMSHE) [20] are improved versions of DSIHE and BBHE algorithms respectively. That is, RMSHE is recursive version of BBHE and RSIHE is recursive version of DSIHE. Instead of dividing image into two sub-histograms (or sub-images), they divide image into sub-histograms until they reach a recursive level, which is usually called r, hence, 2r sub-histograms are created and equalized independently. For RSIHE, it is stated that, as the recursive level increases, it takes more computational time for algorithm to compute different histograms and enhancement becomes ineffective [19]. There are also exposure based HE algorithms are employed such as exposure based sub-image histogram equalization (ESIHE) [20]. ESIHE applies an exposure threshold in order to divide image histogram into two parts (over-exposure and under-exposure). MVSIHE [21] is another technique uses mean and variance values to decompose image histogram into four parts. It also employs histogram bin modification to set balance between high frequency bins and low frequency bins. As a final step, MVSIHE fuses input image and normalized image after enhancement, it uses a δ parameter which is in the range of [0, 1].

Local HE algorithms are the last sub-group that will be explained in this section. Adaptive histogram equalization (AHE) is one of the most simple local HE algorithms. HE is applied to every pixel based on the pixels surrounding that pixel (contextual region). Although it is easy to implement and yet effective, it is slow and it may generate undesired features in the image under certain conditions. Contrast limited adaptive histogram equalization (CLAHE) is a variation of the classical AHE algorithm. CLAHE uses two parameters, which are called number of tiles (NT) and clip limit (CL). The image is divided into M $\times$ N contextual regions according to the NT parameter. CL is applied to prevent histogram bins from exceeding a limit [22]. Performance of CLAHE depends on these two parameters. If the parameters are selected appropriately, better results could be obtained [23]. Some studies reported that the parameters are selected manually [24, 25], although automatic parameter selection techniques for CLAHE are known. Entropy based CLAHE [26] and interior-point constrained optimization algorithm based CLAHE [27] are other methods which tried to iteratively optimize the results of CLAHE. Thus, these two methods are proposed to obtain better results by selecting parameters automatically but they are not very flexible since they support fixed sizes for the NT parameter. In addition to the mentioned methods, approaches that are using metaheuristic algorithms are opted in the literature. A speed-constrained multi-objective particle swarm optimization (SMPSO) based CLAHE method is proposed [28] in order to select parameters of CLAHE by evaluating results with a multi-objective fitness function. The fitness function evaluates entropy and structural similarity index (SSI) of the images and tries to choose optimal parameters of CLAHE for medical images. It is also tried to apply a modified PSO (MPSO) on CLAHE (MPSO-CLAHE) [29]. Even though MPSO-CLAHE uses the same fitness function with PSO based LCM-CLAHE, it also penalizes the particles that exceed the search space limits. A multi-objective cuckoo search (MOCS) based CLAHE (MOCS-CLAHE) [30] is proposed for increasing entropy and preventing noise. A multi-objective fitness function that exploits fast noise variance estimation (FNVE) and entropy is employed. Although the method has an advantage in terms of computational time (CT), some other state-of-the-art methods are competitive in terms of absolute mean brightness error (AMBE), Entropy, peak signal-to-noise ratio (PSNR) and SSI. Some studies are tried to modify CLAHE instead of optimizing parameters. As a consequence as mentioned in the discussion above, each sub-group of HE algorithms are designed for specific purposes, hence, they may have pros and cons as stated. Global HE approaches try to distribute intensity values uniformly as possible whereas it may cause loss of details. Sub-image histogram based HE algorithms may fail for different scenarios although they usually preserve brightness and entropy. Recursive HE algorithms are not effective as the recursive level increases, as stated before. Exposure based algorithms depend on exposure levels, but images with large spans may not be enhanced correctly [31]. Local HE algorithms are concerned with preserving local details whereas providing high entropy. AHE suffers from amplification of noise, thus, CLAHE is devised, which applies clip limit to overcome noise amplification presented by AHE. CLAHE is a widely used algorithm in the literature, especially in medical imaging and deep learning as a preprocessing step. CLAHE is employed for enhancing fundus images [32], optical coherence tomography (OCT) images [33] and magnetic resonance imaging (MRI) images [34]. Moreover, some studies employed CLAHE for enhancing face images for face recognition [35] and for other various deep learning applications [36, 37]. However, if parameters of CLAHE, NT and CL, are not determined appropriately, the resulting images may become subject to artifacts and bad quality. Various methods reviewed in the above paragraph are tried to select CLAHE parameters automatically. Supervised methods consume time for training phase [23], and some other methods [26] do not consider all of the NT parameters. Moreover, some other approaches employing optimization techniques such as SMPSO based CLAHE [28], PSO based LCM-CLAHE [38], MPSO-CLAHE [29] and interior-point constrained optimization based CLAHE [27] are especially proposed and developed for medical images. In this study, a method that covers all category of images with different characteristics is proposed. Since a better selection of CLAHE parameters give rise to better results, with a motivation of this concern, it is aimed at selecting these parameters (NT and CL) appropriately by using multi-objective flower pollination algorithm (MOFPA) [39]. A multi-objective function is used for MOFPA which maximizes entropy and negative FNVE [40] in order to preserve local details and prevent noise. Also, from the experimental results, it is observed that the proposed method shows an outstanding performance as compared with the other state-of-the-art enhancement methods. Visual comparison is also made for sample images. The proposed method is proven to be successful for 825 images belong to 3 different datasets. The metrics used in this study are as follows: (i) entropy, (ii) AMBE, (iii) PSNR, (iv) SSI, (v) CT, which are used to make conclusion about the image quality. The contributions of the proposed MOFPAE-CLAHE method are as follows:

2 Materials and Methods

2.1 Contrast Limited Adaptive Histogram Equalization

CLAHE is a variant of AHE [22] and it has two parameters, namely, NT and CL. NT (or block size) parameter determines the number of tiles (sub-blocks) that the image will be divided into. NT has two elements, which are M and N. M determines the number of tiles in the x-axis and N determines the number of tiles in the y-axis. M and N must be at least 2 and must be smaller than or equal to image size in the x-axis and y-axis. CL is another parameter which allows CLAHE to apply a limit to the histogram of a tile, hence, it helps to prevent over-enhancement and noise amplification. CL is determined in a normalized range of [0, 1]. The pixels which are clipped using CL are called residual are redistributed until no residual pixels are left. The steps of the CLAHE algorithm might be explained as follows:

Step 1: Supply a gray image or luminance matrix of a color image, NT and CL parameters to the CLAHE algorithm.

Step 2: Divide image into M N tiles such that M is the number of tiles in x-axis and N is the number of tiles in y-axis, according to the NT parameter. If the image size is not appropriate for the current NT parameter, pad the image symmetrically (also known as mirroring) on all of the 4 sides.

Step 3: Compute the histogram of each tile regarding to the number of gray levels.

Step 4: Compute the average number of pixels in the current tile according to Eq. 1:

$$P_{avg} = \frac{P_X \times P_Y}{L} \tag{1}$$

where P_{avg} is the number of average pixels in the current tile, P_X is the number of pixels in the x-axis, P_Y is the number of pixels in the y-axis and L is the number of gray levels.

Step 5: Since CL is the normalized value of the actual CL, actual CL has to be computed using Eq. 2:

$$A_{CL} = P_{avg} \times N_{CL} \tag{2}$$

where N_{CL} is the normalized clip limit mentioned before, which is provided as a parameter and A_{CL} is the actual clip limit, which is appropriate for clipping the histogram bins. Then, the total number of pixels to be clipped are calculated using Eq. 3:

$$N_{clipped} = \sum_{i=0}^{L-1} H(i) - A_{CL} \tag{3}$$

where $N_{clipped}$ is the number of clipped pixels, $H(i)$ is the value of the gray level i in the histogram of the current tile. Average bin increment, Inc_{bin} could be calculated according to Eq. 4:

$$INC_{bin} = \frac{N_{clipped}}{L} \tag{4}$$

Then, an upper limit, U_L, is computed for clipping the histogram by using Eq. 5:

$$U_L = \frac{A_{CL}}{Inc_{bin}} \tag{5}$$

By accepting that i is the integer valued gray level in therange of $[0, L-1]$, for each gray level, the clipping must be done. If $H(i)$ is greater than the A_{CL}, then, $H(i)$ is set to A_{CL}. Else, the rule in Eq. 6 applies:

$$H_{clipped}(i) = \begin{cases} A_{CL}, & \text{if } H(i) > U_L \\ H(i) + Inc_{bin}, & \text{otherwise} \end{cases} \tag{6}$$

where $H_{clipped}(i)$ is the value of the gray level i in the clipped (updated) histogram $H_{clipped}$ of the current tile. Similarly, number of the remaining pixels, $N_{premain}$ is initialized with the same value of $N_{clipped}$. Then, $N_{premain}$ is also updated simultaneously while clipping the histogram with Eq. 6, according to Eq. 7:

$$N_{premain} = \begin{cases} N_{premain} + U_L - H(i), & \text{if } H(i) > U_L \\ N_{premain} - Inc_{bin}, & \text{otherwise} \end{cases} \tag{7}$$

Step 6: Redistribute all of the pixels that remain after clipping procedure, until no pixels are left to redistribute. A step size value is computed for redistribution process, according to Eq. 8:

$$R_{stepsize} = Max\left(1, \left[1 + \left(\frac{N_{premain}}{L}\right)\right]\right) \tag{8}$$

where $R_{stepsize}$ is the step size value and $N_{premain}$ is the number of the remaining pixels. Histogram is scanned starting from the minimum level, 0, to the maximum level, $L-1$. $R_{stepsize}$ is repeatedly computed until $N_{premain}$ becomes smaller than 1 and Eq. 9 is employed for this purpose. Simultaneously, histogram values are updated according to Eq. 9 and $N_{premain}$ is updated according to Eq. 10.

$$H_{clipped}(i) = H_{clipped}(i) + R_{stepsize} \tag{9}$$

$$N_{premain} = N_{premain} - R_{stepsize} \tag{10}$$

Step 7: The clipped histogram is matched with a uniform, exponential or Rayleigh distribution. One of the mentioned distributions is preferred and generated in the appropriate range. Histogram matching (or specification) is made between the CDF of the clipped histogram and CDF of the preferred distribution.

Step 8: In order to eliminate artifacts at the boundaries of the tiles, new gray level assignments are made for the pixels in the tiles using bilinear interpolation. Four other tiles surrounding the related pixel is used for this calculation. The bilinear blending function is expressed as in Eq. 11:

$$f_{j,k} = (1-j) \times (1-k) \times f_{00}(I) + j \times (1-k) \times f_{10}(I) + (1-j) \times k \times f_{01}(I) + j \times k \times f_{11}(I) \tag{11}$$

where j and k are in the range of [0,1] and f represents mapping function of the center pixels of other contextual regions.

2.2 Multi-Objective Flower Pollination Algorithm

MOFPA is a nature-inspired algorithm, which imitates the pollination behavior of the flowering plants. There are two main processes which are local pollination process and global pollination process. Local pollination process consists of abiotic and self-pollination. Abiotic pollination includes natural events such as wind and diffusion. Hence, the pollens are transferred by these natural events. Self-pollination is a reproduction strategy of the flowers, which increases the survival chance of the same flower species. The pollens are transferred to the same flower or other flowers of the same plant. However, global pollination process employs biotic and cross-pollination. Some creatures such as insects, birds and bats are involved in biotic pollination. Cross-pollination is a pollination process where pollens are transferred to a different plant. In addition, insects like bees may also develop flower constancy in a period such that their likelihood to visit same flowers (or plants) again are higher in comparison with the probability of visiting others. This is known as flower constancy, which is profitable for some plant species [39]. MOFPA imitates the mentioned behaviors in an appropriate manner. Birds and similar creatures (some insects etc.) use flying strategies like Lévy flight (41–43). Since the travelling behavior of insects (pollinators) is similar to Lévy flight, it is reported that Lévy flight is used to mimic this characteristic [39]. A step size $L(\lambda)$ is determined since pollinators may travel long distances with different step sizes. Hence, step size is drawn from a Lévy distribution such that $L > 0$ and $s > 0$ according to Eq. 12:

$$L \sim \frac{\lambda \Gamma(\lambda)\sin\left(\frac{\pi\lambda}{2}\right)}{\pi} \times \frac{1}{s^{1+\lambda}} \tag{12}$$

where $\Gamma(\lambda)$ is known as the standard gamma function. For updating positions of the pollens/pollinators, an updating formula could be expressed as in Eq. 13:

$$x_i^{t+1} = x_i^t + \gamma L(\lambda)(x_i^t - g_{best}) \tag{13}$$

where x_i^t is the solution (position) vector i at iteration t and γ is a scale factor which is employed for controlling the step size. The best solution found at current iteration is gbest whereas $L(\lambda)$ represents the strength of the pollination and also the step size. For global pollination Eq. 13 is used, in order to model local pollination, Eq. 14 is employed:

$$x_i^{t+1} = x_i^t + \varepsilon(x_j^t - x_k^t) \tag{14}$$

where x_j^t and x_k^t are pollens belong to the different flowers. The ε is generated from a uniform distribution in the range of [0,1]. Furthermore, a probability p is determined which represents the switch probability between local and global pollination.

As it can be seen, local and global pollination processes are applied according to probability p. The ε in Eq. 14 may cause flower constancy for local pollination. Pollens exceeding the boundary limits are set to boundary limits back. If they exceed upper limit, they are set to upper limit and if they fall under the lower limit, they are set to lower limit, in the related dimension. For a multi-objective optimization algorithm, multiple solution vectors are obtained which are non-dominated. These solutions form the Pareto front. No element of X_1 is bigger than the related element of X_2, and at least one element is smaller. This situation could be expressed using Eq. 15:

$$X_1 \geq X_2 \iff X_1 > X_2 \vee X_1 = X_2 \tag{15}$$

where X_1 is one solution vector whereas X_2 is another.

2.3 Proposed Multi-Objective Flower Pollination Algorithm Enhanced Contrast Limited Adaptive Histogram Equalization Method

The purpose of this study is to propose a quick, robust and reliable parameter selection method for CLAHE. Since the performance of the CLAHE depends on its parameters, a better contrast enhancement result could be obtained by selecting these parameters automatically. Hence, it is aimed at selecting NT and CL parameters for CLAHE such that resulting enhanced images provide maximum entropy and minimum noise. In order to achieve our goal, a multi-objective function that employs entropy and negative FNVE is predetermined.

2.4 Multi-Objective Fitness Function Of Multi-Objective Flower Pollination Algorithm

Multi-objective fitness function used for MOFPA consists of 2 fitness functions. First fitness function calculates entropy, which is given in Eq. 16:

$$H(X) = -\sum_{i=0}^{L-1} P_i \log_2 P_i \tag{16}$$

where $H(X)$ is the entropy of the image, P_i is the probability of the gray level i and L is the number of gray levels. There are 256 levels for an 8-bit image. Moreover, the second fitness function is a measure to estimate noise variance in an image, which is called FNVE. FNVE employs the difference between two kernels, namely, L_1 and L_2, which are given in Eq. 17 and Eq. 18 respectively.

$$L_1 = \begin{bmatrix} 0 & 1 & 0 \\ 1 & -4 & 1 \\ 0 & 1 & 0 \end{bmatrix} \tag{17}$$

$$L_2 = \begin{bmatrix} 1 & 0 & 1 \\ 0 & -4 & 0 \\ 1 & 0 & 1 \end{bmatrix} \tag{18}$$

Considering that image elements like edges have strong second order differential components, a noise estimator should be insensitive to Laplacian belong to the image. Since L_1 and L_2 approximate to the Laplacian of the image, difference between these two kernels is computed which results in another kernel to be used as a noise estimator. Noise estimation operator could be given in Eq. 19:

$$N_S = 2(L_2 - L_1) \begin{bmatrix} 1 & -2 & 1 \\ -2 & 4 & -2 \\ 1 & -2 & 1 \end{bmatrix} \tag{19}$$

where N_S is the noise estimation operator. It can be seen that N_S has zero mean and zero variance. The variance of the noise in an image could be computed using Eq. 20:

$$\sigma_n^2 = \frac{1}{36(N-2)(M-2)} \sum_{X=1}^{M} \sum_{Y=1}^{N} (I*N_S)^2 \tag{20}$$

where M and N are number of rows and columns of the image I respectively, x and y are the spatial coordinates. An estimate of $36\sigma_n^2((4^2 + 4.(-2)^2 + 4.1^2)\sigma_n^2)$ could be obtained at each pixel. In order to compute FNVE faster, since Eq. 20 requires one multiplication per pixel, another formula which is given in Eq. 21 is used.

$$\sigma_n = \sqrt{\frac{\pi}{2}} \frac{1}{6(N-2)(M-2)} \sum_{X=1}^{M} \sum_{Y=1}^{N} |I*N_S| \tag{21}$$

Since it is tried to achieve maximum entropy and minimum FNVE, in order to both preserve entropy and prevent noise in the resulting image, maximization is preferred. Hence, first fitness function f_1 maximizes entropy, which is given in Eq. 22:

$$f_1 = H(X) \tag{22}$$

where H(X) is the entropy of image X as given in Eq. 16. Second fitness function f_2 is given in Eq. 23:

$$f_2 = -\sigma_n \qquad (23)$$

where the-σ_n provides minimization of the noise variance.

2.5 Parameter Configuration for MOFPA

MOFPA parameters needs to be set before execution, since it is a parameterized meta-heuristic algorithm. Parameters for MOFPA could be selected according to the problem type. The problem type in this study, on account of CLAHE, requires 3 parameters to be optimized (2 parameters for NT and 1 parameter for CL). Used parameters are as follows: (i) number of dimensions (d), (ii) population size (N), (iii) number of iterations (t), (iv) upper bounds (Ub), lower bounds (Lb) and (v) switch probability (p). Values of the parameters are given in Table 1. Number of dimensions is selected as 3 since we have a three-dimensional (two for NT and one for CL) problem. Population size and number of iterations are selected relatively low as compared to numbers such as 100 or 200, in order to increase the speed and efficiency of the MOFPA. Upper bounds, lower bounds and switch probability are determined experimentally, which gave rise to better results according to preliminary experiments that were carried out.

Table 1. Parameter configuration for MOFPA.

Parameter	Value
Number of dimensions (d)	3
Population size (N)	10
Number of iterations (t)	5
Upper bounds (U_b)	[8,8,0.00600]
Lower bounds (L_b)	[2 2 0.00080]
Switch probability (p)	0.7

2.6 Methodology for Parameter Optimization of CLAHE

The proposed methodology, MOFPAE-CLAHE, follows the steps given below in order to optimize CLAHE parameters:

Step 1: Acquire gray image/luminance matrix for supplying to MOFPA.
Step 2: Run MOFPA to find optimal parameters until termination criteria is met. Apply CLAHE to the image with each solution (parameters) that a pollen includes, then, compute fitness. Select the pollen n/2 as the best among the Pareto front solutions to provide balance between entropy and FNVE at each iteration. Termination criteria is the number of iterations, and the probability p is fixed.
Step 3: Obtain the resulting image.

The illustration of the proposed method is given in Fig. 1.

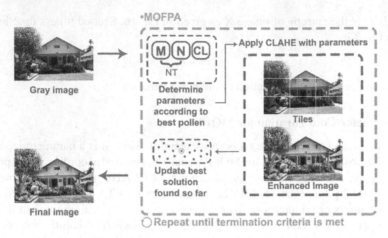

Fig. 1. The illustration of the proposed MOFPAE-CLAHE method.

2.7 Datasets

Performance evaluation of the proposed method and other state-of-the-art methods is made on 821 images. Pasadena-Houses 2000 dataset consists of 241 house images. The Faces 1999 dataset includes 450 images belong to male and female contributors. The last dataset, DIARETDB0, includes 130 retinal images. The datasets Pasadena-Houses 2000 and Faces 1999 can be accessed by using the link in [44] whereas DIARETDB0 can be accessed using the link in [45]. The details for the datasets are given in Table 2. The images in the datasets are converted to gray for the experiments.

Table 2. Details of the datasets

Dataset	Number of images	Size	Type
Pasadena-Houses 2000	241	1760 × 1168	JPG
Faces 1999	450	896 × 592	JPG
DIABETR0	130	1500 × 1152	PNG

2.8 Evaluation Metrics

Performance evaluation of the output images, which are enhanced using the proposed method and other state-of-the-art methods, is made using entropy, AMBE, PSNR, SSI and CT.

3 Results and Discussion

3.1 Performance Evaluation

The performance of the proposed method and other state-of-the-art methods are given in Table 3 for comparison. It can be seen that the proposed method outperformed most of the other methods in terms of evaluation metrics and competitive in some cases with its pros and cons. Visual results for a sample face image is given in Fig. 2. It can be seen that the proposed method provided a balanced solution and did not introduce artifacts as like some other algorithms.

Table 3. Performance results for all datasets.

Dataset name	Used method	Evaluation metrics				
		Entropy	AMBE	PSNR	SSI	CT
Pasadena-Houses 2000	HE	7.26	15.50	21.61	0.90	**1.76**
	BBHE	7.27	6.66	25.15	0.93	1.83
	DSIHE	7.27	6.86	25.13	0.93	1.84
	RSIHE (r = 2)	7.31	**2.58**	29.87	0.96	1.81
	ESIHE	7.35	4.09	**30.27**	**0.97**	1.86
	MVSIHE (δ = 0.6)	7.40	**1.55**	**34.69**	**0.98**	1.82
	AHE (63 × 63 window size)	**7.81**	23.60	9.00	0.41	50.18
	CLAHE (NT = 8 × 8, CL = 0.1)	7.75	15.27	13.73	0.66	**0.07**
	MOCS-CLAHE	7.62	7.80	21.83	0.90	6.32
	MOFPAE-CLAHE	7.61	6.64	23.16	0.93	6.25
Faces 1999	HE	7.28	21.39	18.72	0.83	**0.47**
	BBHE	7.29	8.24	22.19	0.89	0.48
	DSIHE	7.28	8.55	21.46	0.87	0.49
	RSIHE (r = 2)	3.53	27.07	13.66	0.94	0.48
	ESIHE	7.39	**6.15**	**26.39**	**0.96**	0.48
	MVSIHE (δ = 0.6)	7.40	**1.98**	**32.65**	**0.98**	0.49
	AHE (63 × 63 window size)	**7.87**	21.10	11.36	0.39	12.98
	CLAHE (NT = 8 × 8, CL = 0.1)	**7.90**	19.52	13.59	0.54	**0.03**
	MOCS-CLAHE	7.68	8.91	21.45	0.87	2.19
	MOFPAE-CLAHE	7.66	7.88	22.84	0.92	2.07

(continued)

Table 3. (*continued*)

Dataset name	Used method	Evaluation metrics				
		Entropy	AMBE	PSNR	SSI	CT
DIARETDB0	HE	5.97	75.11	9.55	0.53	1.40
	BBHE	5.93	45.45	11.61	0.60	1.36
	DSIHE	5.93	32.17	12.90	0.63	1.37
	RSIHE (r = 2)	5.90	14.57	<u>20.58</u>	0.76	**1.11**
	ESIHE	6.03	28.64	17.14	<u>0.79</u>	1.36
	MVSIHE (δ = 0.6)	6.01	**8.66**	20.25	**0.89**	<u>1.39</u>
	AHE (63 × 63 window size)	**7.38**	43.71	10.90	0.16	41.35
	CLAHE (NT = 8 × 8, CL = 0.1)	7.24	50.37	12.38	0.33	**0.06**
	MOCS-CLAHE	<u>6.33</u>	<u>13.78</u>	**24.68**	0.82	5.17
	MOFPAE-CLAHE	6.24	**9.86**	**26.83**	<u>0.89</u>	5.08

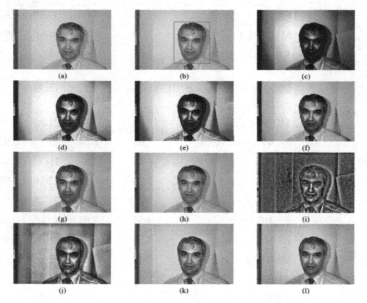

Fig. 2. Visual results for image_0105: (a) Original Image, (b) Important Regions (c) HE, (d) BBHE, (e) DSIHE, (f) RSIHE (r = 2), (g) ESIHE, (h) MVSIHE (δ = 0.6), (i) AHE (63 × 63 window size), (j) CLAHE (NT = 8 × 8, CL = 0.1), (k) MOCS-CLAHE, (l) MOFPAE-CLAHE.

3.2 Limitations and Further Studies

The proposed method is successful with handling a wide variety of images according to the experimental results. Although, it is not fast enough for using in real-time applications, it could be used as a preprocessing technique for applications such as medical image enhancement before training supervised models. Also, it could be used to enhance any kind of image to provide high visual quality by improving contrast and reducing noise.

4 Conclusion

In this paper, a novel method to determine parameters of the CLAHE algorithm is proposed. The proposed method developed to provide high entropy values and prevent noise in the resulting images. The experimental results obtained on 3 different datasets that include 821 images in total. Since images that belong to different categories are used, the experimental results of the proposed method show that MOFPAE-CLAHE can be applied on a wide variety of images. Both visual and performance results indicate that the proposed method provides best or at least competitive results for preventing noise and enhancing contrast of images. It also preserves local details since it employs CLAHE for enhancing the contrast. The proposed MOFPAE-CLAHE method is applicable in the fields of computer vision, supervised learning and medical imaging for the future studies.

References

1. Tsai, C.Y., Chou, C.H.A.: Novel simultaneous dynamic range compression and local contrast enhancement algorithm for digital video cameras. Eurasip J. Image Video Process **2011**(1), 1–19 (2011)
2. Rao, B.S.: Dynamic histogram equalization for contrast enhancement for digital images. Appl. Soft Comput. J. **89**, 106114 (2020)
3. Feng, M.L., Tan, Y.P.: Contrast adaptive binarization of low quality document images. IEICE Electron. Express **1**, 501–506 (2004)
4. Moon, Y.S., Gyu Han, B., Seok Yang, H., Gyeong Lee, H.: Low contrast image enhancement using convolutional neural network with simple reflection model. Adv. Sci. Technol. Eng. Syst. **4**, 159–164 (2019)
5. Muslim, H.S.M., Khan, S.A., Hussain, S., Jamal, A., Qasim, H.S.A.: A knowledge-based image enhancement and denoising approach. Comput. Math. Organ. Theory **25**, 108–121 (2019)
6. Gu, K., Zhai, G., Lin, W., Liu, M.: The analysis of image contrast: from quality assessment to automatic enhancement. IEEE Trans. Cybern. **46**, 284–297 (2016)
7. Celik, T.: Two-dimensional histogram equalization and contrast enhancement. Pattern Recognit. **45**, 3810–3824 (2012)
8. Lidong, H., Wei, Z., Jun, W., Zebin, S.: Combination of contrast limited adaptive histogram equalisation and discrete wavelet transform for image enhancement. IET Image Process **9**, 908–915 (2015)
9. Demirel, H., Ozcinar, C., Anbarjafari, G.: Satellite image contrast enhancement using discrete wavelet transform and singular value decomposition. IEEE Geosci. Remote Sens. Lett. **7**, 333–337 (2010)

10. Kim, S.E., Jeon, J.J., Eom, I.K.: Image contrast enhancement using entropy scaling in wavelet domain. Signal Process. **127**, 1–11 (2016)
11. Agaian, S.S., Silver, B., Panetta, K.A.: Transform coefficient histogram-based image enhancement algorithms using contrast entropy. IEEE Trans. Image Process **16**, 741–758 (2007)
12. Bhateja, V., Misra, M., Urooj, S.: Human visual system based unsharp masking for enhancement of mammographic images. J. Comput. Sci. **21**, 387–393 (2017)
13. Sundaram, M., Ramar, K., Arumugam, N., Prabin, G.: Histogram modified local contrast enhancement for mammogram images. Appl. Soft Comput. J. **11**, 5809–5816 (2011)
14. Atta, R., Abdel-Kader, R.F.: Brightness preserving based on singular value decomposition for image contrast enhancement. Optik (Stuttg) **126**, 799–803 (2015)
15. Gonzalez, R.C., Woods, R.E., Masters, B.R.: Digital image processing, third edition. J. Biomed. Opt. **14**, 029901 (2009)
16. Pawar, M., Talbar, S.: Local entropy maximization based image fusion for contrast enhancement of mammogram. J. King Saud Univ. Comput. Inf. Sci. **33**, 150–160 (2021)
17. Kim, Y.T.: Contrast enhancement using brightness preserving bi-histogram equalization. IEEE Trans. Consum. Electron. **43**, 1–8 (1997)
18. Wang, Y., Chen, Q., Zhang, B.: Image enhancement based on equal area dualistic sub-image histogram equalization method. IEEE Trans. Consum. Electron. **45**, 68–75 (1999)
19. Sim, K.S., Tso, C.P., Tan, Y.Y.: Recursive sub-image histogram equalization applied to gray scale images. Pattern Recognit. Lett. **28**, 1209–1221 (2007)
20. Singh, K., Kapoor, R.: Image enhancement using exposure based sub image histogram equalization. Pattern Recognit. Lett. **36**, 10–14 (2014)
21. Zhuang, L., Guan, Y.: Image enhancement via subimage histogram equalization based on mean and variance. Comput. Intell. Neurosci. **2017**, 1–12 (2017)
22. Pizer, S.M., et al.: Adaptive histogram equalization and its variations. Comput. Vis. Graph Image Process **39**, 355–368 (1987)
23. Campos, G.F.C., et al.: Machine learning hyperparameter selection for contrast limited adaptive histogram equalization. Eurasip J. Image Video Process **59**, (2019)
24. Rahmi-Fajrin, H., Puspita, S., Riyadi, S., Sofiani, E.: Dental radiography image enhancement for treatment evaluation through digital image processing. J. Clin. Exp. Dent. **10**, e629–e634 (2018)
25. Tripathy, S., Swarnkar, T.: Unified preprocessing and enhancement technique for mammogram images. Proc. Comput. Sci. **167**, 285–292 (2020)
26. Min, B.S., Lim, D.K., Kim, S.J., Lee, J.H.: A novel method of determining parameters of CLAHE based on image entropy. Int. J. Softw. Eng. its Appl. **7**, 113–120 (2013)
27. Qiu, J., Harold Li, H., Zhang, T., Ma, F., Yang, D.: Automatic x-ray image contrast enhancement based on parameter auto-optimization. J. Appl. Clin. Med. Phys. **18**, 218–223 (2017)
28. More, L. G., Brizuela, M. A., Ayala, H. L., Pinto-Roa, D. P., Noguera, J. L. V.: Parameter tuning of CLAHE based on multi-objective optimization to achieve different contrast levels in medical images. In Proceedings of International Conference Image Process ICIP, pp. 4644–4648. IEEE, Quebec City, Canada (2015)
29. Aurangzeb, K., et al.: Contrast enhancement of fundus images by employing modified PSO for improving the performance of deep learning models. IEEE Access **9**, 47930–47945 (2021)
30. Kuran, U., Kuran, E. C.: Parameter selection for CLAHE using multi-objective cuckoo search algorithm for image contrast enhancement. Intell. Syst. Appl. **12**, 200051 (2021)
31. Majeed, S.H., Isa, N.A.M.: Iterated adaptive entropy-clip limit histogram equalization for poor contrast images. IEEE Access **8**, 144218–144245 (2020)
32. dos Santos, J.C.M., et al.: Fundus image quality enhancement for blood vessel detection via a neural network using CLAHE and Wiener filter. Res. Biomed. Eng. **36**, 107–119 (2020)

33. Saya Nandini Devi, M., Santhi, S.: Improved Oct image enhancement using CLAHE. Int. J. Innov. Technol. Explor. Eng. **8**, 1351–1355 (2019)
34. Gajula, S., Rajesh, V.: MRI brain image segmentation by fully convectional U-Net. Rev. Gestão Inovação e Tecnol. **11**, 6035–6042 (2021)
35. Ayyavoo, T., John Suseela, J.: Illumination pre-processing method for face recognition using 2D DWT and CLAHE. IET Biometrics **7**, 380–390 (2018)
36. Yang, D., Liu, G., Ren, M., Xu, B., Wang, J.: A multi-scale feature fusion method based on u-net for retinal vessel segmentation. Entropy **22**, 811 (2020)
37. Yang, D., Liu, G.R., Ren, M.C., Pei, H.Y.: Retinal blood vessel segmentation method based on multi-scale convolution kernel u-net model. J. Northeast. Univ. **42**, 7–14 (2021)
38. Mohan, S., Mahesh, T.R.: Particle swarm optimization based contrast limited enhancement for mammogram images. In: 7th International Conference on Intelligent Systems and Control, pp. 384–388. IEEE, Coimbatore, India (2013)
39. Yang, X.S., Karamanoglu, M., He, X.: Multi-objective flower algorithm for optimization. Proc. Comput. Sci. **18**, 861–868 (2013)
40. Immerkær, J.: Fast noise variance estimation. Comput. Vis. Image Underst. **64**, 300–302 (1996)
41. Yang, X.S., Deb, S.: Cuckoo search via levy flight. In: 2009 World Congress on Nature and Biologically Inspired Computing, pp. 210–214. IEEE, Coimbatore, India (2009)
42. Roy, S., Sinha Chaudhuri, S.: Cuckoo search algorithm using lèvy flight: a review. Int. J. Mod. Educ. Comput. Sci. **5**, 10–15 (2013)
43. de Moura Meneses, A.A., da Silva, P.V., Nast, F.N., Araujo, L.M., Schirru, R.: Application of cuckoo search algorithm to loading pattern optimization problems. Ann. Nucl. Energy **139**, 107214 (2020)
44. Computer Vision Group at CALTECH Computational Vision: [Data Sets]. http://www.vision.caltech.edu/archive.html. Accessed 07 Jan 2022
45. Kauppi, T., et al.: DIARETDB0. https://www.it.lut.fi/project/imageret/diaretdb0/diaretdb0_v_1_1.zip. Accessed 07 Jan 2022

Multi Channel EEG Based Biometric System with a Custom Designed Convolutional Neural Network

Kaan Bakırcıoglu[1]([✉]) (ID), Musa Bindawa Tanimu[1] (ID), Nalan Özkurt[2] (ID),
Mustafa Seçmen[2] (ID), Cüneyt Güzeliş[3] (ID), and Osman Yıldız[4] (ID)

[1] Graduate School, Yasar University, Izmir 35100, Turkey
20500015001@stu.yasar.edu.tr
[2] Department of Electrical and Electronics Engineering, Yasar University, Izmir 35100, Turkey
[3] Yaşar University, Izmir 35100, Turkey
[4] EDS Elektronik Destek San. ve Tic. Ltd., Şti, Istanbul 34785, Turkey

Abstract. In this study, a convolutional neural network (CNN) is designed to identify multi-channel raw electroencephalograph (EEG) signals obtained from different subjects. The dataset contains 14 channel EEG signals taken from 21 subjects with their eyes closed at a resting state for 120 s with 12 different stimuli. The resting state EEG waves were selected due to better performance in classification. For the classification, a Convolutional Neural Network (CNN) was custom designed to offer the best performance. With the sliding window approach, the signals were separated into overlapping 5 s windows for training CNN better. fivefold cross-validation was used to increase the generalization ability of the network. It has been observed that, while the proposed CNN is found to give a correct classification rate (CCR) of 72.71%, the CCR reached the level of average 83.51% by using 4 channels. Also, this reduced the training time from 626 to 306 s. Therefore, the results show that usage of specific channels increases the classification accuracy and reduces the time required for training.

Keywords: Electroencephalograph · Biometric systems · Multi-channel · Convolutional · Neural networks

1 Introduction

In biometric applications, EEG is known to carry genetically-specific information [1–3]. The capacity of EEG-based biometrics was demonstrated by the effective identification of individuals using features extracted from EEG data collected during resting states or mental tasks [2]. The existence of individual features in EEG data has yet to be studied, but it has the essential advantages of implicit features that cannot be forgotten or lost and cannot be casually obtained or stolen by external observers. It has resistance to forced extraction because under stress brain activity changes, and this causes failure in the authentication. Another advantage of using EEG based biometric system is that

M. N. Seyman (Ed.): ICECENG 2022, LNICST 436, pp. 124–134, 2022.
https://doi.org/10.1007/978-3-031-01984-5_10

it can be used by disabled patients or users missing some physical trait [4]. With the low-cost sensors and the fast development of machine learning algorithms researchers have been doing more studies about biometric systems which are using resting state EEG signals [5, 6]. Besides, with different types of stimuli like visual evoked potential [7, 8], different types of classifiers were employed such as support vector machine [6], polynomial regression [5] convolutional encoders [9] and CNN-GRU [10].

Several methods in literature have been used in attempt to solve the challenges faced by EEG-Based biometrics. Below, this paper puts forward some deep learning techniques used in improving the methods, saving time in training.

Chen et al. [11] proposed a GSLT-CNN model to compare raw EEG and extracted feature performances. This model achieved better result than traditional methods like SVM, LDA and bagging trees. Di et al. [12] a CNN with 3 convolutional layers, a fully connected layer and an output layer to analyze the network for multi-classification. High classification accuracies were achieved. The performance of this model however was not compared with other models. Maiorana [13] explored multiple deep learning techniques for EEG-Based biometric recognition, getting results better than traditional methods (LDA, SVM). The work emphasizes on the useful of CNNs and RNNs.

Özdenizci et al. [9] uses adversarial model learning with Convolution Network architecture to learn session-invariant individual features for EEG-Based biometrics. However, the model used in this work was based on the assumption that the lack of consistency in data is only caused by collecting recordings in different sessions, which is a disadvantage.

Wilaiprasitporn et al. [10] uses a convolution neural network with a recurrent neural network to get both spatial and temporal information from EEG to perform identification. This work shows the strengths of CNN in this field, but it only focuses on the effects of different electrode positions, affective state, frequency bands.

Although, the studies on this topic have reached a certain stage, there are still several main difficulties. The practicality is one of the most important challenges in this area and there is still work to be done in the EEG-Based biometry to improve accuracy, privacy, usability, etc. for individual identification in Brain Computer Interface (BCI) systems. Therefore, in this study, a biometric identification system using custom-designed CNN was proposed to increase the accuracy. By using deep learning approach, the feature extraction step was omitted, and a computationally efficient system was employed. Also, the effect of selection of the channels on the accuracy and training time were examined. The dataset used in this study was specifically recorded [14] for EEG based biometric research. It was captured in a controlled environment to avoid artifacts from external environment. The dataset was carefully studied, to be used as input to the designed CNN architecture.

The following section summarizes properties of EEG signals and the basic characteristics of EEG based biometry systems briefly. Section 3 explains the used dataset and methodology, where the experimental study and results were given in the next section. Finally, the conclusions were drawn.

1.1 Electroencephalograph (EEG) Based Biometry

Electrical changes that are known as brain waves macroscopically detected by an electrode on the scalp. Then, these waves can be pictured in an electroencephalogram(EEG) in which time is a horizontal axis and voltage is vertical axis [15]. To begin the measure signals, the electrodes need to be allocated to regions on the scalp by the standards of the globally accepted 10/20 system like shown in Fig. 1. The recorded signals generally have amplitudes that are within the range of some micro volts to 100 μV estimates with frequency reading from 0.5 to 30–40 Hz. Also, there are common EEG noises that interfere with the signal, such as EOG from eye muscle, EMG from muscle motion or shifts in the electrode placements and movements in the cables.

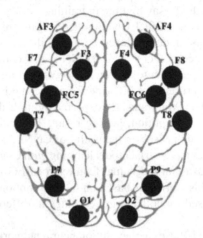

Fig. 1. Globally accepted 10/20 electrode placement system.

Poulos et al. initially suggested EEG signals to be used for recognition of person [16]. After those studies in EEG based authentication gained growing interest. Logically, some information specific to individuals is supposed to be contained by EEG signals. It is still not certain if intended or non-intended mental functions produce the best or most efficient signals. This issue is closely linked to which area of the scalp can include the biometric identification signals. The mental functions or motor movements generally used to activate EEG signals for biometric systems in the research literature may be divided into three major categories:

- Resting state, without actions done physically and mentally, with eyes kept open or closed. Only one (Fp1) electrode channel was used to get data by Su et al. from 40 healthy participants keeping their eyes closed and this study reached 97.5% correct recognition rate (CRR) [17].
- Event-Related Potential (ERP) signals stimulated from visual input or motor event. 78% identification accuracy was reached by Singh al et al. from single channel raw signals recorded off 10 healthy participants [18].
- Intentional Mental Activities, such as counting in the mind or motor imagery. Marcel et al. used 8 electrodes to record signals from 9 participants while they were imagining hand movements. They reported a 7.1% half total error rate [3].

The resting state with eyes closed modality was chosen for the purpose of this research because the creators of the dataset [14] claimed it to give the best results which is also supported with the literature studies.

A good biometrics system must meet some standards like universality, uniqueness, permanence and performance [19]. Just like the other methods, EEG Based biometrics has its own pros and cons. When EEG compared with other modalities like face, fingerprint, EEG has a clear advantage in universality and uniqueness. Therefore, the aim of this study is to propose an EEG-based biometry system that overcomes the other challenges of biometric identification such as permanence and performance.

2 Material and Method

"Biometric EEG Database" (BED) [14] was chosen for this study. BED is a new dataset for EEG-based biometric using a low-cost EEG device. BED is a collection of EEG recordings by 21 healthy subjects while they experience 12 different stimuli. The images provided are aimed at extracting specific emotions, flashing Visual Evoked Potentials (VEP) with flashing black color with frequencies 3, 5, 7 and 10 Hz respectively and mathematical computations VEP at 3, 5, 6, and 10 Hz and resting state with eyes open and close. EEG signals are collected in 3 section each separated by one week to allow for the analysis of the template ageing. EEG signals collected from 14 channels with Emotiv EPOC + portable EEG headset. Sensors were placed according to 10/20 system to AF3, F7, F3, FC5, T7, P7, O1, O2, P8, T8, FC6, F4, F8, AF4 [14]. According to studies it was understood that best performance for biometric is taken from the resting state with eyes closed [20, 21].

2.1 Preparing the Raw EEG signals as Input to the Convolutional Neural Network

Raw EEG signals from resting with eyes closed were used in this study. These signals are 120 s long, to get better results using the data in its best performance, the sliding window approach was applied. 5 s was chosen for window size overlap period is 2.5 s shown in Fig. 2. 14 channels are shown in Fig. 3 every color represent different channel. Resting Data from three recording sessions were used to obtain a $14 \times 1280 \times 2870$ data sample for classification, where 14 is the number of channels, 1280 is the size of windows, and 2870 is the number of samples.

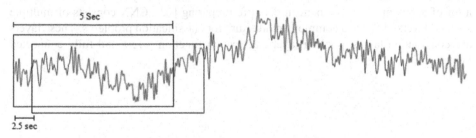

Fig. 2. Windowing size and overlapping.

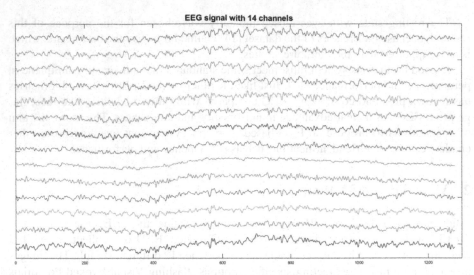

Fig. 3. Raw 14 channels EEG signal after windowing.

The data was then normalized because some of the data are differently scaled, and machine learning algorithms find trends by comparing features from data points. Normalization fixes this scale problem, and the normalized data was fed as input to the CNN.

To improve accuracy and computation time, the usage of lower number of channels was also considered. F3, F4, O1 and O2 channels which are shown to be more dominant in EEG biometrics [20], were isolated and used as input data to the same structure CNN with different input size.

Due to limited sample number, fivefold cross validation method was only used. After the whole dataset was mixed once, it was divided into two parts as 20% for test and 80% for training, which are selected in distinctly in each trial.

2.2 Designed Convolutional Neural Network Architecture

The Convolutional Neural Network is an architecture of deep learning that is an alteration of standard Neural Network for handling multiple arrays of data such as pictures, signals, and languages. One significant feature of CNN, which separates it from other machine learning calculations, is its capacity to pre-process the data by itself. In this manner, a lot of assets may not be spent in data pre-preparing [22]. CNN consists of multiple stacked layers to create a complex architecture for classification problems. These layers are convolution layers, pooling layers, activation function layers and fully connected layers [23].

There are batch normalization layer and ReLU layer, following the convolutional layer. The Softmax layer and a classification layer follow the fully connected layer because it contains a softmax function, which can be also considered as a multi-class generalization of the logistic sigmoid function. The optimum values of the number of layers and parameters were obtained heuristically in network architecture as shown in Fig. 4 for the given problem.

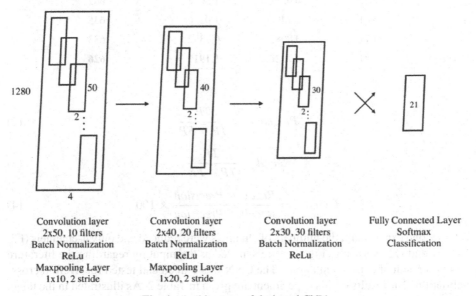

Convolution layer	Convolution layer	Convolution layer	Fully Connected Layer
2x50, 10 filters	2x40, 20 filters	2x30, 30 filters	Softmax
Batch Normalization	Batch Normalization	Batch Normalization	Classification
ReLu	ReLu	ReLu	
Maxpooling Layer	Maxpooling Layer		
1x10, 2 stride	1x20, 2 stride		

Fig. 4. Architecture of designed CNN.

3 Results and Discussion

As described in the previous section, the dataset was prepared for fivefold, and stochastic gradient descent with momentum (SGDM) is chosen to train the network with an initial learning rate of 0.01. Maximum number of epochs are chosen as 15. Herein, an epoch means full training cycle on the whole training data set and the data is shuffled in every epoch. Mini-batch size of 64 is chosen, and the stride number of 2 is selected for each max pooling layer.

Table 1 summarizes the correct classification rate (CCR) loss of the classification along with the training time for 14 channel input classification experiment and F1 score which is calculated from precision and recall. This metrics' equations are given in Eq. (1) to Eq. (4). True positive (TP), true negative (TN), false positive (FP) and false negative (FN) are used in these equations from confusion matrix.

$$CCR = \frac{Correct\ Classification}{Total\ Samples} \times 100 \qquad (1)$$

Table 1. Experimental results with 14 channels input

K-Fold	CCR (%)	F1 Score	Loss (Cross Entropy)	Time Elapsed (seconds)
1	75.26	0.7485	1.1925	629
2	68.12	0.6798	1.4934	631
3	62.89	0.6278	1.5098	602
4	75.61	0.7485	1.0236	635
5	81.71	0.8085	0.7392	633
Average	**72.71**	**0.7226**	**1.1917**	**626**

$$Precision = \frac{TP}{TP + FP} \tag{2}$$

$$Recall = \frac{TP}{TP + FN} \tag{3}$$

$$F1score = \frac{Recall \times Precision}{Recall + Precision} \times 100 \tag{4}$$

As a second experiment, the numbers of channels were reduced and only 4-channels (F3, F4, O1 and O2), shown in Fig. 4, were selected as the input by regarding the literature and as a result of experimentations. The CNN was trained and tested for fivefold cross-validation. The results of this experiment are given in Table 2. As illustrated in the table, the elapsed time is almost halved as expected but there is no a linear relationship between number of channel and training time, while channel number is decreasing 3.5, time is decreasing almost 2 times. since the data collected from all channels were interrelated, the network struggles to reach the valuable information. Thus, the accuracy rates increase approximately 10%, which shows that the proposed CNN is more successful in extracting meaningful information from the selected channels (Fig. 5).

Table 2. Experimental Results with 4 Channels input

K-Fold	CCR (%)	F1 score	Loss (Cross Entropy)	Time elapsed (seconds)
1	87.28	0.8746	0.4913	305
2	85.89	0.8366	0.5746	305
3	81.18	0.8179	0.7041	298
4	80.49	0.8063	0.8049	300
5	82.75	0.8333	0.7006	326
Average	**83.51**	**0.8137**	**0.5951**	**306**

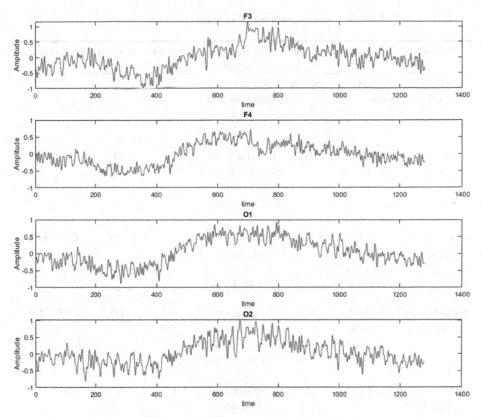

Fig. 5. Raw EEG signals from 4 channel

Table 3 presents a comparison of recent EEG biometric classification studies.

The first three studies [5, 7, 8] have high correct classification rate however, they do feature extraction preprocessing before feeding the classifiers, which increases complexity. In [9], raw data directly as input to a convolutional encoder which is similar to our first experiment and reaches the similar CCR. Comparing the results of previous studies with the same dataset [14, 20], our study outperforms in terms of CCR of 83.5%, thanks to learning abilities of CNN.

Table 3. A comparison with the existing works in literature

Reports	Features	Task	Classification Method	Electrode	Subject	Performance
Rocca et al. [5]	AR Coefficients	Resting	Polynomial regression classifier	5	45	CCR: 95
Yazdani et al. [7]	AR Coefficients & PSD	VEP	Fisher's linear Discriminant & K nearest neighbor classifier	64	20	CCR: 100
Su and Xia [8]	AR Coefficients & PSD	Resting	K-NN Kohonen's LVQ FDA	1	40	CCR: 97.5
Su and Farzin [17]	EEMD-based InsAmp	VEP	Linear discriminant analysis & 3 nearest neighbor classifier	1	118	CCR: 95.9
Özdenizci el al.[9]	Raw EEG	VEP	Convolutional Encoder	16	10	CCR: 72
Gonzales el al.[14]	MFCC	Resting (EC)	Hidden Marko models	1	21	CCR: 40.25
Katsigiannis et al.[20]	MFCC	VEP	Auto-regressor model	1	21	CCR: 29.69
Our Study (14 Ch.)	Raw EEG	Resting (EC)	Convolutional Neural Network	14	21	CCR: 72.71
Our Study (4 Ch.)	Raw EEG	Resting (EC)	Convolutional Neural Network	4	21	CCR: 83.51

4 Conclusion

In this study, it has been demonstrated that CNN can be a promising classification tool for this problem with the ability of representing data without any feature extraction steps. Thus, a more efficient system can be designed with CNN. A custom CNN is designed with three convolution layers, two Max Pooling layers, one fully connected layer and a Softmax layer. The proposed method does not require feature extraction hence, saving computational time. A relatively high classification accuracy is achieved in this work compared to other models. This work also shows that reducing the number of electrode channels improves accuracy and decreases computation time.

In future studies, the effect of each channel on the classification task will be examined, the effects of combining CNN with other deep learning techniques like RNN will be also explored.

Acknowledgements. This study is funded by the Scientific and Technological Research Council of Turkey (TUBITAK-2244) Grant no: 119C171.

References

1. Paranjape, R.B., Mahovsky, J., Benedicenti, L., Koles, Z.: The electroencephalogram as a biometric. Can Conf. Electr. Comput. Eng. **2**, 1363–1366 (2001)
2. Poulos, M., Rangoussi, M., Alexandris, N., Evangelou, A.: Person identification from the EEG using nonlinear signal classification. Methods Inf. Med. **41**, 64–75 (2002)
3. Marcel, S., Millan, J.R.: Person authentication using brainwaves (EEG) and maximum a posteriori model adaptation. IEEE Trans. Pattern Anal. Mach. Intell. **29**, 743–748 (2007)
4. Damaševičius, R., Maskeliunas, R., Kazanavičius, E., Woźniak, M.: Combining cryptography with EEG biometrics. Comput. Intell. Neurosci. **2**, 1–11 (2018)
5. Rocca, D.L., Campisi, P., Scarano, G.: EEG biometrics for individual recognition in resting state with closed eyes. In: 2012 BIOSIG-Proceedings of the International Conference, IEEE, Darmstadt, Germany (2012)
6. Dan, Z., Xifeng, Z., Qiangang, G.: An identification system based on portable EEG acquisition equipment. In: Proceedings of 2013 3rd International Conference on Intelligence Systems and Design Engineering, Appl ISDEA, pp. 281–284. IEEE, Kong, China (2013)
7. Yazdani, A., et al.: Fisher linear discriminant based person identification using visual evoked potentials. In: International Conf Signal Process Proceedings, ICSP, pp. 1677–1680. IEEE, Beijing, China (2008)
8. Su, F., et al.: EEG-based personal identification: from proof-of-concept to a practical system. In: 2010 20th Proceedings of International Conference on Pattern Recognition, pp. 3728–3731. IEEE, Istanbul, Turkey (2010)
9. Özdenizci, O., Wang, Y., KoikeAkino, T., Erdoğmuş, D.: Adversarial deep learning in EEG biometrics. IEEE Signal Process Lett. **26**, 710 (2019)
10. Wilaiprasitporn, T., et al.: Affective EEG-based person identification using the deep learning approach. IEEE Trans. Cogn. Dev. Syst. **12**, 486–496 (2020)
11. Chen, J.X., Mao, Z.J., Yao, W.X., Huang, Y.F.: EEG-based biometric identification with convolutional neural network. Multimed. Tools App. **79**, 10655–10675 (2020)
12. Di, Y., et al.: Using convolutional neural networks for identification based on EEG signals. In: 2018 10th International Conference on Intelligence Human-Machine System and Cybernetics IHMSC, pp. 119–122. IEEE, Hangzhou, China (2018)

13. Maiorana, E.: Deep learning for EEG-based biometric recognition. Neurocomputing **410**, 374–386 (2020)
14. Arnau-Gonzalez, P., Katsigiannis, S., Arevalillo-Herraez, M., Ramzan, N.B.: A new data set for EEG-based biometrics. IEEE Internet Things J. **8**, 12219–12230 (2021)
15. Nakanishi, I., Baba, S., Miyamoto, C.: EEG based biometric authentication using new spectral features. In: Proceedings of ISPACS 2009 International Symposium on Intelligent Signal Processing and Communication Systems, pp 651–654. IEEE, Kanazawa, Japan (2009)
16. Poulos, M., Rangoussi, M., Alexandris, N.: Neural network based person identification using EEG features. In: ICASSP, IEEE International Conference Acoustic Speech Signal Process, pp. 1117–1120. IEEE, Phoenix, USA (1999)
17. Yang, S., Deravi, F., Hoque, S.: Task sensitivity in EEG biometric recognition. Pattern Anal. Appl. **21**, 105–117 (2018)
18. Singhal, G.K., Ramkumar, P.: Person identification using evoked potentials and peak matching. In: 2007 Biometrics Symposium, BSYM. IEEE, Baltimore, USA (2007)
19. Goudiaby, B., Othmani, A., Nait-ali, A.: EEG biometrics for person verification. In: Nait-ali, A. (ed.) Hidden Biometrics, pp. 45–69. Springer, Singapore (2020). https://doi.org/10.1007/978-981-13-0956-4_3
20. Katsigiannis, S., Arnau-Gonzalez, P., Arevalillo-Herraez, M., Ramzan, N.: Single-channel EEG-based subject identification using visual stimuli. In: 2021 IEEE EMBS International Conference on Biomedical and Health Informatics, pp. 1–4. IEEE, Athens, Greece (2021)
21. Ma, L., Minett, J.W., Blu, T., Wang, W.S.Y.: Resting state EEG-based biometrics for individual identification using convolutional neural networks. In: Annual International Conference of the IEEE Engineering in Medicine and Biology Society, pp. 2848–2851. IEEE, Milan, Italy (2015)
22. Team, D.: Convolutional Neural Networks tutorial - Learn how machines interpret images - DataFlair. https://data-flair.training/blogs/convolutional-neural-networks-tutorial/. Accessed 16 Apr 2020
23. Neapolitan, R.E., Jiang, X.: Artificial Intelligence : With an Introduction to Machine Learning. 2nd edn. Chapman and Hall/CRC, London (2018)

A Hybrid Machine Learning Approach to Fabric Defect Detection and Classification

Swash Sami Mohammed and Hülya Gökalp Clarke$^{(\boxtimes)}$

Ondokuz Mayıs University, 55270 Samsun, Turkey
hulya.gokalp@omu.edu.tr

Abstract. This paper proposes a novel approach to detect and classify defects in fabric. Fabric defects may cause a roll of fabric to be graded as second or worse in quality checks, and may affect sales. Traditionally, fabrics are inspected by skilled workers at an inspection platform, which is a long and tiring process, and error-prone. Automated detection of defects in fabric has the potential to eliminate human errors and improve accuracy; therefore it has been an area of research over the last decade. This paper proposes a novel model to detect and classify defects in fabric by training and evaluating our model using the AITEX data set. In the proposed model, the images of fabrics are first fed into U-Net, which is a convolutional neural network (CNN), to determine whether the fabric is defect-free or not. VGG16 and random forest are then used to classify the defects in the fabrics. The training settings of the model were chosen as initial learning rate = 0.001, $\beta1 = 0.9$ and $\beta2 = .999$. The proposed approach achieved accuracy of 99.3% to detect defects, with high accuracy to classify sloughed filling (100%), broken pick (97%), broken yarn (80%) and fuzzy ball (74%), but low for nep (12.5%) and cut selvage (0%).

Keywords: Fabric defects · Convolutional Neural Network · U-Net · CNN · VGG16 · Random forest · Accuracy · Recall · Precision · F1 score

1 Introduction

In the textile industry, reports on fabric defects are used as a measure of quality of a fabric roll. Such reports also serve the purpose of eliminating cause of defects, hence improve production quality. The conventional approach is human inspection to determine the location, type and size of the defects. However, this approach is prone to human errors, optical illusions and has the risk of missing small defects. It also suffers from low accuracy rate, poor consistency among inspectors, and poor efficiency. Therefore, computer enabled automated defect detection based on image processing emerged as a promising approach to improve efficiency and accuracy, and has been an active research area over the last decade. Camera systems mounted on textile production machines together with advanced data processing and machine learning technology can potentially improve accuracy of fabric defect detection and classification. However, deployment of

© ICST Institute for Computer Sciences, Social Informatics and Telecommunications Engineering 2022
Published by Springer Nature Switzerland AG 2022. All Rights Reserved
M. N. Seyman (Ed.): ICECENG 2022, LNICST 436, pp. 135–147, 2022.
https://doi.org/10.1007/978-3-031-01984-5_11

such systems requires significant work on development and performance improvement as compared to the current practice.

A flaw on the manufactured fabric is known as a fabric defect. Defects may be caused by textile machine/process malfunction or oils from the machinery or faulty yarns or improper mixing of dye stuff in the dye solution. Fabric defects can be classified as minor, major and critical defects. Major defects may affect the sale of the product, and critical defects may result in the entire roll to be rated as second or worse in the quality check process. There are more than 60 defect are given in the document on Standard Test Methods for Visually Inspecting and Grading Fabrics [1]. The fabric defect can be classified into seven main classes, named as yarn, weaving, isolated, pattern, wet processing, raising and milling defects. Some of these are due to surface colour change, and others are due to local texture irregularity.

It is very important to detect these fabric defects because of the financial loss concerns that may arise from faulty production [2]. Considering the fact that 85% of the faults in the clothing industry are caused by fabric faults; if the companies producing woven fabrics use an effective quality control system to produce the desired quality fabric and sell it in this way, they will have adopted the most accurate production system [3]. Traditionally, fabric defect detection is carried out by a skilled worker who tries to detect defects in 2–2.5 m length fabric rolls that are passed at a speed of 8–10 m per minute through an illuminated inspection platform. The employee who detects the error stops the machine and marks the area containing the defect and records it. At the end of this process, acceptance/rejection decision is performed according to the total defect rate in the roll. Defect detection is a long and tiring process. Defect inspectors who constantly look at the same point can audit for a maximum of 1 h due to eyestrain. In traditional systems, the error rate is still around 60%. In addition, the risk of Alzheimer's disease has increased in workers who do this type of work. For these reasons, automated/computerized fabric defect detection systems have been researched.

Automated real-time inspection system is usually composed of camera, light, im-age capturing and processing unit. Defect detection techniques vary from conventional image processing techniques to machine learning techniques. In [4], algorithms developed for detecting fabric defects were divided into three groups, namely statistical [5–7], spectral [8–10] and model-based approaches [11–13].

Recently, machine learning approaches have attracted a lot of attention and been applied in detection of fabric defects, as well as in many different fields. For example, neural network and deep learning network approaches were used in [14, 15], while the convolutional deep learning approach was used in [16–18]. In traditional convolutional deep learning models, a large dataset is necessary for successful performance. However, for some classification problems, the amount of data that can be collected is limited in practice, leading to a small dataset. It has been shown that, with small datasets, U-Net gives better results than classical models in pixel-based image segmentation problems.

In this paper, we are proposing a hybrid classification model which employs U-Net to determine whether image contains any defects. If a defect is detected, then defect classification is carried out by using a hybrid model made up of VGG16 and Random Forest. We used the AITEX dataset [19] for training and validation purposed. The results show that the proposed model resulted in 99.8% accuracy for detecting defects which is better than those presented in the literature.

2 Dataset and Experimental Work

We used the AITEX fabric defects dataset [19] for training and testing our model. The original AITEX dataset consists of 245 images of 4096 × 256 pixels captured from seven different fabric structures. The fabrics in the dataset are mainly plain. There are 140 defect-free images, i.e. 20 images for each of fabric structure type. The remaining 105 images contain 12 different types of fabric defects which commonly appear in the textile industry. After data enhancement and decomposition of the original dataset into smaller 256 × 256 pixels images, we obtained a data set of 165 defected samples of 256 × 256 pixels. Then we carried out augmentation on the 165 samples (90° clockwise rotation, 180° clockwise rotation and 270° clockwise rotation), we obtained a set of 660 defected samples. Table 1 shows the numbers of occurrences of the defect types before and after the augmentation. Table 2 shows samples of images for different defect types and corresponding numbers of occurrences after augmentation. We used 592 images corresponding to the seven most common defect types as our data set. This dataset was randomly divided into training set (85%) and validation set (15%).

Table 1. Defective sample counts before and after data augmentation.

Defect type	Original sample count	Count after augmentation
Broken pick	55	220
Fuzzy ball	38	152
Nep	14	56
Sloughed filling	14	56
Cut selvage	9	36
Broken end	9	36
Broken yarn	9	36
Weft curling	6	24
Crease	5	20
Warp ball	4	16
Knots	1	4
Contamination	1	4

Our tests were conducted on a computer with a processor of 'Intel Core i7-11800H', a graphics card of 'RTX 3070 8 GB' and operating system of Windows10. Our source code was developed in Python programming environment.

Table 2. Enhanced AITEX fabric defects dataset.

Defect Name	Sample count	Defected sample	Grayscale mask
Broken pick	220		
Fuzzy ball	152		
Nep	56		
Sloughed filling	56		
Cut selvage	36		
Broken end	36		
Broken yarn	36		
Weft curling	24		
Crease	20		
Warp Ball	16		
Knots	4		
Contamination	4		

3 Defect Detection and Classification

A two-stage classification approach is used in the proposed model. Images of fabrics are first applied to a customized U-Net to determine whether the fabric is defected or not. Images of defected fabrics are then put through a classification process where VGG16 is used for extracting features and a random forest is used to determine defect type. Following subsections describe U-Net, VGG16 and random forest methods used.

3.1 Defect Detection Using a Customized U-Net

U-Net, a type of Convolutional Neural Networks (CNN) approach, was first developed in 2015 by Olaf Ronneberger, Phillip Fischer, and Thomas Brox to perform better segmentation on biomedical images [20]. Different from traditional convolutional deep learning models which require a large dataset for successful performance, U-Net performs well with small datasets. Since data sets available for fabric defects are small, U-Net was used for defect detection in this work.

The architectural structure of the proposed U-Net is shown in Fig. 1. The number of filters in the original U-Net has been reduced from 64,128, 256, 512, 1024 to 16, 32, 64, 128, 256, respectively. The reduction in the number of filters speeds up the training process and reduces the computational load. As seen in Fig. 1, in the encoder side or in the feature extraction side of the U-Net, different numbers and sizes of features are extracted along the convolutional neural network model, and the pooling process of their height and width dimensions is carried out using the pooling layer.

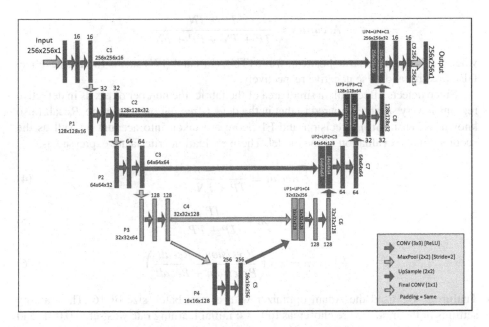

Fig. 1. Architectural structure of the proposed U-Net.

The second half of the model serves to increase the size, hence the resolution of the image at the output of the model in accordance with the input image. In order to reduce complexity and computation time, each convolution output in the Encoder part is combined with the corresponding upsampling layers.

Loss Function. The number of fabric defects is usually small and the total area affected by the defects is quite small compared to the defect-free part of the fabric. Using an ordinary loss function such as standard cross entropy may cause the model to fall into its local optimum points. To overcome this imbalance problem, cross entropy and Dice binary loss function are used together. Dice function is a frequently used performance criterion to evaluate success in biomedical images, and will be used in this work. The Cross-entropy (C) and Dice (D) loss functions are expressed as follows;

$$C(p, q) = -\sum_{x \in X} p(x) \log q(x) \tag{1}$$

$$D(p, q) = \frac{2\sum_i^N p_i q_i}{\sum_i^N p_i^2 + \sum_i^N q_i^2} \tag{2}$$

where p(x) and q(x) in (1) represents distribution functions of predicted and actual sets, the values p_i and q_i values in (2) are the pixel values of prediction and ground truth, respectively.

Training Evaluation Metrics. In traditional binary segmentation problems, accuracy metric is typically used. The Accuracy metric is defined as follows

$$Accuracy = \frac{TP + TN}{TP + TN + FP + FN} \tag{3}$$

where (TP) represents true positive, while (TN), (FP) and (FN) stands for true negative, false positive and false negative respectively.

Since defects affect only a small area of the fabric, the number of pixels in defective regions is very small compared to that in the defect-free region. Therefore, Recall (also known as sensitivity), precision and F1 Score are taken into account as well as the accuracy in the evaluation of the model. These evaluation criteria are expressed as,

$$Recall = \frac{TP}{TP + FN} \tag{4}$$

$$Precision = \frac{TP}{TP + FP} \tag{5}$$

$$F1score = 2 * \left(\frac{Precision * Recall}{Precision + Recall} \right) \tag{6}$$

Training. We used the Adam optimizer with a mini-batch size of 16. The training settings of the model were chosen as follows: initial learning rate was set to 0.001, and exponential decay rates for the estimates of mean and variance were set to $\beta 1 = 0.9$ and $\beta 2 = 0.999$, respectively. We trained the model for 100 epochs. Table 3 lists the results

Table 3. Performance comparison of the proposed model

Model	PTIP [21]	U-Net	Mobile U-Net [17]	Improved U-Net [18]	Our U-Net
Accuracy (%)	85.6	89.3	93.5	98.3	99.2
Recall (%)	90.1	85.1	90.4	92.7	94.3

from our model and compares them with other models. Accuracy for our model is 99.2% and recall is 94.3%, both of which are superior as compared to other models.

Then, we trained the model for 500 epochs. Figures 2, 3, 4 and 5 present the results of accuracy, recall, F1-Score and precision for training and testing phases. As can be seen, the proposed model showed superior performance after being trained for 500 rounds. The accuracy was 99.8% for the training phase and 99.3% for the validation phase. Corresponding values were 98.5% and 90.2% for recall, 96.2% and 91.3% for F1, and 96.5% and 92.2% for precision.

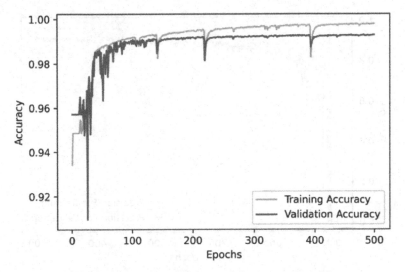

Fig. 2. Accuracy performance of the proposed model.

The loss function performance figures of the proposed model for the training and validation phases are shown in Fig. 6. As can be seen in the figure, values of the loss functions were reduced to very small values, i.e. being 0.0095 for Training-Loss and 0.0529 for Validation-Loss.

We tested the trained model on numerous images from the validation data set. For this we randomly selected an image from the validation data set and applied it to the input of the model, and obtained the model output. We have seen that our model successfully detected the defects in all the images. Figure 7 shows two sample images of defective

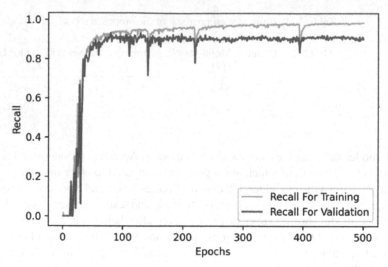

Fig. 3. Recall performance of the proposed model.

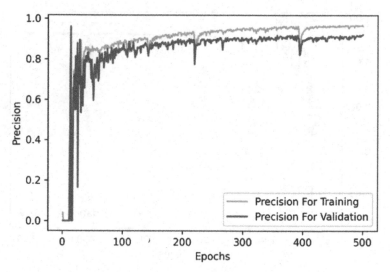

Fig. 4. Precision performance of the proposed model.

fabrics on the left column, and model output on the right, and shows that the defects were detected successfully by the model.

3.2 Hybrid Model for Defect Classification

We used a hybrid model for fabric defect classification in this work. Images of fabrics are first applied to the customized U-Net to determine whether the fabric is defected. Images of defected fabrics are then put through a classification process where VGG16 is used for extracting features and a random forest to determine defect type.

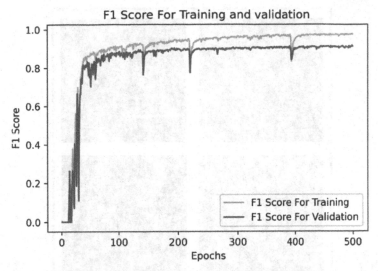

Fig. 5. F1-score performance of the proposed model.

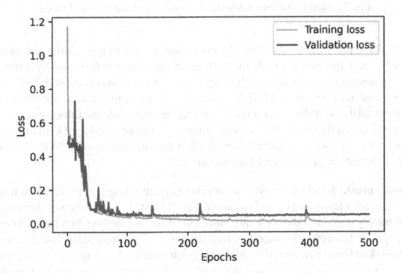

Fig. 6. Loss performance of the proposed model.

VGG16. VGG16 is a convolutional neural network model proposed in an article by K. Simonyan and A. Zisserman from Oxford University [22]. In VGG architecture, the image is passed through a series of convolutional layers which followed by three Fully-Connected (FC) layers. Filters with a very small receptive field (3 × 3) are used in the convolutional layers. The convolution stride is fixed to 1 pixel; the spatial padding of convolutional layer input is used to preserve spatial resolution after convolution, i.e. the padding is 1-pixel for 3 × 3 convolutional layers. Max-pooling follows every stack of convolutional layers, and performs spatial pooling over a 2 × 2 pixel window, with

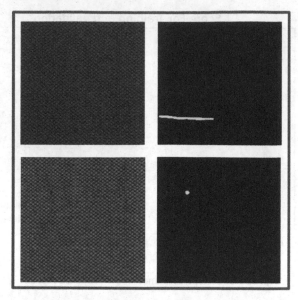

Fig. 7. Samples of defect detection test results of the proposed model.

stride 2. Three Fully-Connected (FC) layers follow a stack of convolutional layers with 4096, 4096 and 1000 channels. Each fully connected layer is followed by a nonlinear activation function, such as ReLU, The final layer is the soft-max layer which normalizes output real values from the last fully connected layer to target class probabilities. In our work, we used the VGG16 only for feature extraction, therefore the fully connected layer which used in original model for classification is removed (see Fig. 8), and the feature set of 8 × 8 × 512 which obtained from the last convolution layer of VGG16 were fed to random forest for fabric defect classification.

Random Forest. Random Forest is a supervised learning algorithm. As the name suggests, it creates a forest in a random manner. The "forest" is a collection of decision trees that are mostly trained by the "bagging" method. With this method, hundreds of decision trees are created and each decision tree makes an individual prediction. The structure of a simple random forest consists of multiple decision trees as shown in Fig. 9 and combines them to get a more accurate and stable prediction. For example, in regression problems, average of the predictions of the decision trees is used. In classification problems, most voted one is chosen among the predictions. The biggest advantage of the random forest is that it does not cause an over-learning/overfitting problem that is often experienced in traditional machine learning methods.

3.3 Testing the Model

We tested our model by using images of fabrics with seven most common defect types (namely broken pick, fuzzy ball, nep, sloughed fill, cut selvage, broken end and broken

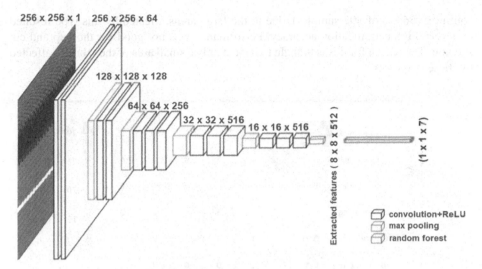

256 x 256 x 1   256 x 256 x 64

128 x 128 x 128

64 x 64 x 256

32 x 32 x 516

16 x 16 x 516

Extracted features (8 x 8 x 512)

(1 x 1 x7)

convolution+ReLU
max pooling
random forest

Fig. 8. Architectural structure of VGG16 used.

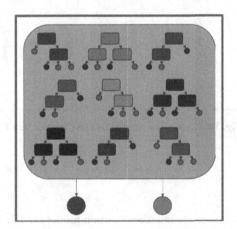

Fig. 9. Simple random forest.

yarn). We had 592 samples images for the seven most common defect types. The proposed model performed well on the limited data set of fabric defects; U-Net detected fabric defects with high accuracy (99.3%). The confusion matrix for classification performance of our model is given in Fig. 10. It can be seen that the proposed hybrid model classifies sloughed filling type with 100% accuracy, broken pick type with 97% accuracy, broken yarn type with 80% accuracy and fuzzy ball type with 74% accuracy. However, the model could classify nep type only with 12.5% accuracy, and confused this type with fuzzy ball and broken end types. The model failed to classify cut selvage type, and confused it with broken pick. High accuracy for the broken pick defect is attributed to the fact that this defect type is the most occurring type in the data set (220 out of 592 samples) and the area affected by defect is not small. The sloughed fill, although not so common (56 out of 592 samples), due to the large areas affected by this type resulted in a very high classification accuracy. Performance was not good for the nep and cut selvage. The reason for this is thought to be that only a small area of the fabric is affected by these two types.

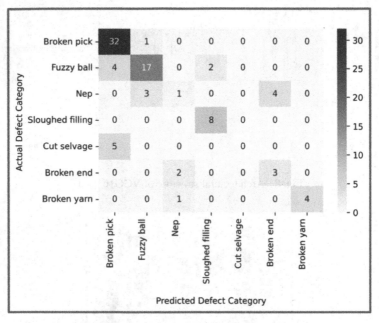

Fig. 10. Confusion matrix for classification results.

4 Conclusions

We proposed a hybrid detection and classification model for fabric defects. The model first detects defects by using a customized U-Net, and then carries out classification on defected fabrics by using VGG16 for feature extraction and random forest for classification. AITEX data set was used for training and testing purposes. We applied data enhancement, decomposition, augmentation on the data set, and obtained 660 images of 256×256 pixels for defected fabrics and used 592 of those corresponding to the seven most common defect types. The customised U-Net performed well on binary classification of defected and defect-free images, giving accuracy level of 99.3%. On the defect classification side of our model, we achieved high accuracy for defect types of broken pick, sloughed fill, broken yarn and fuzzy ball. On the other hand, exhibited poor classification performance for types of cut selvage and nep. Our results show that defects that affect large area on the fabric surface can be detected with high accuracy. Future research efforts can be directed towards improving the classification performance for defects with small size. The developed model will be evaluated by collecting data in real field trials at a company producing textile machinery in Turkey.

References

1. Standard Test Methods for Visually Inspecting and Grading Fabrics. D5430–13 (2017)
2. İzbudak, H., Alkan, A.: Denim fabric defect detection by using correlation method. In: National Conference on Electrical, Electronics and Computer Engineering, Bursa, Turkey (2010)
3. Dorrity, J.L., Vachtsevanos, G., Jasper, W.: Real-time fabric defect detection and control in weaving processes. Natl. Textile Center Ann. Report G94-2 (1996)
4. Hanbay, K., Talub, M.F., Özgüven, Ö.F.: Fabric defect detection systems and methods—a systematic literature review. Optik **127**, 11960–11973 (2016)
5. Zhang, Y.F., Bresee, R.R.: Fabric defect detection and classification using image analysis. Text. Res. J. **65**(1), 1–9 (1995)
6. Chetverikov, D., Hanbury, A.: Finding defects in texture using regularity and local orientation. Pattern Recogn. **35**(10), 2165–2180 (2002)
7. Jasper, W.J., Potlapalli, H.: Image analysis of mispicks in woven fabric. Text. Res. J. **65**(11), 683–692 (1995)
8. Tsai, D.M., Hsieh, C.Y.: Automated surface inspection for directional textures. Image Vis. Comput. **18**(1), 49–62 (1999)
9. Chan, C.H., Pang, G.K.: Fabric defect detection by Fourier analysis. IEEE Trans. Ind. Appl. **36**(5), 1267–1276 (2000)
10. Escofet, J., Navarro, R.F., GarciaVerela, M.S.M., Pladellorens, J.M.: Detection of local defects in textile webs using Gabor filters. Opt. Eng. **37**(8), 2297–2307 (1998)
11. Kumar, A.: Neural network based detection of local textile defects. Pattern Recogn. **36**(7), 1645–1659 (2003)
12. Cohen, F.S., Fan, Z., Attali, S.: Automated inspection of textile fabrics using textural models. IEEE Trans. Pattern Anal. Mach. Intell. **13**(08), 803–808 (1991)
13. Odemir, S., Baykut, A., Meylani, R., Erçil, A., Ertuzun, A.: Comparative evaluation of texture analysis algorithms for defect inspection of textile products. In: 14th International Conference on Pattern Recognition (Cat. No. 98EX170), vol. 2, pp. 1738–1740. IEEE, Brisbane, QLD, Australia (1998)
14. Campbell, J.G., Fraley, C., Murtagh, F., Raftery, A.E.: Linear flaw detection in woven textiles using model-based clustering. Pattern Recogn. Lett. **18**(14), 1539–1548 (1997)
15. Şeker, A., Peker, K.A., Yüksek, A.G., Delibaş, E.: Fabric defect detection using deep learning. In: 24th Signal Processing and Communication Application Conference (SIU), pp. 1437–1440. IEEE, Zonguldak, Turkey (2016)
16. Mei, S., Wang, Y., Wen, G.: Automatic fabric defect detection with a multi-scale convolutional denoising autoencoder network model. Sensors **18**(4), 1064 (2018)
17. Jing, J.F., Ma, H., Zhang, H.H.: Automatic fabric defect detection using a deep convolutional neural network. Color. Technol. **135**(3), 213–223 (2019)
18. Rong-qiang, L., Ming-hui, L., Jia-chen, S., Yi-bin, L.: Fabric defect detection method based on improved U-Net. J. Phys. Conf. Ser. **1948**(1), 012160 (2021)
19. Silvestre-Blanes, J., Albero, T., Miralles, I., PérezLlorens, R., Moreno, J.: A public fabric database for defect detection methods and results. Autex Res. J. **19**(4), 363–374 (2019)
20. Ronneberger, O., Fischer, P., Brox, T.: U-net: convolutional networks for biomedical image segmentation. In: Navab, N., Hornegger, J., Wells, W.M., Frangi, A.F. (eds.) MICCAI 2015. Lecture Notes in Computer Science, vol. 9351, pp. 234–241. Springer, Cham (2015). https://doi.org/10.1007/978-3-319-24574-4_28
21. Wang, Z., Jing, J.: Pixel-wise fabric defect detection by CNNs without labelled training data. IEEE Access **8**, 161317–161325 (2020)
22. Simonyan, K., Zisserman, A.: Very deep convolutional networks for large-scale image recognition. arXiv preprint arXiv:1409.1556 (2014)

A Method of CNN Deep Learning for Indonesia Ornamental Plant Classification

Dewi Agushinta Rahayu(✉) ⓘ, Hustinawaty ⓘ, Ihsan Jatnika ⓘ, and Baby Lolita

Gunadarma University, Jl. Margonda Raya No. 100, Pondok Cina, Depok 16424,
West Java, Indonesia
dewiar@staff.gunadarma.ac.id

Abstract. Indonesia is considered one of the most biodiverse regions in the world,
with 670 mammal species, 1,604 birds, 787 reptiles, and 392 amphibian species
as per the IUCN. Flower ornamental plants count among the potential commodities that can be developed both on a small and large scale, as evidenced by the
increasing public interest in agribusiness. Many people are still not familiar with
the existing types of flower ornamental plants. Several flower ornamental plants
only grow or live in some parts of the area. Technological developments can help
provide knowledge to the public. The technology currently being widely used is
the Deep Learning technique. Deep Learning is a type of artificial neural network
algorithm that uses metadata as input and processes it with many hidden layers,
using the Convolutional Neural Network (CNN) method. The Convolutional Neural Network (CNN) method can classify objects, essentially images, and recognise
them. This study will explore a CNN Deep Learning method that can classify various types of Indonesian ornamental plants object images. The results should pave
the way for a prototype that can easily recognise Indonesian ornamental flowers
in the future.

Keywords: Convolutional Neural Network · Deep Learning · Ornamental plants

1 Introduction

Indonesia is located on the line 6° North–11° South Latitude and 95°–141° East Longi-
tude. Thus, it has a tropical climate and is crossed by the equator. This location causes
Indonesia to have high and abundant biodiversity. Indonesia is considered one of the
world's most biodiverse regions [1]. There are billions and even trillions of flora and
fauna that coexist in the area. According to the Royal Botanic Gardens, Kew, England
in 2017, the country boasted approximately 391,000 vascular plant species known to
science. Around 369,000 species, or 94%, are flowering plants. Every year, 2,000 new
ornamental plant species are discovered or described, many of which are already on the
verge of extinction. Scientists say that, based on the best estimates available at present,
21% of all ornamental plants are currently endangered. Some parts of the world still have
a diverse plant population, including some rare species [2]. Unfortunately, only a few
of these species are legally protected, and few of us are aware of it. Many Indonesians
people as well as internationals are still unfamiliar with the types of ornamental plants

M. N. Seyman (Ed.): ICECENG 2022, LNICST 436, pp. 148–156, 2022.
https://doi.org/10.1007/978-3-031-01984-5_12

available or the fact that several types of flowers are only grown or live in certain parts of the world. Despite these issues, it is expected that planters can preserve this biodiversity. The urgency of this research resides in the fact that flower ornamental plants count among the potential commodities that can be developed both on a small and large scale, as evidenced by the increasing public interest in agribusiness. People need to know the various kinds of flower ornamental plants available and thus encourage an increasing number of operators, flower ornamental plant products, and new development areas. Flower ornamental plants have high economic value and the potential to be developed.

In international trade, one species of ornamental plant, the chrysanthemum, is the second most important cut flower ornamental plant after roses and carnations [3]. Chrysanthemums, roses, tuberoses and orchids are Indonesia's largest cut flower commodities. Over time, the demand for chrysanthemums in Indonesia has increased by 25%. According to the Ornamental Plant Research Centre, the market demand has grown by 31.62% since 2003. Additionally, statistics provided by from the Central Bureau in 2010 showed that the demand for chrysanthemum flowers in 2008 was 99,158,942 pieces, and that number has increased to 107,847,072 in 2009 until now.

However, chrysanthemum flowers are very vulnerable in handling. It is therefore important to find out how to transport this plant properly. The optimization of transportation routes for chrysanthemum flowers has been enforced using the Genetic Algorithm method [4, 5].

As the data provided by the Central Bureau of Statistics in 2018 further shows, the orchid harvested area has increased by 2.66%, and production has increased by 23.31%. The need for flower ornamental plants in general increases from time to time. The amount of public interest in flower ornamental plants is closely related to population growth, increased income, and living standards. Furthermore, the construction of residential buildings, office buildings and gardens in cities creates opportunities for business development in the field of ornamental plants. The built database is therefore expected to assist the Ministry of Agriculture in identifying and storing information on all types of Indonesian flower ornamental plants.

The technology currently being widely used is the Deep Learning technique. Several supervised learning techniques are available for Deep Learning, including Recurrent Neural Networks (RNNs), Convolutional Neural Networks (CNNs), and Deep Neural Networks (DNNs). Furthermore, the RNN category includes approaches such as gated recurrent units (GRUs) and long short-term memory (LSTM) [6].

Deep Learning is based on an artificial neural network algorithm that uses metadata as input and processes it in many hidden layers, using the Convolutional Neural Network (CNN) method. The CNN method is one of the Deep Learning methods that can carry out an unaccompanied learning process for object recognition, object extraction, and classification. The CNN method is expected to recognise Indonesian flower ornamental plants and classify them according to their names. CNN implementation is utilized in several agricultural fields [7–9]. Unfortunately, CNN research for plant classification, particularly in ornamental plants, is still rare. The study of CNN methods implementation for plant classification in high-resolution imagery uses five classes of plant species, namely rice, onion, coconut, banana, and chili plants [10]. The network learning process yields 100% accuracy in terms of training data. Tests on validation data resulted in 93%

accuracy, whereas test data yielded an 82% accuracy. This study result indicates that the CNN method can perform better classification.

This paper introduces the design of one method of ornamental plant classification, i.e., the powerful Deep Learning method called CNN. The objects used will be Indonesian flower ornamental plants. This paper will consist of several parts. The first part explains why it is important for an algorithm to recognise Indonesian flower ornamental plants and why they represent a promising commodity. The second part presents the CNN-based method used to identify and classify such plants, followed by a discussion. The last part refers to future work and conclusions.

2   Method

This section explains the steps in developing a prototype of classifying flower ornamental plants using the CNN architecture method. Figure 1 illustrates a framework of the research method. It will start from problem identification, review some research works, gather data, model design, pre-processing, and the CNN method processing.

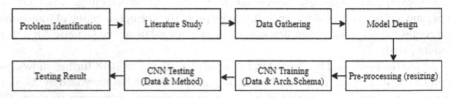

Fig. 1. Research methods.

2.1 Problem Identification

The problem identified is how to make the architecture of the CNN method for classifying flower images to get the information needed on them.

Convolutional Neural Network (CNN or ConvNet) is a well-known Deep Learning algorithms. This learning model is to perform classification tasks directly from images, videos, text, or sounds. Deep learning is an advanced result of the Multi-Layer Perceptron (MLP) designed to process data into two-dimensional forms, such as images or sound. CNN is used to classify labeled data using the supervised learning method. There are trained data and targeted variables so that the purpose of this method is to group data into existing data (www.Mathworks.com).

2.2 Data Gathering

Several flower images with a total of around 3000 data will be used for training. Each data is different in their number. The objects were obtained from google images and the flower dataset [11].

The sample used in this research will consist of 30 types of flower images found in the world. Some of the research objects used are represented in Fig. 2. Image data will be processed for training and testing. Each type of image data will be saved into a labelled folder, then retrieve and show its scientific data at the end process.

Fig. 2. Research object.

2.3 Model Design

The model design is used to set the interface and/or appearance of the application. The model design consists of several detailed flow diagrams. These diagrams are process flows that explain how image processing goes on the application prototype created.

There are some process flows designed, the CNN architecture training process, entering information data, and testing the CNN architecture, explained in the next sub sections.

2.4 Preprocessing Phase

This phase begins by selecting the flower ornamental plant images that ought to undergo manipulation, translation, colour transformation, and dimensional change of camera angles.

The segmentation results for feature extraction determine the distance of Euclid at the time of making the index image shape. All of these pre-processing image data results will be input and stored in the database. The image to be trained as the training image data will be resized into 28 × 28 pixels. Furthermore, the processed image will be trained into the network, formed, and stored as training image data. The database aims to store all the information resulting from the image analysis. The information or data stored in the database consists of an image ID and data related to flower ornamentals in an image. The database formation stage consists of the test image database formation and the training image database formation. The training database is the data that already exists. Segmentation using histogram, image manipulation such as rotation, and predefined class will also be conducted. The test image database is data classed and labelled to calculate the accuracy of the classification model to be formed.

2.5 CNN Training

Each neuron on CNN is presented in two-dimensional form, so this method is suitable for processing with image input [12]. The input, feature extraction, classification, and output processes create the CNN structure. The components of the CNN extraction process break into several hidden layers – the convolution layer, activation function (ReLU), and pooling.

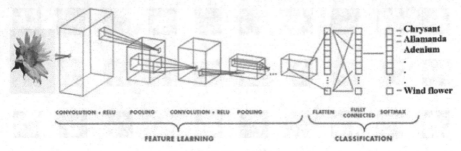

Fig. 3. CNN architecture.

As seen in Fig. 3, CNN works hierarchically, with the output of the first convolution layer utilized as the input for the next convolution layer. The classification process is based on fully connected and activation functions (softmax) with a classification result as the output [13].

Deep Learning technique with CNN method which popularized with AlexNet architecture was tested with ImageNet dataset [14]. The architecture design produced substantial results, with a test error rate of 17% in the testing set four. These results are exceptional, as the objects in the dataset are very intricate and numerous. In addition, a similar study using 16 to 19 convolution layers was performed [15]. The results showed a good performance with greater accuracy than the architecture stated previously. This proves that the network depth is an equally crucial component which stimulates good performance in image recognition. It can be said that the more layers used, the deeper a network architecture is.

The flow for the CNN training is presented in Fig. 4. The first CNN training process contains training data prepared with each label name. Then, the image is resized by 28 × 28 pixels and the labels or folder names are counted. The training process is run using the created CNN architecture, by input the image and the adjusted value of the convolution filter, ReLU, and pooling. After this process, the value data is saved as training data.

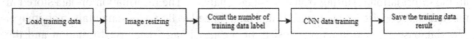

Fig. 4. CNN training.

The input information data process in Fig. 5 will first load all the data contained in the database. Afterwards, it will display the number of the last data input into the database after loading all the data. The information data input entities are flower name, kingdom, division, class, order, family, genus, and description. The data will be saved in the created database and will be used for testing the data image at a later stage.

2.6   CNN Testing of Data and Method

The AlexNet model can be improved by increasing the convolution layer size in the middle of the model array and reducing the size of the first layer filter in the existing

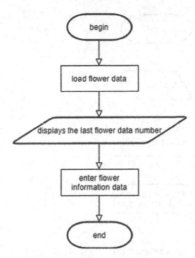

Fig. 5. Input data information.

hyperparameter architecture [16]. The results show that when new data is retrained with the softmax classification, it provides a good model for many other data sets. This result is very likely because it beats previous research with Caltech-101 and Caltech-256 datasets. Afterwards, the AlexNet model is examined [17]. The contribution reduces the number of parameters in the network from 60 million to about 4 million, which is a significant improvement.

Figure 6 shows the CNN testing flow. In the first testing process, the image is resized by 28 × 28 pixels. The image that has gone through the resizing process will then be added to the CNN architecture to calculate the convolution filter, ReLU, and pooling values. Then it will compare with the training data stored from the calculated results. Then it will look for information data that is under the test results. If the data is correct, it will display the valid flower data from the database, but if not, it will display data that does not match the flower image tested otherwise.

We will set the parameters for the Deep Learning method to determine how many neurons receive input and add weight from the images of flower ornamental plants. These parameters are meant to classify the flower ornamental plant. The CNN model is used to detect and recognise objects based on the results of feature extraction.

The CNN network architecture will adjust with 22 layers. It will consist of one image input layer, five convolutional filter layers, five batch normalization layers, five ReLU layers, three pooling layers, one fully connected layer, one softmax layer, and one classification layer. One output target will be set.

The learning process is carried out using the trainNetwork function, with the parameters trainData, layer, and options. We will test the model by confirming the information it yields with experts. This way, we will be able to evaluate the CNN model and establish the accuracy of the flower ornamental plant classification.

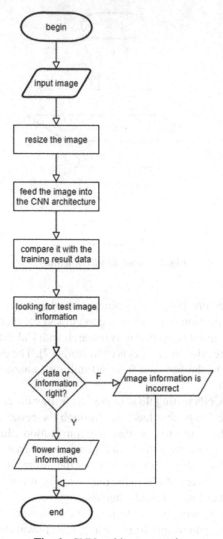

Fig. 6. CNN architecture testing.

2.7 Testing Result

From all the adjusted parameters, optimal values will be achieved so that the reference value is obtained for testing the CNN architecture. The CNN training will get the best training performance value using a predetermined parameter reference.

The image results tested with the CNN method will be recorded in order to evaluate the accuracy percentage for the total image number as well as for each classified image. This research will produce new basis method of the CNN to classify and find out the type of ornamental plants that fits the output.

3 Future Work

The data used comes from the Indonesian Ornamental Plants Research Center (BALITHI) under the Research and Development Centre of the Ministry of Agriculture. It is also possible to obtain such data from international databases. The application prototype will be developed using the Python or MATLAB programming language. This prototype is expected to help the Indonesian Ornamental Plants Research Centre to build a database for Indonesian ornamental plants, particularly flowers. The expected goal is to produce a prototype for recognising various types of Indonesian flower ornamental plants. The application prototype will provide information on Indonesian flower ornamental plants more quickly and accurately, using the CNN Deep Learning.

4 Conclusion

This CNN model will be developed and implemented to build an ornamental plants classification prototype. Indonesian flower ornamental plants will be the objects used for training. An implemented application prototype implemented will assist the Research Centre in obtaining exhaustive information regarding the wealth and variety of Indonesian ornamental plants. Researchers are expected to continue to enrich the database and image classification methods of ornamental flower plants in Indonesia. Databases or datasets of Indonesian flower ornamental plants can also be generated so that researchers can obtain more varied data. The work needed to implement this application prototype will be finished at a later stage.

Acknowledgements. This work is partially supported by the Directorate General of Higher Education, Ministry of Education and Culture, Research and Technology Republic of Indonesia Grant No. 309/E4.1/AK.04.PT/2021 on July 12, 2021, and to the Research Center of Ornamental Plants, as the partner.

References

1. Mittermeier, R.A., Da Fonseca, G.A.B., Rylands, A.B., Brandon, K.: A brief history of biodiversity conservation in Brazil. Conserv. Biol. **19**(3), 601–607 (2005)
2. Fonseca, C.R., Venticinque, E.M.: Biodiversity conservation gaps in Brazil: a role for systematic conservation planning. Perspect. Ecol. Conserv. **16**(2), 61–67 (2018). https://doi.org/10.1016/j.pecon.2018.03.001
3. Nxumalo, S.S., Wahome, P.K.: Effects of application of short-days at different periods of the day on growth and flowering in chrysanthemum (Dendranthema grandiflorum). J. Agric. Soc. Stud. **6**(2), 39–42 (2010)
4. Bahar, E., Agushinta, R.D., Septy, W.R.: Solusi Algoritma Genetika Pada Permasalahan Transportasi Komoditas Bunga Krisan. 2nd edn. Gunadarma, Jakarta (2016)
5. Agushinta R.D., Bahar, E., Septy, W.R.: Penerapan Algoritma Genetika Pada Permasalahan Distribusi dan Rute Kendaraan. Gunadarma, Jakarta (2016)
6. Alzubaidi, L., et al.: Review of Deep Learning: concepts, CNN architectures, challenges, applications, future directions. J. Big Data **8**, 53 (2021). https://doi.org/10.1186/s40537-021-00444-8

7. Yalcin, H., Razavi, S.: Plant classification using convolutional neural networks. In: 2016 Fifth International Conference on Agro-Geoinformatics (Agro-Geoinformatics), pp. 1–5. IEEE, Tianjin, China (2016). https://doi.org/10.1109/Agro-Geoinformatics.2016.7577698

8. Jadhav, S.B., Udupi, V.R., Patil, S.B.: Convolutional neural networks for leaf image-based plant disease classification. IAES Int. J. Artif. Intell. (IJ-AI) 8(4), 328–341 (2019). https://doi.org/10.11591/ijai.v8.i4.pp328-341

9. Valarmathia, G., Suganthi, S.U., Subashini, V., Janaki, R., Sivasankari, R., Dhanaseka, S.: CNN algorithm for plant classification in Deep Learning. Proc. Mater. Today 46(9), 3684–3689 (2021). https://doi.org/10.1016/j.matpr2021.01.847

10. Arrofiqoh, E.N., Harintaka: Implementation of convolutional neural network methods for plant classification in high-resolution imagery. Geomatika 24(2), 61–68 (2018)

11. Nilsback, M., Zisserman, A.: 102 Category Flower Dataset. http://www.robots.ox.ac.uk/~vgg/data/flowers/102/. Accessed 20 Aug 2021

12. Maggiori, E., Tarabalka, Y., Charpiat, G., Alliez, P.: Convolutional neural networks for large-scale remote-sensing image classification. IEEE Trans. Geosci. Remote Sens. 55(2), 645–657 (2016). https://doi.org/10.1109/TGRS.2016.2612821

13. Katole, A.L.: Hierarchical Deep Learning architecture for 10K objects classification. Comput. Sci. Inf. Technol. (CS & IT), pp. 77–93 (2015). https://doi.org/10.5121/csit.2015.51408

14. Krizhevsky, A., Sutskever, I., Hinton, G.E.: ImageNet classification with deep convolutional neural networks. In: NeurIPS Proceedings: Advances in Neural Information Processing Systems, pp. 84–90. ACM, Lake Tahoe, USA (2012)

15. Simonyan, K., Vedaldi, A., Zisserman, A.: Deep Inside Convolutional Networks: Visualizing Image Classification Models and Saliency Maps (2013). CoRR. abs/1312.6034

16. Zeiler, M.D., Fergus, R.: Visualizing and understanding convolutional networks. In: Fleet, D., Pajdla, T., Schiele, B., Tuytelaars, T. (eds.) ECCV 2014. Lecture Notes in Computer Science, vol. 8689, pp. 818–833. Springer, Cham (2014). https://doi.org/10.1007/978-3-319-10590-1_53

17. Szegedy, C., et al.: Going deeper with convolutions. In: Proceedings of 2015 IEEE Conference on Computer Vision and Pattern Recognition (CVPR), pp. 1–9. IEEE, Boston, MA (2015)

Computing

Quantum Data Classification by a Dissipative Protocol with a Superconducting Quantum Circuit Implementation

Ufuk Korkmaz[(✉)] [iD], Cem Sanga[iD], and Deniz Türkpençe[iD]

Istanbul Technical University, Istanbul 34469, Turkey
{ufukkorkmaz,sanga,dturkpence}@itu.edu.tr

Abstract. Artificial intelligence (AI) and machine learning (ML) have begun to include promising methods for solving real-world problems. However, the power of these methods is limited by the CPU capabilities of the current computers. Quantum computing (QC) appears to be not only an alternative route for more powerful computers but also the introduction of a new computing paradigm. Much more powerful AI protocols are predicted to be developed by the QC implementations. In this study, we present a binary classification of quantum data implemented by superconducting quantum circuits. Binary classification of data is a subroutine of both AI and ML. Therefore, much effort has been spent on the development of AI and ML strategies to be implemented on quantum computers. In our framework, we adopt a dissipative protocol for the classification of quantum information. The dissipative model of quantum computing has already been proven to be well-matched to the circuit model of quantum computing. More specifically, we introduce repeated interactions-based model with distinct quantum reservoirs as strings of pure qubits representing the quantum data. In the scenario, a probe qubit repeatedly interacts with the reservoir units and the binary classification is encoded in the steady quantum state of the probe qubit. We also present analytical results including system and reservoir parameters. We use realistic parameters for the implementation of the proposal with superconducting quantum circuits which are the leading platform for building universal quantum computers.

Keywords: Information reservoir · Quantum neuron · Superconducting circuits · Collisional model

1 Introduction

Perceptron is a mathematical model that inspired by the biological neuron cell, which is the basic unit of the neurocomputing [1–3]. Artificial neural networks (ANN) have various applications in data processing [1, 2, 4–13]. Binary classification is a subroutine for ANN based ML algorithms [14, 15]. Moore's law defines a linear growth to the number of transistors against a linear timescale by use of the semiconductors state-of-the-art [16]. Chip crisis has been appearing to be the harbinger of the end of Moore's

© ICST Institute for Computer Sciences, Social Informatics and Telecommunications Engineering 2022
Published by Springer Nature Switzerland AG 2022. All Rights Reserved
M. N. Seyman (Ed.): ICECENG 2022, LNICST 436, pp. 159–170, 2022.
https://doi.org/10.1007/978-3-031-01984-5_13

law restricting the power of current CPU technology. The number of studies on adapting the advantages of quantum computing to ML algorithms has increased recently [17–22]. There are also studies involving quantum algorithms using quantum classifiers through unitary gates [23–27]. In the QC circuit model, it is assumed that the system of interest is completely isolated from the environmental degrees of freedom. However, encoding classical data into a quantum register is a challenge and requires time-optimized unitary operations.

Considering some studies, we see that quantum reservoirs can be evaluated as communication channels where information is transmitted and they are not trash cans where valuable information is thrown [28–32]. In the light of these ideas, we consider the classification task of quantum data by use of non-unitary dynamics. It was reported that the dissipative model of QC is equivalent to the standard circuit model [33]. Non-trivial quantum steady states could be obtained by dissipation assisted methods [34] reminiscent of quantum reservoir engineering [35–38].

In this work, we show that a single probe qubit interacting weakly with distinct quantum information environments can classify quantum data in a steady state. Here, strings of ideal qubits in pure quantum states with certain parameters are dubbed reservoirs of quantum information [39, 40]. In this scheme, the probe qubit goes through a dissipation process, interacting sequentially with the subunits of the distinct information reservoirs [34]. This repeated interaction task is referred to as a collision model. Next, using the trace-out operations, we acquire the steady-response of the probe qubit where the classification result is encoded. The steady-state magnetization is chosen as an identifier of classification. The additivity [41] and divisibility [42, 43] properties of quantum dynamic maps allow one to obtain the weighted contribution of each reservoir in the collisional description open quantum systems.

In this study, the quantum master equation was developed according to the collision model, considering the repeated interaction process, and a summary of the analytical results obtained by this equation was presented. The details of the analytical and numerical results obtained from this equation are included in our study [29]. Finally, we consider the physical application of the quantum classifier in superconducting circuits [44]. Superconducting circuits became the leading platform for the realization of quantum information processing. Therefore, we follow the multi-superconducting qubit architecture [45, 46] for our open quantum classifier model. Here, we simulate the dissipative dynamics with three transmon qubits interacting via a resonator bus [47]. As we mentioned earlier, the reservoirs are formed by the iterative interaction scheme. Superconducting qubit is also called an artificial atom, since the energy level spectra can be managed and configured by the circuit element parameters [48]. We only examine the classification analysis of the model, excluding the training and learning of the model from our scope.

2   Model and Theory

The simplest binary classifier is the perceptron, which is the primary processing unit of biological neuron inspired artificial neural networks [3]. First, weighted combination of input parameters defined as $z = f\left(x^T w\right)$ where $x = [x_1, \cdots x_N]^T$ is a vector defining the input instances and $w = [w_1, \cdots w_N]^T$ is the corresponding weights. Here, f is an activation function modulating the response. The binary classification is defined as $z \equiv 0$ if $z = f(x^T w) \geq 0$ and $z \equiv 1$, else. The input weighted summation can also be represented as

$$x^T w = \sum_i w_i x_i. \tag{1}$$

Inspired by this classical perspective, we express our open quantum model as

$$\Lambda_t[\varrho_0] = \sum_i P_i \Phi_t^{(i)}[\varrho_0], \tag{2}$$

where each dynamical map stands for the readout qubit coupling to respective reservoirs. Here, ϱ_0 is the density matrix of the readout (probe) qubit, and P_i is the probability that the probe qubit will experience from the respective reservoir.

The maps used above are expressed as completely positive trace preserving (CPTP) quantum dynamic maps as follows

$$\Phi_t^{(i)}[\varrho_0] = Tr_{\mathcal{R}_i}\left[U_t(\varrho_0 \otimes \varrho_{\mathcal{R}_i})U_t^\dagger\right]. \tag{3}$$

Here, U_t is a unitary propagator that moves through the probe and the information reservoir degrees of freedom and $\varrho_{\mathcal{R}_i}$ is the density matrix that expresses the quantum state of the ith information reservoir. If a dynamical map satisfying $\Phi_{t+s} = \Phi_t(\Phi_s[\varrho])$ complete positivity (CP) for t and $s \geq 0$, this is named as a CP divisible map [42]. Equation (2) can be used as the open quantum equivalent of Eq. (1). However, in order to use Eq. (2) in this form, quantum dynamic maps must satisfy the additivity and divisibility conditions [41–43]. In addition, the weak coupling condition is also provided, thanks to the divisibility and full positivity conditions of the quantum dynamic maps [43].

We build our model as an open quantum system, and quantum information units, which we characterize with qubits, also called information reservoirs, will be used as input data. Considering the Bloch sphere representation, a qubit is expressed as $|\psi(\theta, \varnothing)\rangle = \cos(\frac{\theta}{2})|e\rangle + e^{i\varnothing}\sin(\frac{\theta}{2})|g\rangle$ in terms of polar and azimuth angles. Along this work, we parameterize the 'quantum features' with θ and take $\varnothing = 0$. We examined our model in the structure of open quantum dynamics in the process of a repeated interaction [49]. When we examine the applications of the collisional model, we see that the identical units (ancillas) of an information reservoir do not interact with each other. Each interaction is defined through a unitary operation in a small-time scale τ. This standard collisional model leads to memoryless Markovian open quantum evolution. We denote the system (the probe qubit) by S and the nth unit of a single information reservoir by $\mathcal{R}_n$. We initially expressed the system plus reservoir $S\mathcal{R}$ state as the product state $\varrho(0) = \varrho_S(0) \otimes \varrho_\mathcal{R}$, where $\varrho(0) = |+\rangle\langle+|$ and $\varrho_\mathcal{R} = |\psi_\theta\rangle\langle\psi_\theta|$. Our open system evolution is Markovian. Because, as we mentioned above, we use the standard collisional model where there is no interaction/correlation between the subunits of the reservoirs. In the course of the evolution, the system state transforms to be equivalent to the reservoir ancilla states. Such a situation is called quantum homogenization [50]. When we reformulate Eq. (3) as stepwise partial trace operations, the system reaches steady state with the definition of dynamic maps via collision model as follows

$$\Phi_{n\tau}[\varrho_0] = Tr_n\left[U_{0n} \cdots Tr_1\left[U_{01}\left(\varrho_0 \otimes \varrho_{\mathcal{R}_{i_1}}\right)U_{01}^\dagger\right] \otimes \cdots \otimes \varrho_{\mathcal{R}_n}U_{0n}^\dagger\right] \tag{4}$$

using the trace-out dynamics. Here, $n\tau$ is the time passed for n collisions, $U_{0i} = exp[-iH_{0i}\tau/\hbar]$ are unitary propagators that define collisions between each ancilla and probe qubit. It is the Hamiltonian that defines the whole system in the form of $H_{0i} = H_{free}^i + H_{int}^i$, where H_{free}^i is free terms of the Hamiltonian as

$$H_{free}^i = \frac{\hbar\omega_0}{2}\sigma_0^z + \frac{\hbar\omega_i}{2}\sum_{i=1}^{N}\sigma_i^z. \tag{5}$$

Here, $\hbar$ is the Planck constant, $\sigma_{0,i}^z$ are the Pauli-z operators for the system space of the ith reservoir and $\omega_{0,i}$ are the frequencies of the probe and the reservoir qubits, respectively. Assuming $\omega_0 = \omega_i$, H_{int}^i interaction Hamiltonian is as follows

$$H_{int}^i = \hbar\sum_{i=1}^{N}J_i(\sigma_0^+\sigma_i^- + H.c.) \tag{6}$$

where J_i is the coupling strength to the ith reservoir, $\sigma^{+,-}$ are the Pauli raising and lowering operators, respectively.

In order to connect our dynamic model to real physical systems, we derive a microscopic master equation reminiscent of micromaser master equations depending on random and repeated interactions [29, 32]. In this case, the $U(\tau) = exp[-iH_{int}\tau/\hbar]$ is obtained as the unitary operator

$$U(\tau) = 1 - i\tau(\sigma_0^+ S_{j_i}^- + \sigma_0^- J_j^+) - \frac{\tau^2}{2}(\sigma_0^+\sigma_0^- S_{j_i}^- S_{j_i}^+ + \sigma_0^-\sigma_0^+ S_{j_i}^+ S_{j_i}^-), \tag{7}$$

which we evaluate up to the second order in τ after constructing the system unitary evolution in the interaction picture where $S_{j_i}^\pm = \sum_{i=1}^{N}J_i\sigma_i^\pm$ are collective operators weighted by J_i. It is presumed that the initial system is factored $\varrho(t) = \varrho_S(0) \otimes \varrho_{\mathcal{R}_i}$ and the reservoir states are return to their original states after each interaction. Thanks to the micro-maser theory, considering random interactions with the Poisson process, the evolution can be states as

$$\varrho(t + \delta t) = r\delta t U(\tau)\varrho(t)U^\dagger(\tau) + (1 - r\delta t)\varrho(t) \tag{8}$$

in the time interval δt. Here, $r\delta t$ is an interaction event probability at a rate r and $1 - r\delta t$ is the probability of occurring a non-interaction state. In the time limit $\delta t \to 0$ and for the reduced dynamics of the probe qubit, the main equation is obtained as

$$\dot{\varrho}_0(t) = rTr_{\mathcal{R}_i}\left[U(\tau)\varrho(t)U^\dagger(\tau) - \varrho(t)\right]. \tag{9}$$

After some algebra, the master equation we get for our model is

$$\dot{\varrho}_0 = - i[H_{eff}, \varrho] + \sum_{i=1}^{N}J_i^2(\varsigma^+\mathcal{L}[\sigma_0^+] + \varsigma^-\mathcal{L}[\sigma_0^-])$$
$$+ \sum_{i<j}^{N'}J_iJ_j(\varsigma_s^+\mathcal{L}_s[\sigma_0^-] + \varsigma_s^-\mathcal{L}_s[\sigma_0^+]). \tag{10}$$

Here, $H_{eff} = r\tau\sum_i^N J_i(\langle\sigma_i^-\rangle\sigma_0^+ + \langle\sigma_i^+\rangle\sigma_0^-)$ is the effective Hamiltonian describing a coherent drive on the probe qubit, $\langle\mathcal{O}_i\rangle = Tr[\mathcal{O}\varrho_{\mathcal{R}_i}]$ are averages calculated over identical reservoir units, $\mathcal{L}[o] \equiv 2o\varrho o^\dagger - o^\dagger o \varrho - \varrho o o^\dagger$ is the standard Lindblad term and $\mathcal{L}_s[o] \equiv 2o\varrho o - o^2\varrho - \varrho o^2$ denotes a squeezing effect by the reservoir, respectively. $\zeta^\pm = \frac{r\tau^2}{2}\langle\sigma_i^\pm\sigma_i^\mp\rangle$ coefficients contain diagonal inputs and $\zeta_s^\pm = 2r\tau^2\langle\sigma_i^\pm\rangle\langle\sigma_j^\pm\rangle$ include non-diagonal inputs. These terms represent information transferred from information reservoirs. $N' = N(N-1)/2$ is a total number of terms.

When we take $\dot{\varrho}_0 = 0$, the steady quantum state of the system is

$$\varrho_0^{ss} = \frac{1}{\sum_i^N J_i^2} \sum_{i=1}^N J_i^2 (\langle\sigma_i^+\sigma_i^-\rangle|e\rangle\langle e| + \langle\sigma_i^-\sigma_i^+\rangle|g\rangle\langle g|$$
$$+ i\gamma_1^-(\langle\sigma_i^+\sigma_i^-\rangle - \langle\sigma_i^-\sigma_i^+\rangle)|e\rangle\langle g| + H.c.) \tag{11}$$

where $\gamma_1^- = r\tau \sum_{i=1}^N J_i\langle\sigma_i^-\rangle$.

2.1 The Quantum Classifier

The classification rule will be made through the $\langle\sigma_0^z\rangle^{ss}$ steady-state magnetization of the probe qubit, since probe qubit amplitude parameter determined as the classification descriptive value. Thus, the binary decision of the classifier in this case is as follows

$$Decision : \begin{cases} 0, \langle\sigma_0^z\rangle^{ss} = \frac{1}{\sum_i^N J_i^2} \sum_{i=1}^N J_i^2\langle\sigma_i^z\rangle \geq 0 \\ 1, \; else. \end{cases} \tag{12}$$

Here, $\langle\sigma_i^z\rangle$ is the ancilla magnetization of the ith information reservoir and J_i is the coupling strength of the system to the corresponding reservoir. Our master equation, which we derive from the collision model, allows us to derive the decision rule for the classifier through a weighted combination of the reservoir parameters with J. When we also define magnetization as $\langle\sigma_i^z\rangle = \langle\sigma_i^+\sigma_i^-\rangle - \langle\sigma_i^-\sigma_i^+\rangle = \cos\theta_i$, the binary classification rule reads 0, $\frac{1}{\sum_i^N J_i^2} \sum_{i=1}^N J_i^2 \cos\theta_i \geq 0$, and, else in the form of the information reservoir amplitude parameter.

3 Superconducting Transmon Qubits

In this section, the QuTip software package [51, 52] was used to simulate the transmon qubit system for implementation of the quantum classifier. Figure 1 shows schematically the interactions of the three qubits through the coplanar waveguide (CPW), which effectively acts as a harmonic oscillator [28, 32]. Here, Q2 and Q3 represent the reservoir qubits and Q1 represents the system qubit with which they interact. The remaining two are reservoir qubits which are characterized by their respective starting angles. We assume that the information content is buried inside these starting angles, namely, θ_1 and θ_2. After the parameters are defined according to the realistic parameters [53] in the light of the collision model. When we look at the flow followed in the simulation, it is based on obtaining the stable quantum state of the system by taking a partial trace over the reservoir degrees of freedom by writing the Hamiltonian by using the density matrix formulation that expresses the quantum classifier.

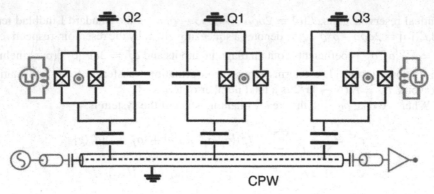

Fig. 1. A schematic representation of the quantum classifier in our physical model via a Lumped-element circuit diagram [28]. Three transmon qubits (Q_1 : probe qubit and $Q_{2,3}$: *reservoir qubits*) are coupled via a CPW resonator. Blue colored pulses indicate the controllability of the reservoir qubits by external inputs.

The effective Hamiltonian of the designed system is given below

$$H_{eff} = \frac{\hbar}{2} \sum_{i=1}^{3} \omega_i \sigma_i^z + \hbar \left(\omega_r + \sum_{i=1}^{3} \chi_i \sigma_i^z \right) a^\dagger a + \sum_{i=2,3} J_{1,i} \left(\sigma_1^+ \sigma_i^- + H.c. \right)$$

(13)

where w_1, w_2 and w_3 are respective qubit frequencies, w_r is the CPW resonator frequency of coupling, σ_z is the Pauli-z operator, $\sigma^+ (\sigma^-)$ is the Pauli raising(lowering) operator and $a(a^\dagger)$ is the bosonic annihilation(creation) operator. The effective coupling of flip-flop type between qubits is denoted by J and given in terms of qubit-CPW coupling parameters as

$$J_{1,i} = \frac{g_1 g_i}{2} \left(\frac{1}{\Delta_1} + \frac{1}{\Delta_i} \right)$$

(14)

where g_i is the coupling strength of the qubit to the CPW, Δ_i is described as $|w_i - w_r|$ and $\chi_i = (g_i)^2 / \Delta_i$ is the frequency shift of the respective qubit.

Initially, the system is put into the product state given as below

$$\varrho = \varrho_{th}^{res} \otimes \varrho_{q_1}(0) \otimes \varrho_{q_2} \otimes \varrho_{q_3}$$

(15)

where ρ_{th}^{res} is the thermal harmonic oscillator density matrix of CPW. Also, $\hat{n} = 0.008$, which corresponds to 100 mK and used to calculate ρ_{th}^{res}, is a thermal excitation number [54]. The probe and the two reservoir transmon qubits are initially $\varrho_{q_1}(0) = |+\rangle\langle+|$ and $\varrho_{q_2} = \varrho_{q_3} = |\psi(\theta, \phi)\rangle\langle\psi(\theta, \phi)|$, respectively. To apply the collision model, we raise the given Hamiltonian Eq. (13) to an exponential and interact the system with this propagator. Following the collision model, the propagator should be applied a large number of times. After each iteration, the probe qubit should be disconnected from other density matrices by means of information exchange. Furthermore, the reservoir qubits must be returned to their original state before each interaction. The cutting-edge technology of today allows for an energy dissipation time in the $T_1 \approx 50 - 100$ μs time scale while single qubit reset times (t_r) can reach the order $1 - 10$ ns. Inspired with these values, we take $w_1/2\pi = 4.86$ GHz, $w_2/2\pi = 5.73$ GHz, $w_3/2\pi = 4.94$ GHz, $w_r/2\pi = 6.73$ GHz and $g_{1,2,3}/2\pi = 250$ MHz. We scale these parameters by dividing them with w_r. The resulting dimensionless values are $J_{1,2} = 0.007126$, $J_{1,3} = 0.005077$, $\Delta_1 = 0.2778$, $\Delta_2 = 0.1485$, $\Delta_3 = 0.2659$, $\chi_1 = 0.004966$, $\chi_2 = 0.009286$, and $\chi_3 = 0.005188$. The interaction time is $\tau = 1.2$ ns corresponding to $\tau = 8.076$ when scaled.

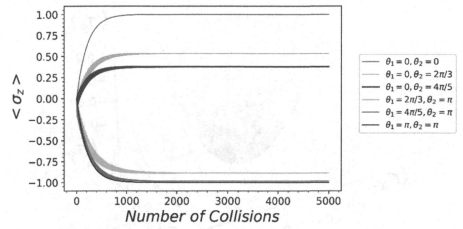

Fig. 2. Variation of probe qubit orientation against the number of collisions with different values for the reservoir qubit initial angles θ_1 *and* θ_2. The probe qubit starts at in the state $|+\rangle = (|e\rangle + |g\rangle)/\sqrt{2}$. The reservoir qubit values are initialized as $\rho_{q2} = \rho_{q3} = |\psi(\theta, \phi)\rangle\langle\psi(\theta, \phi)|$ for the values for theta are $\theta = 0, 2\pi/3, 4\pi/5, \pi$ with indicated combinations given in figure legend. The couplings between the probe qubit and the reservoir qubits are $J_{1,2} = 0.007126$, $J_{1,3} = 0.005077$ by Eq. (14). We scale these parameters by dividing them with w_r.

The probe qubit ends up in equilibration state when it interacts with the reservoirs. The equilibration curves are given in Fig. 2. The continuous variation of the evolution curve verifies that the dynamics obeys Markov evolution. At smaller angles around zero expectation value, the curves broaden as a result of oscillations, showing that it is harder to get equilibration. From the evolution of probe qubit, it is clear that the steady state is reached after $n = 1.5 \times 10^3$ collisions. Since each interaction time was 1.2 ns, the equilibration time for probe qubit is $n\tau = 1.8$ μs, which is much smaller than the experimental value of T_1. This shows that the architecture design in this work is feasible to build using physical systems. If there were more information reservoir qubits for information exchange, the equilibration time would be shorter due to aggregate effects.

The dynamics of the probe qubit Bloch vector under the interactions of collision model is given in Fig. 3. As a result of the parameters we used, it was observed that the dynamical behavior of the probe qubit in Bloch representation expresses a reasonable open quantum channel in the presence of two information reservoirs.

Randomly chosen data pairs in terms of azimuthal Bloch angles $\theta_{1,2}$ acted as two different information reservoirs. The steady state magnetization $\langle \sigma_0^z \rangle^{ss}$ of the probe qubit returns a binary decision class '0' for $\langle \sigma_0^z \rangle^{ss} \geq 0$ and class '1' else. As is evident in Fig. 4, our model successfully classifies quantum information with state-of-the-art superconducting quantum circuits. Each point represents a steady-state classification response of the probe transmon qubit.

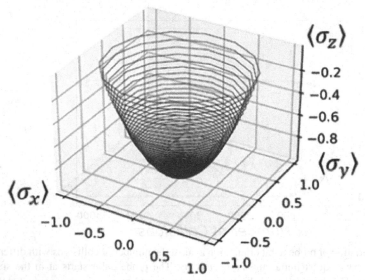

Fig. 3. 3D visualization of the Bloch sphere trajectory of the probe qubit during the open system evolution in the presence of two information reservoirs. The effective couplings between the probe qubit and the reservoir qubits as $J_{1,2} = 0.007126$, $J_{1,3} = 0.005077$. We scale these parameters by dividing them with w_r. The interaction time is $\tau = 1.2$ ns.

In Fig. 3, we observe that 1000 collisions are sufficient to equilibrate the probe qubit to a steady value. Since each collision takes 1.2 ns as indicated above, the classification response should take 1.2 μs. This is much shorter than the energy dissipation time. In other words, our quantum data classification model based on dissipative quantum dynamics is possible with current superconducting quantum technology. The prominent advantage of dissipative models is that the optimized time-dependent control is not needed to encode the input data to the quantum register.

The success of linear classification of the proposed model is illustrated in Fig. 4.

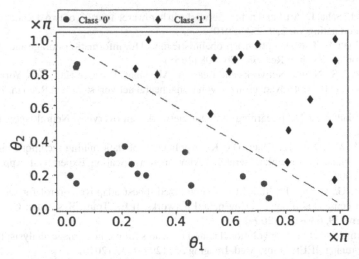

Fig. 4. Linearly separable classification pattern of the probe qubit in the steady state. The couplings of the probe to the information reservoirs were taken equal. The classification implemented for 32 amplitude parameter pairs randomly in range $0 < \theta_{1,2} < \pi$.

4 Conclusion

We have shown that the simple open quantum model we created within the framework of the collision model can classify quantum data. This model refers to the theoretical example containing a single probe (system) qubit in contact with the qubits (ancillas) that we consider to be information reservoirs. Likewise, the reservoirs and physical qubits we obtain through recursive interaction are transmon qubits that interact via the resonator variance, which also works for qubit readout.

A possible application of the suggested physical model with quantum classifier and superconductor circuits is numerically discussed. Based on the numerical results obtained, it has been shown that the collision model can rightly simulate CP divisibility and open quantum dynamics in the Markov approximation. We observed that the physical model that we used realistic parameters, worked faster than the classical models. Therefore, we have shown that an open quantum system can have useful information in the stable quantum states from the classification point of view, contrary to the point that mixed quantum states are useless.

Acknowledgment. We would like to express our gratitude for the support of this study from TUBITAK (Grant No. 120F353).

References

1. McCulloch, W.S., Pitts, W.: A logical calculus of the ideas immanent in nervous activity. Bull. Math. Biophys. **5**(4), 115–133 (1943). https://doi.org/10.1007/BF02478259

2. Misra, J., Saha, I.: Artificial neural networks in hardware: a survey of two decades of progress. Neurocomputing **74**, 239–255 (2010)
3. Rosenblatt, F.: The perceptron: a probabilistic model for information storage and organization in the brain. Psychol. Rev. **65**, 386–408 (1958)
4. Haykin, S.S.: Neural Networks and Learning Machines. Prentice Hall, New York (2009)
5. Gu, J., et al.: Recent advances in convolutional neural networks. Pattern Recogn. **77**, 354–377 (2018)
6. Schmidhuber, J.: Deep learning in neural networks: an overview. Neural Netw. **61**, 85–117 (2015)
7. Ngai, E.W.T., Xiu, L., Chau, D.C.K.: Application of data mining techniques in customer relationship management: a literature review and classification. Expert Syst. Appl. **36**, 2592–2602 (2009)
8. Hou, Z.-G., Cheng, L., Tan, M.: Decentralized robust adaptive control for the multiagent system consensus problem using neural networks. IEEE Trans. Syst. Man Cybern. Part B (Cybern.) **39**, 636–647 (2009)
9. Tajbakhsh, N., et al.: Convolutional neural networks for medical image analysis: full training or fine tuning. IEEE Trans. Med. Imaging **35**, 1299–1312 (2016)
10. Tang, J., Deng, C., Huang, G.-B.: Extreme learning machine for multilayer perceptron. IEEE Trans. Neural Netw. Learn. Syst. **27**, 809–821 (2016)
11. Shi, B., Bai, X., Yao, C.: An end-to-end trainable neural network for image-based sequence recognition and its application to scene text recognition. IEEE Trans. Pattern Anal. Mach. Intell. **39**, 2298–2304 (2017)
12. Mutuk, H.: Energy levels of one-dimensional anharmonic oscillator via neural networks. Mod. Phys. Lett. A **34**, 1950088 (2019). https://doi.org/10.1142/S0217732319500883
13. Mutuk, H.: Cornell potential: a neural network approach. Adv. High Energy Phys. **2019**, e3105373 (2019)
14. Lorena, A.C., de Carvalho, A.C.P.L.F., Gama, J.M.P.: A review on the combination of binary classifiers in multiclass problems. Artif. Intell. Rev. **30**(1–4), 19–37 (2009). https://doi.org/10.1007/s10462-009-9114-9
15. Galar, M., Fernández, A., Barrenechea, E., Bustince, H., Herrera, F.: An overview of ensemble methods for binary classifiers in multi-class problems: experimental study on one-vs-one and one-vs-all schemes. Pattern Recogn. **44**, 1761–1776 (2011)
16. Moore, G.E.: Cramming more components onto integrated circuits **38**, 4 (1965)
17. Schuld, M., Petruccione, F.: Learning with quantum models. In: Schuld, M., Petruccione, F. (eds.) Supervised Learning with Quantum Computers, pp. 247–272. Springer, Cham (2018)
18. Schuld, M., Sinayskiy, I., Petruccione, F.: The quest for a quantum neural network. Quantum Inf. Process. **13**(11), 2567–2586 (2014). https://doi.org/10.1007/s11128-014-0809-8
19. Rebentrost, P., Mohseni, M., Lloyd, S.: Quantum support vector machine for big data classification. Phys. Rev. Lett. **113**, 130503 (2014)
20. Banchi, L., Pancotti, N., Bose, S.: Quantum gate learning in qubit networks: Toffoli gate without time-dependent control. npj Quantum Inf. **2**, 1–6 (2016)
21. Lloyd, S., Weedbrook, C.: Quantum generative adversarial learning. Phys. Rev. Lett. **121**, 040502 (2018)
22. Huang, H.-Y., et al.: Power of data in quantum machine learning. Nat Commun. **12**, 2631 (2021)
23. Yamamoto, A.Y., Sundqvist, K.M., Li, P., Harris, H.R.: Simulation of a multidimensional input quantum perceptron. Quantum Inf. Process. **17** (2018). Article number: 128. https://doi.org/10.1007/s11128-018-1858-1
24. Tacchino, F., Macchiavello, C., Gerace, D., Bajoni, D.: An artificial neuron implemented on an actual quantum processor. npj Quantum Inf. **5**, 1–8 (2019)

25. Torrontegui, E., García-Ripoll, J.J.: Unitary quantum perceptron as efficient universal approximator. EPL **125**, 30004 (2019)
26. Abbas, A., Schuld, M., Petruccione, F.: On quantum ensembles of quantum classifiers. Quantum Mach. Intell. **2** (2020). Article number: 6. https://doi.org/10.1007/s42484-020-000 18-6
27. Mangini, S., Tacchino, F., Gerace, D., Bajoni, D., Macchiavello, C.: Quantum computing models for artificial neural networks. EPL **134**, 10002 (2021)
28. Türkpençe, D., Akıncı, T.Ç., Şeker, S.: A steady state quantum classifier. Phys. Lett. A **383**, 1410–1418 (2019)
29. Korkmaz, U., Türkpençe, D.: Transfer of quantum information via a dissipative protocol for data classification. Phys. Lett. A **426**, 127887 (2022)
30. Blume-Kohout, R., Zurek, W.H.: A simple example of "Quantum Darwinism": redundant information storage in many-spin environments. Found. Phys. **35**(11), 1857–1876 (2005). https://doi.org/10.1007/s10701-005-7352-5
31. Zwolak, M., Zurek, W.H.: Redundancy of einselected information in quantum Darwinism: the irrelevance of irrelevant environment bits. Phys. Rev. A **95**, 030101 (2017)
32. Korkmaz, U., Sanga, C., Türkpençe, D.: Mimicking an information reservoir by superconducting quantum circuits. In: 2021 5th International Symposium on multidisciplinary Studies and Innovative Technologies (ISMSIT), pp. 105–109 (2021)
33. Verstraete, F., Wolf, M.M., Ignacio Cirac, J.: Quantum computation and quantum-state engineering driven by dissipation. Nat. Phys. **5**, 633–636 (2009)
34. Poyatos, J.F., Cirac, J.I., Zoller, P.: Quantum reservoir engineering with laser cooled trapped ions. Phys. Rev. Lett. **77**, 4728–4731 (1996)
35. Altintas, F.: Dissipative dynamics of atom–field entanglement in the ultrastrong-coupling regime. Phys. Scr. **2014**(T160), 014002 (2014)
36. Wang, C., Gertler, J.M.: Autonomous quantum state transfer by dissipation engineering. Phys. Rev. Res. **1**, 033198 (2019)
37. Marshall, J., Campos Venuti, L., Zanardi, P.: Classifying quantum data by dissipation. Phys. Rev. A **99**, 032330 (2019)
38. Du, Y., Hsieh, M.-H., Liu, T., Tao, D., Liu, N.: Quantum noise protects quantum classifiers against adversaries. Phys. Rev. Res. **3**, 023153 (2021)
39. Deffner, S., Jarzynski, C.: Information processing and the second law of thermodynamics: an inclusive, hamiltonian approach. Phys. Rev. X **3**, 041003 (2013)
40. Deffner, S.: Information-driven current in a quantum Maxwell demon. Phys. Rev. E **88**, 062128 (2013)
41. Kołodyński, J., Brask, J.B., Perarnau-Llobet, M., Bylicka, B.: Adding dynamical generators in quantum master equations. Phys. Rev. A **97**, 062124 (2018)
42. Wolf, M.M., Cirac, J.I.: Dividing quantum channels. Commun. Math. Phys. **279**, 147–168 (2008). https://doi.org/10.1007/s00220-008-0411-y
43. Filippov, S.N., Piilo, J., Maniscalco, S., Ziman, M.: Divisibility of quantum dynamical maps and collision models. Phys. Rev. A **96**, 032111 (2017)
44. Wendin, G.: Quantum information processing with superconducting circuits: a review. Rep. Prog. Phys. **80**, 106001 (2017)
45. Majer, J., et al.: Coupling superconducting qubits via a cavity bus. Nature **449**, 443–447 (2007)
46. Filipp, S., et al.: Multimode mediated qubit-qubit coupling and dark-state symmetries in circuit quantum electrodynamics. Phys. Rev. A **83**, 063827 (2011)
47. Koch, J., et al.: Charge-insensitive qubit design derived from the Cooper pair box. Phys. Rev. A. **76**, 042319 (2007)
48. Krantz, P., Kjaergaard, M., Yan, F., Orlando, T.P., Gustavsson, S., Oliver, W.D.: A quantum engineer's guide to superconducting qubits. Appl. Phys. Rev. **6**, 021318 (2019)

49. Bruneau, L., Joye, A., Merkli, M.: Repeated interactions in open quantum systems. J. Math. Phys. **55**, 075204 (2014)
50. Scarani, V., Ziman, M., Štelmachovič, P., Gisin, N., Bužek, V.: Thermalizing quantum machines: dissipation and entanglement. Phys. Rev. Lett. **88**, 097905 (2002)
51. Johansson, J.R., Nation, P.D., Nori, F.: QuTiP: an open-source Python framework for the dynamics of open quantum systems. Comput. Phys. Commun. **183**, 1760–1772 (2012)
52. Johansson, J.R., Nation, P.D., Nori, F.: QuTiP 2: a Python framework for the dynamics of open quantum systems. Comput. Phys. Commun. **184**, 1234–1240 (2013)
53. Deng, X.-H., Barnes, E., Economou, S.E.: Robustness of error-suppressing entangling gates in cavity-coupled transmon qubits. Phys. Rev. B **96**, 035441 (2017)
54. Liao, J.-Q., Dong, H., Sun, C.P.: Single-particle machine for quantum thermalization. Phys. Rev. A **81**, 052121 (2010)

Sensor Application Ontology for Internet of Things

Alpay Doruk(✉) ⓘD

Bandirma Onyedi Eylul University, 10200 Balıkesir, Turkey
adoruk@bandirma.edu.tr

Abstract. More and more devices are connected over the internet and the sensor data they receive from the environment is monitored by other applications or end users. This technology is called the Internet of Things. Sensors used in the Internet of Things can be very diverse. When a sensor, of a certain type or has certain characteristics to be used in different Internet of Things applications, is required to be found over the Internet, this search process can be very difficult to do because of the excess of sensors and the fact that sensor information is located in different structures over the Internet. In order to solve this problem, the use of Semantic Web technologies was considered and a study was carried out within this scope. With this study, a data model was created by first deriving the characteristics and values of certain types of sensors, and then a sensor application ontology was created using the OWL language. An application program was then developed using the Java programming language and the sensor application ontology developed was queried through the SPARQL query language.

Keywords: Ontology · Sensor · Internet of Things · Semantic Web

1 Introduction

Today, an unprecedented number of physical objects are connected to the Internet of Things (IoT). Such objects can be of many different types, such as thermostats for creating smart home systems, HVAC (Heating, Ventilation and Air Conditioning) monitoring and control systems, autonomous vehicle and robot systems, sensors that display the condition of a machine running in a factory, wearable technologies (smartwatches, smart health products, etc.). There are many different areas and environments where the Internet of Things can play a remarkable role and improve our quality of life. These applications include transportation, health, industrial automation and emergency response to natural and human-caused disasters where it is difficult for people to make decisions, etc. The common characteristics of all these systems are that they use various sensors to interact with the environment.

Ontologies in Semantic Web contains the concepts, data, attributes and relationships between entities on a domain. They include the classes, their attributes, and also the instances of the classes. An ontology can be queried by using query languages.

M. N. Seyman (Ed.): ICECENG 2022, LNICST 436, pp. 171–177, 2022.
https://doi.org/10.1007/978-3-031-01984-5_14

When an application or a system is to be developed for the Internet of Things, it is very important to find and select sensors that are suitable and having the right features for the work to be done. A wide range of sensors are available on the market, and a search over the internet is usually required to find the correct and most suitable sensor necessary for the job. However, an useful environment, where sensor data is available collectively and expressed with the same format, is not fully available over the internet.

When this problem was addressed, the idea of creating a structure consisting of sensor types and information emerged as a solution. In line with this idea, the use of Semantic Web technologies was considered. Firstly, the sensor types are investigated, after this work an application ontology is developed according to the sensor types and with use of a developed application, this ontology was queried.

In the second chapter of the paper the background in this context is introduced, in the third chapter the material and method used in the research are explained, and the fourth chapter concludes the paper.

2 Background

In order to develop an ontology in the subject of sensors, it was first investigated whether there is an ontology prepared in this regard.

S. Avancha, et al. [1], has developed a comprehensive sensor node ontology for adaptive sensor networks. This ontology is used to adapt a wireless sensor network to operating conditions with changing the parameters while the communication and calibration of the network stay maintained.

M. Eid, R. Liscano, and A. E. Saddik [2, 3], has proposed a framework to develop a sensor ontology. Their framework references the Standard Upper Merged Ontology (SUMO) [4], which forms a starting point for developing IEEE Standard Upper Ontology [5], a general-purpose, large and formal ontology.

A prototype sensor information store compatible with the Semantic Web infrastructure called OntoSensor was developed using ISO (International Standards Organization) and OGC (Open Geospatial Consortium) models by D. J. Russomanno, C. R. Kothari, and O. a. Thomas [6].

In another study, M. Compton et al. [7], developed an ontology called SSN Ontology, which defines sensors as capabilities, measurement processes, observations and deployments.

In another study conducted by E. Maleki, F. Belkadi, B. J. van der Zwaag, and A. Bernard [8], a sensor ontology was developed that enables the implementation of a service application in Industrial Product-Service Systems.

In recent years, SSN ontology has been revisited and an ontology called SOSA has been developed to model the interaction between entities involved in Sensor, Observation, Sample and Actuator (SOSA) ontology, observation, operation and sampling actions by Armin Haller et al. [9] and K. Janowicz, A. Haller, S. J. D. Cox, D. Le Phuoc, and M. Lefrançois [10]. SSN and SOSA were developed by a joint working group created by W3C (World Wide Web Consortium) and OGC (Open Geospatial Consortium) Web Spatial Data (SDW) to identify sensors, actuators, samplers and their observations, operation and sampling activities. These ontologies are published as both the W3C recommendation and the OGC standard of implementation. Also OGC (Open Geospatial Consortium) has developed a generic data model, named SensorML [11], in UML (Unified Modeling Language) to capture the classes and their relations for all types of sensors.

3 Material and Method

3.1 Tools and Languages

At the beginning of the study the tools and programming languages to be used in the development of Sensor Application Ontology and the creation of the querying application have been decided. In this context, to use the W3C standard OWL [12] as the ontology development language and the Protégé [13] tool, a free, open-source ontology editor and framework developed by Stanford University as an ontology development environment was chosen. The Apache Jena [14] library was used to parse the ontology and SPARQL [15] querying language was used to query the developed Sensor Application Ontology.

While developing the application, the Java programming language was used on the Netbeans development tool and it was provided to work web-based through Apache Tomcat [16].

3.2 Method

Firstly, during the ontology development phase, the sensor types, to be used to restrict sample application, were selected and in this context, the 6 most widely used sensor types in Internet of Things applications were decided. These sensor types are Flow, Pressure, Level, Infrared, Speed and Proximity and Displacement sensors.

In the second step of the study, the samples of the selected sensor types were examined and their characteristics were extracted. Some of these features are seen in Table 1. These characteristics were used to develop the classes in the ontology and also to develop the attributes of the classes.

After this stage, the development of ontology was carried out using the Protege development environment and the OWL ontology language. It was decided that all sensor types were subclasses of a master class called Sensor derived from owl: Thing, and the implementation was realized (Fig. 1).

The features seen in Table 1 were also developed as attributes of sensor types (Fig. 2).

In the next phase of the study, sample sensors from the selected sensor types were included in the ontology and the development of Sensor Application Ontology was completed (Fig. 3).

Table 1. Sensor types and features.

Sensor type	Sensor features
Flow sensor	operatingVoltage operatingCurrent flowOfSensor housing …
Pressure sensor	pressureMeasurementRange maxPressure accuracy operatingVoltage …
Level sensor	maxPressure bodyMaterial floatMaterial …
Infrared sensor	speed speedUnit detectionDistance operatingVoltage …
Speed sensor	measuringAngleDegree measuringAngleDegreeUnit operatingRange operatingDelay …
Proximity displacement sensor	operatingFrequency operatingFrequencyUnit detectionDistance detectionRange …

At the last stage of the study, Sensor Application Ontology has been queried with the use of developed application program. The application program was developed using Apache Jena Library, Java Programming Language and Apache Tomcat. SPARQL query language was used to query the developed Sensor Application Ontology (Fig. 4).

While making a query firstly the Sensor Type is selected, secondly the desired Sensor Attribute is selected and the third step is selecting the range of the attribute and writing the desired value. After pushing the Search Button, the name of the Sensor and desired attribute values are listed as output (Fig. 4).

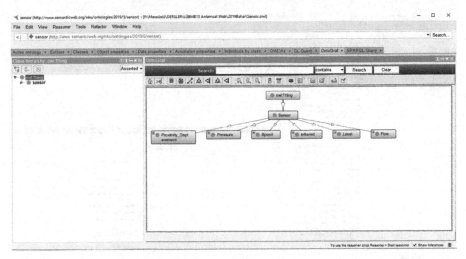

Fig. 1. The classes of the developed Sensor Application Ontology shown in the Protégé tool.

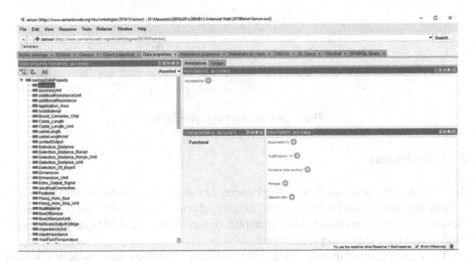

Fig. 2. Examples of attributes of sensor types shown in the Protégé tool.

The tool had been developed using many different technologies and the Sensor Querying Application is an easy to use tool. But also there must be done some improvements to the tool as user interface.

Fig. 3. Some examples of the instances of selected sensor types shown in the Protégé tool.

Fig. 4. Sensor querying application.

4   Conclusion

At the end of the study, a Sensor Application Ontology, that could be used to search sensors that can be used in Internet of Things applications and to find the properties of these sensors, was developed. Also, an application program that could query the Sensor Application Ontology was programmed.

The missing part of the study is that the application ontology includes only a limited type of sensors and sensor instances. In future studies, it is planned to increase both the sensor types and the sensor samples included in the application ontology.

Another development in the study may be in the process of determining sensor characteristics. In the current method, sensor features are manually added to ontology. In the later stages of the study, it is planned to determine the sensor characteristics from sensor information over the internet and add them to the ontology automatically.

References

1. Avancha, S., Patel, C., Joshi, A.: Ontology-driven adaptive sensor networks. In: The First Annual International Conference on Mobile and Ubiquitous Systems: Networking and Services (MobiQuitous), pp. 194–202. IEEE, Boston, USA (2004)

2. Eid, M., Liscano, R., Saddik, A.E.: A novel ontology for sensor networks data. In: IEEE International Conference on Computational Intelligence for Measurement Systems and Applications, pp. 75–79. IEEE, La Coruna, Spain (2006)
3. Eid, M., Liscano, R., Saddik, A. E.: A universal ontology for sensor networks data. In: IEEE International Conference on Computational Intelligence for Measurement Systems and Applications, pp. 59–62. IEEE (2007)
4. Pease, A., Niles, I., Li, J.: The suggested upper merged ontology: a large ontology for semantic web and its applications. In: Working Notes of the AAAI-2002 Workshop on Ontologies and the Semantic Web. Edmonton, Canada (2002)
5. Pease, A., Niles, I.: IEEE standard upper ontology: a progress report. Knowl. Eng. Rev. **17**(1), 65–70 (2002)
6. Russomanno, D.J., Kothari, C.R., Thomas, O.A.: Building a sensor ontology: a practical approach leveraging ISO and OGC Models. Dep. Electr. Comput. Eng. Univ. Memphis **1**, 637–643 (2005)
7. Compton, M., et al.: The SSN ontology of the W3C semantic sensor network incubator group. J. Web Semant. **17**, 25–32 (2012)
8. Maleki, E., Belkadi, F., van der Zwaag, B.J., Bernard, A.: A sensor ontology enabling service implementation in industrial product-service systems. IFAPapersOnLine **50**(1), 13059–13064 (2017)
9. Haller, A., et al.: The modular SSN ontology: a joint W3C and OGC standard specifying the semantics of sensors, observations, sampling, and actuation. Semant. Web **10**, 1–19 (2018)
10. Janowicz, K., Haller, A., Cox, S.J.D., Le Phuoc, D., Lefrançois, M.: SOSA: a lightweight ontology for sensors, observations, samples, and actuators. J. Web Semant. **56**, 1–10 (2019)
11. Botts, M., Robin, A.: OpenGIS® Sensor Model Language (SensorML) Implementation Specification, Version 1.0.0. Wayland, MA, Open Geospatial Consortium, 180p. (2007). (OGC 07–000)
12. Web Ontology Language (OWL). https://www.w3.org/OWL/. Accessed 06 Jan 2021
13. Protege Web Page. https://protege.stanford.edu/. Accessed 06 Jan 2021/01/06
14. Apache Jena. https://jena.apache.org/. Accessed 06 Jan 2021
15. SPARQL Query Language for RDF. https://www.w3.org/TR/rdf-sparql-query/. Accessed 06 Jan 2021
16. Apache Tomcat. http://tomcat.apache.org/. Accessed 06 Jan 2021

Response Times Comparison of MongoDB and PostgreSQL Databases in Specific Test Scenarios

Emin Güney$^{(\boxtimes)}$ ⓘ and Nurdoğan Ceylan ⓘ

Sakarya University of Applied Sciences, 54050 Sakarya, Turkey
{eminguney,nurdoganceylan}@subu.edu.tr

Abstract. Today, phones, tablets, commercial software, and many different devices are constantly generating data. These produced data should be accessed later on, such as software in business processes or business intelligence. Therefore, these generated data must be stored. There are many popular ways to store data constantly growing in size. All these options come with certain advantages and disadvantages. In this study, a performance comparison will be made between the PostgreSQL database, which is one of the relational databases used for data storage for many years, and the MongoDB database, which is one of the document databases, which has become increasingly popular in recent years, in certain test scenarios. In addition, the properties of relational databases and document databases are given. As a result of the study, similar data and test scenarios created in two databases and different test scenarios in terms of performance were examined, and response times were compared.

Keywords: PostgreSQL · MongoDB · Relational database · NoSQL database

1 Introduction

There has been a very rapid production of data from many sources such as web pages, social media, forums, blogs, and sensors in recent years. This rapid data production has caused institutions and organizations to change their perspective on data production. In addition, this rapid data production has revealed the concept of big data. The processing, storage, and reporting of all this big data have been the subject of many studies [1]. One of the essential steps for data is to be stored in a suitable format for later access. There are many ways for this storage process. Relational databases and document databases can be counted as some of them. Both methods have many advantages and disadvantages.

E. F. Codd invented the relational database concept at IBM in 1970. In 1974, the prototype relational database work started at IBM. However, the Oracle database, whose work was completed in 1979, was the first relational database product. Subsequently, many database tools such as DB2, Informix, Silver Surfer have been developed. In a relational database model, data is stored in one or more tables. Each table has related columns. The data is kept in multiple rows in the tables, and there is a special and

M. N. Seyman (Ed.): ICECENG 2022, LNICST 436, pp. 178–188, 2022.
https://doi.org/10.1007/978-3-031-01984-5_15

unique value field for each row. Another table establishes the relationship between the tables by using the value of the particular column in this table. Primary and foreign keys provide this relationship. According to their intended use, there is more than one type of relationship in the relational database model. These are one-to-one relationships, one-to-many relationships, and many-to-many relationships. There are index structures to access data faster [2]. NoSQL databases are specifically designed for specific data models and have flexible schemas for building modern applications. It has started to be used by a broad audience worldwide with many easy and practical features. NoSQL databases are used in many applications thanks to their flexible structures. Thanks to its flexible structures, it is very suitable for unstructured or semi-structured data. It has a distributed and easily expandable hardware structure instead of permanent and expensive servers.

With its less controlled structure, faster transactions can be enabled. It contains many data types and offers a functional structure. It also essentially eliminates relational databases' transformation problems and costs with Object Oriented Programs (OOP). It is designed for OLTP for various data access patterns involving low latency applications. Transaction and schema structures of relational databases are not among the primary purposes of NoSQL databases. Data is held in collection structures as a key-value relationship. Collections are stored in JSON-like file systems. Since there are no schema and constraint controls, adding, deleting, and updating operations can be quickly and effectively. The document data model is an increasingly popular database management system today. There is a structure for indexing data and documents for faster searches. Thus, fast query operations can be performed in relational databases [3, 4].

PostgreSQL is a free and open-source relational database product. It can run on many leading operating systems. The geographical data types part is very developed. There is also a document database section. It is used by many companies such as Apple, BioPharm, Etsy, IMDB, Macworld, Debian, Fujitsu, Red Hat, Sun Microsystems, Cisco, Skype [5].

MongoDB is a general-purpose, document-based, distributed database built for modern application developers and cloud computing. MongoDB stores data in binary JSON format, and data structures created for collections are not predefined. It is used by many companies such as Google, UPS, Facebook, Cisco, eBay, Bosch, Adobe, SAP, Forbes [6, 7].

2 Literature Review

There are many comparison studies in the literature to analyze the performance of databases. Some of these studies are given below. Politowski et al. made a runtime comparison for reading and writing operations of MongoDB as a document-oriented database and PostgreSQL as a relational database. They noted a significant performance difference between the databases tested, especially in search operations [8]. Jung et al. compared the performance of insert, select, update, and delete operations to evaluate performance differences between RDBMS (Relational Database Management System) and NoSQL. For this purpose, PostgreSQL and MongoDB databases were chosen, and they said that MongoDB's insert, select, update, and delete processing speed is generally faster than PostgreSQL. However, PostgreSQL's selection process can be improved by using indexes [9].

Tang and Fan describe the experimental results by analyzing the data model and mechanism of each database using a measurement tool called YCSB (Yahoo! Cloud Serving Benchmark) of five NoSQL clusters (Redis, MongoDB, Couch-base, Cassandra, HBase) [10]. To compare the performance of MongoDB and Post GIS, Agarwal et al. have demonstrated in their study that MongoDB performs better for large amounts of data by comparing the data in the indexed and non-indexed datasets [11]. Sharma et al. performed performance analyses of PostgreSQL, MongoDB, and N4j databases to find the appropriate NoSQL database for Geographical information system (GIS) application. Their Java-based application stated that MongoDB performs well in case of the large number of records [12]. Hajjaji et al. performed performance analyzes of three databases, Apache Cassandra, Apache HBase, and MongoDB. As a result of their research, they concluded that Cassandra is the most suitable database model for sizeable remote sensing data management [13]. From current studies, Makris et al. compared the response times of two datasets (relational and NoSQL) to find the appropriate dataset for industrial applications. Performance evaluations were performed to measure the performance of MongoDB and PostgreSQL databases in the storage system in different business scenarios. By confirming the performance of PostgreSQL to a large extent, they concluded that the use of PostgreSQL in industrial applications would be efficient [14].

In this study, performance analyzes were performed in different scenarios to compare two types of databases that are popularly used for data storage. The first of these two databases is PostgreSQL, a relational database, and the other is the MongoDB database, a document database.

Based on these two databases, the general features of relational and document databases were examined and compared. Table 1 gives the general features of Post-greSQL and MongoDB databases. Based on the table given, this article compares the speeds of these two databases for data insertion, grouping, fetching, and other operations. It is aimed to make the study original by working with different current technologies. The technologies used are described in the next section. In the study performed by producing synthetic data, test results for PostgreSQL and MongoDB databases were presented and interpreted.

Table 1. Comparison of the work performed with licensed applications.

	PostgreSQL	MongoDB
Licensing	Open source	Open source
Developed language	C	C, C++, Javascript
First release	1996	2009
Definition	Relational database	Document database
Developer	PostgreSQL development group	MongoDB Inc.
Orientation	Object based	Document based
Transaction	There is the concept of transaction	Transaction concept purposes not

(continued)

Table 1. (*continued*)

	PostgreSQL	MongoDB
Schema	There is the concept of schema	Schema concept not goals
Syntax	Similar to other relational databases	Different from relational databases
Official website	postgresql.org	mongodb.com

3 Technology Overview

First of all, to compare the two databases, a suitable test environment should be created. In order to create a suitable test environment, the same type of test data and hardware of the same power must be provided in the two databases. It was tried to prevent the operation of processes that would tire the hardware during the test process, except for the database tested in the background. Many technologies today have been used for a suitable and fair testing environment. These technologies are shown in Fig. 1.

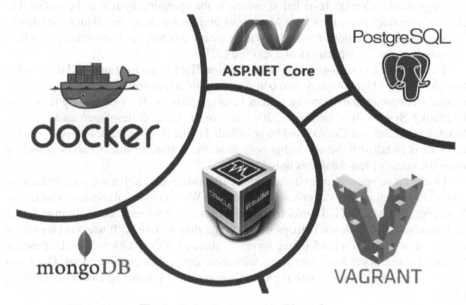

Fig. 1. Technologies used in this study.

After the appropriate test environment was prepared, the performance test was carried out by applying the determined test scenarios. Free and open-source programs were generally used for the test environment. Afterward, synthetic data was created on the established virtual server and programs. The performance test was completed by measuring with many different test scenarios, explained in detail in the following sections.

Virtual Box is a program that creates a virtual system within the system, which is used to install one or more operating systems by creating a virtual machine within the operating system. It is a free program developed by Oracle. It supports guests and hosts on different platforms, including Windows, Linux, Oracle Solaris, and macOS X. Voted virtualization app of the year by the Linux community. It is portable as it can be developed, tested, and demonstrated across multiple operating systems. It supports up to 32 virtual servers. It can connect with multiple network options. Video and 3D accelerators are available. DevOps processes of institutions and companies can be accelerated with VirtualBox. Folders can be shared between guests and the host system. Windows can be easily resized in fullscreen viewing modes. The servers created for the test environment are defined as virtual servers on the Virtual Box. All installations are built on Virtual Box [15, 16].

Vagrant is an open-source software product for creating and maintaining portable virtual software development environments. With Vagrant, which operating systems will be installed in the virtual server environment, which programs will be installed afterward, and which container structure these programs will be installed with can be defined declaratively. It will be elementary for users who want to do this test themselves to set up the test environment by using the test's vagrant file after installing Virtual Box. Instead of taking the image of the complete test environment and distributing it, the test environment can be raised with a simple and small-sized Vagrant file. In the Vagrant file, CentOS installation, which is the operating system to be tested. The Docker container program where MongoDB and PostgreSQL installations are made, and declarative definitions are made. With Vagrant, this test has been made portable in the simplicity and compactness of a text file [17].

CentOS is a Linux distribution based on Red Hat Enterprise Linux (RHEL), a distribution of Red Hat company, and compatible with this distribution. Developed by an independent group, the operating system's name stands for The Community Enterprise Operating System. In a January 7, 2014 statement, CentOS developer lead Karanbir Singh announced that CentOS had been included in the RedHat team. It is open source. CentOS is installed to be accessible only from the command line. CentOS is built to meet the needs of test databases only [18].

Docker is an open-source virtualization platform developed for software developers and system developers. Docker can run Linux and Windows virtual containers on Linux, Windows, and MacOSX. Thanks to this platform, the platform can easily install, test, and distribute web systems. Perhaps its most important feature is "It was working on my computer, why didn't it work on the server?" eliminating the problem. The databases to be tested with Docker have been set up with their appropriate configurations. Databases can be started and stopped with the CentOs command system and Docker commands [19, 20].

.NET Core was developed with this library to test two databases..NET Core is an open-source, general-purpose development platform maintained on GitHub by Microsoft and the NET Community. The "StopWatch" class was used during the testing phase while applying the scenarios. This class provides a set of methods and properties that you can use to measure elapsed time accurately. In the mini-application developed to implement the test scenarios, all-time measurements were made with this class [21].

Visual Studio Code is a powerful source code editor that can run on Windows, macOS or Linux. It is used for scripting and writing test codes. At the same time, CentOS,

Docker, Vagrant commands are also provided with this application. Visual Studio Code was chosen for its accessible, compact, and easy-to-use features.

Official.NET core providers were used while writing test codes on the relevant databases. These NpgSQL 4.1.2 and MongoDB Driver 2.10.0 libraries are used. Queries and database operations were performed in the simplest form through standard query languages in both databases.

First of all, a test environment was created to test the two databases. This test environment of the virtual servers has two processors (i7 2.6 GHz), 5 GB RAM, and 50 GB SSD disk space. In addition to this, the characteristics of the computer on which the virtual servers is installed are given in Table 2. In order to test, 1.6 Million synthetic data of the same type were added to the two databases. Test scenarios were carried out during the insertion phase and similar query processes in Fig. 2. The data model created jointly in the two databases is shown. Test scenarios were applied on this data model and synthetic data more than once and averaged. The data model consists of personnel, unit, occupation tables, or collections.

Table 2. Characteristics of the test computer.

Name	Properties
Operation System (OS)	Windows 10
Virtual Machine Operating System	Cent OS (Red Hat)
Central Processing Unit (CPU)	Intel Core i7 6700 HQ
Graphics Processing Unit (GPU)	Nvidia Geforce GTX 950 M 4 GB
RAM	8 GB
Memory (SSD)	512 GB SSD (M2 SATA)

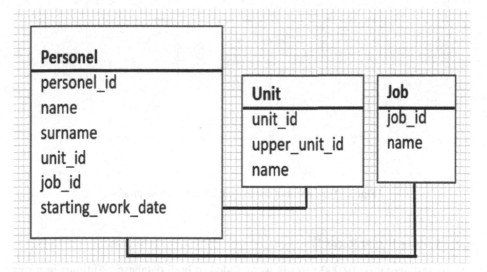

Fig. 2. Data diagram created to test the models.

4   Experimental Results

Test scenarios can be listed as follows;

- Adding 25,000 records
- Adding 10,000 records
- Fetching all records
- Number of personnel grouped by unit
- Number of personnel grouped by occupation

4.1   Adding 25,000 Records

In this test scenario, 25,000 records were added to both databases 16 times in a row. In Fig. 3, the duration and average duration of these trials in seconds are given. Test results showed that NoSQL databases have much less control than relational databases, so multiple record insertion operations are seen to be up to 20 times faster on average.

It is seen that additions to NoSQL databases are faster since the collections do not have a clear schema concept in NoSQL databases, the collection columns are not based on a clear template, and there is no explicit column type control. It is set to generate id fields in two databases automatically. Data is added synchronously in a loop.

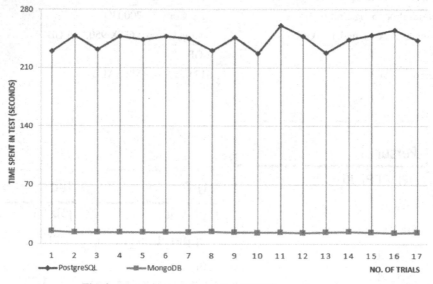

Fig. 3. Time spent of the adding 25,000 records process.

4.2   Adding 10,000 Records

In this test scenario, 10,000 records were added to both databases 20 times in a row. In Fig. 4, the duration and average duration of these trials in seconds are given. The test results showed that since NoSQL databases have much less control than relational databases, multiple record insertion operations are seen to be up to 8 times faster on average.

It is seen that additions to NoSQL databases are faster due to the fact that the collections do not have a clear schema concept in NoSQL databases, the collection columns are not based on a clear template, and there is no explicit column type control. It is set to generate id fields in two databases automatically. Data is added synchronously in a loop. In the first two tests, it was seen that NoSQL databases were much faster in adding data. NoSQL databases outperformed relational databases in the data insertion test.

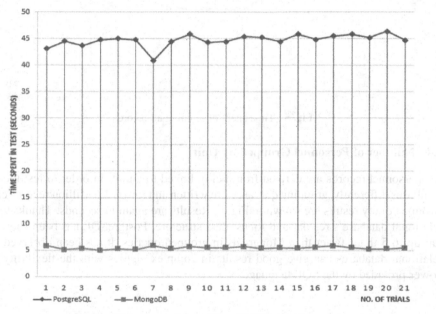

Fig. 4. Time spent of the adding 10,000 records process.

4.3 Fetching All Records

There are 1.6 Million records in each of the two tables. These records were brought 10 times in two databases. The average and all times in seconds are shown in Fig. 5. No action was taken on the returned data. The PostgreSQL database has been observed to give results two times faster on average. Small delays may have been caused because NoSQL databases keep other data in JSON files besides table data and the increase in the size of the queried data. PostgreSQL data, kept in a more regular format, seems to be brought faster. As a result, PostgreSQL, a relational database, was able to present the same amount of data to the end-user more quickly. Results are shown in seconds. All trials gave similar results.

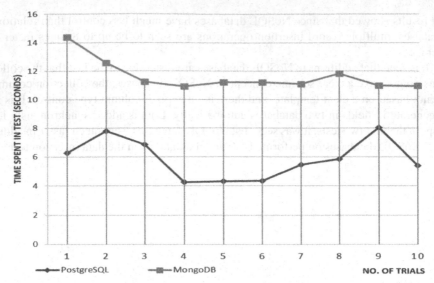

Fig. 5. Time spent of fetching all records.

4.4 Number of Personnel Grouped by Unit

All personnel records are derived from being linked to a unit. In order to test the two databases differently, grouping queries were written and run on 1.6 Million records each. Grouped query results are shown in Fig. 6. Results are again in seconds. Thanks to the relational database's regular and robust data structure, PostgreSQL has been shown to run up to 5 times faster than MongoDB in grouped queries. It has been observed that relational databases can give good results in complex queries with the flexibility and power provided by the SQL language.

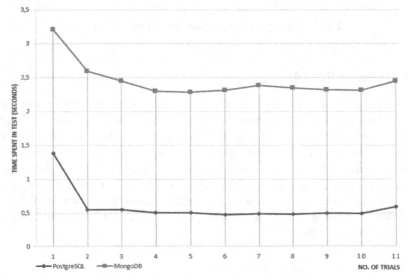

Fig. 6. Number of personnel grouped by unit.

4.5 Number of Personnel Grouped by Occupation

All personnel records are derived from being linked to a unit. In order to test the two databases differently, grouping queries were written and run on 1.6 Million records each. Grouped query results are shown in Fig. 7. Results are again in seconds. Thanks to the relational database's stable and robust data structure, PostgreSQL has been shown to run up to 5 times faster than MongoDB in grouped queries. It has been observed that relational databases can give good results in complex queries with the flexibility and power provided by the SQL language.

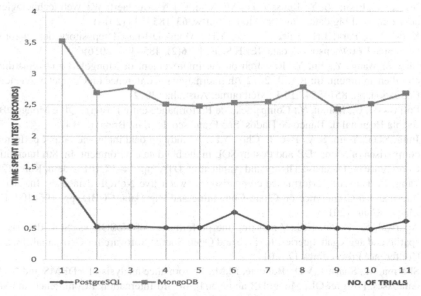

Fig. 7. Number of personnel grouped by occupation.

5 Result and Discussion

In our study, PostgreSQL and MongoDB were tested with different test scenarios. According to the test results, in some cases MongoDB and in other cases PostgreSQL outperformed. For example, since there is no schema structure, no collection column data type control and no template, MongoDB database has achieved much faster results in data insertion processes. On the other hand, PostgreSQL showed successful results in bulk data fetching and more complex query operations.

The result of this comparison showed that for a comprehensive software ecosystem, relational databases such as PostgreSQL should be used when necessary, and a document database such as MongoDB when necessary. For example, relational databases seem more suitable for sensitive transactions such as banking. NoSQL databases seem to be a very suitable option with their fast structure in an application where there are too many record adding operations such as logging operations. Now, NoSQL databases should be considered as a good option besides traditional relational databases at the point of data storage.

References

1. Doğan, K., Arslantekin, S.: Büyük Veri: Önemi, Yapısı ve Günümüzdeki Durum. Ankara Univ. J. Faculty Langu. History Geogr. **56**(1), 15–36 (2016)
2. Codd, E.F.: A relational model of data for large shared data banks. Commun. ACM **13**(6), 377–387 (1970)
3. Ward, M.: NoSQL database in the cloud: MongoDB on AWS. Amazon Web Serv. E-J. 1–13 (2013)
4. Baron, J., Kotecha, S.: Storage options in the AWS cloud traditional vs . cloud - based storage alternatives. Amazon Web Serv. 1–34 (2013)
5. Vitolo, C., Elkhatib, Y., Reusser, D., Macleod, C.J.A., Buytaert, W.: Web technologies for environmental big data. Environ. Model. Softw. **63**, 185–198 (2015)
6. Kang, Y.S., Park, I.H., Rhee, J., Lee, Y.H.: MongoDB-based repository design for IoT-generated RFID/sensor big data. IEEE Sens. J. **16**(2), 485–497 (2016)
7. Liu, Y., Wang, Y., Jin, Y.: Research on the improvement of MongoDB Auto-Sharding in cloud environment. In: ICCSE 2012 7th International Conference on Computer Science and Education, pp. 851–854. IEEE, Melbourne, Australia (2012)
8. Politowski, C., Maran, V.: Comparação de Performance entre PostgreSQL e MongoDB. In: Escola Regional de Banco de Dados. Sao Francisco do Soul, Brazil (2014)
9. Jung, M.G., Youn, S.A., Bae, J., Choi, Y.L.: A study on data input and output performance comparison of MongoDB and PostgreSQL in the big data environment. In: 8th International Conference on Database Theory and Application DTA, pp. 14–17. IEEE, Jeju, Korea (2015)
10. Tang, E., Fan, Y.: Performance comparison between five NoSQL databases. In: 2016 7th International Conference on Cloud Computing and Big Data, CCBD, pp. 105–109. IEEE, Macau, China (2016)
11. Agarwal, K., Rajan, K.S.: Analyzing the performance of NoSQL vs. SQL databases for spatial and aggregate queries. In: Free and Open-Source Software for Geospatial (FOSS4G) Conference Proceedings 17 (2017)
12. Sharma, M., Sharma, V.D., Bundele, M.M.: Performance analysis of RDBMS and No SQL databases: PostgreSQL, MongoDB and Neo4j. In: 3rd International Conference and Workshops on Recent Advances and Innovations in Engineering ICRAIE, pp. 22–25. IEEE, Jaipur, India (2018)
13. Hajjaji, Y., Farah, I.R.: Performance investigation of selected NoSQL databases for massive remote sensing image data storage. In: 2018 4th International Conference on Advanced Technologies for Signal and Image Processing ATSIP, pp. 1–6. IEEE, Sousse, Tunisia (2018)
14. Makris, A., Tserpes, K., Spiliopoulos, G., Zissis, D., Anagnostopoulos, D.: MongoDB Vs PostgreSQL: a comparative study on performance aspects. GeoInformatica **25**(1), 241–242 (2021)
15. Virtualbox website. https://www.oracle.com/tr/virtualization/virtualbox/. Accessed 09 Jan 2022
16. Dordevic, B., Timcenko, V., Pavlovic, O., Davidovic, N.: Performance comparison of native host and hyper-based virtualization VirtualBox. In: 2021 20th International Symposium INFOTEH, pp. 17–19. IEEE, East Sarajevo, Bosnia and Herzegovina (2021)
17. Vagrantup website. https://www.vagrantup.com/. Accessed 01 Jan 2022
18. Centos website. https://www.wikizero.com/tr/CentOS. Accessed 12 Jan 2022
19. Anderson, C.: Docker. IEEE Softw. **32**(3), 102–105 (2015)
20. Merkel, D.: Docker: lightweight Linux containers for consistent development and deployment docker : a little background under the hood. Linux Journal **2014**(239), 2–7 (2014)
21. Dotnet website. https://docs.microsoft.com/tr-tr/dotnet/core/. Accessed 10 Jan 2022

MIMD-Simulators Based on Parallel Simulation Language

Volodymyr Svjatnij[1]([✉]) [iD], Artem Liubymov[1] [iD], Oleksandr Miroshkin[2] [iD],
and Volodymyr Kushnarenko[3] [iD]

[1] Donetsk National Technical University, Shybankova Square 2, 85300 Pokrovsk, Ukraine
vsvjatnyj@gmail.com
[2] Ulm University, Helmholtzstraße 16, 89081 Ulm, Germany
[3] HLRS Universität Stuttgart, Nobelstrasse 19, 70569 Stuttgart, Germany

Abstract. The analysis of available tools for Complex Dynamic Systems (CDS) simulation showed that modern parallel tools lag behind the level of service of sequential Block-, Equation- and Object-Oriented (BO, EO, OO) simulation languages: developers of MIMD-simulators are forced to work on a programming language level. A concept of parallel modeling languages development based on the analogy between the principles of the functioning of consecutive languages and paradigm of MIMD-parallelism is proposed in the paper. An equation systems solving in any sequential language corresponds to MIMD-parallelism and can be interpreted as a virtual assignment "One functional language element – one MIMD-process". A transformation of a CDS simulation-model's BO-specification into a structure of MIMD-processes is shown by an example of a model of a Network Dynamic Object with Lumped Parameters (NDOLP). It was defined that the principles of equation systems solving by BO-language corresponds to MIMD-parallelism. Each block of the BO-language corresponds to a MIMD-process that accurately performs the block operation(s), also a set of processes was obtained, that are connected by a communication graph, which is synthesized on the base of the connection scheme between the outputs and inputs of the BO-simulator blocks.

Keywords: Complex Dynamic System · Simulation-model · Modeling language · Functional block · MIMD-simulator · MIMD-process · Devirtualization

1 Introduction

A mathematical model of CDS [1] is an equation or a system of equations of the studied dynamic processes and a formal description of the system topology (technological schemes, graphs, structures of automation systems, secondary topologies as a result of

M. N. Seyman (Ed.): ICECENG 2022, LNICST 436, pp. 189–200, 2022.
https://doi.org/10.1007/978-3-031-01984-5_16

approximation of systems with distributed parameters, etc.). A model that is reduced to a form adopted to computational methods and also software and hardware needs to solve the equation system is called a simulation-model of CDS. Taking into account the complexity indicators (high orders of equation systems, spatial distribution and multi-connectivity of parameters, hierarchy of structures, different physical nature of interacting processes, various methods of approximating models with respect to spatial coordinates, etc.), it should be noted that the construction of CDS simulation-models is a non-trivial task and requires significant computer support. The choice of a certain computational method determines the discrete CDS simulation-model, that in the process of hardware-software implementation is transformed into a CDS simulator.

Sequential CDS simulators have gone from implementation by methods of programming languages [2] to means of Block- (BO), Equation- (EO) and Object-Oriented (OO) modeling languages [3–5]. The development of parallel MIMD-simulators is carried out, as before, with the help of programming languages using the tools of the MPI and OpenMP libraries for data exchange and synchronization of MIMD-processes. As a result, subject matter experts who develop parallel simulators are forced to work with the tools of previously traditional second and third generation modeling systems [2], which are inferior to sequential modeling languages in terms of service level and user friendliness. The main stages and methods of Complex Dynamic Systems (CDS) modeling are shown in Fig. 1. In the theory and practice of Parallel Simulation Technologies (ParSimTech), one of the key problems is a development of Distributed Parallel Simulation Environments (DPSE) with full-featured software for the development, debugging and operation of parallel CDS simulators (Parallel Modeling and Simulation Software).

In order to approach the level of service to the fifth generation of modeling tools [1, 2], it is necessary to have parallel modeling languages in DPSE that ensure the transformation of the CDS model specifications into executable software modules of parallel simulators and exempt subject matter experts from the issues of choosing computational methods, constructing discrete CDS simulation-models and their software implementation. The analysis shows that the developed and experimentally studied pairs "topological analyzers - generators of equations" [1] of simulation-model allow to directly apply the principles of BO-, OO- and EO-simulation languages to solve systems of equations. The concept of parallel modeling languages development is considered.

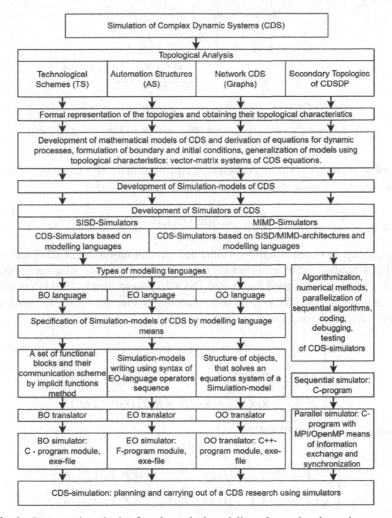

Fig. 1. Stages and methods of mathematical modeling of complex dynamic systems.

2 Block Diagrams for Solving Differential Equations in Modeling Languages and MIMD-Parallelism

The main component of the block-oriented modeling language [3] is a functional block (Fig. 2), which is implemented in software. The block has n inputs ($n \geq 1$) and 1 output; the coefficients of the input variables and the initial conditions for the output variable, which is the result of a certain operation, can be set in it:

$$Y = F(X_1, X_2, \ldots, X_n, a_1, a_2, \ldots, a_k, T), \tag{1}$$

where Y – function – the result of operations of input parameters, X_1–X_n – incoming parameters, a_1–a_k – initial conditions for the output variable, T – time.

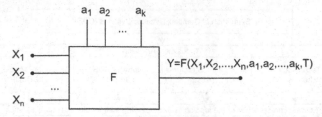

Fig. 2. Example of the functional block used in BO-modeling language.

To solve a system of ordinary differential equations in the BO-language of modeling, the following set of basic mathematical operations is provided:

$$F \in \left\{ \sum_{i-1}^{n} a_i x_t; \int \sum_{i-1}^{n} a_i x_i dt; f(x_i), \varphi(x_i x_k); f(t), x_i * x_k, x_i / x_k \right\} \qquad (2)$$

The analogy between the BO-specification simulation-model of CDS and MIMD-principle of parallelization is shown on the example of a model of a simple Network Dynamic Object with Lumped Parameters (NDOLP), described by the system of Eq. (3) with air flows in branches X, Y_1, Y_2, coefficients of flows inertia K_x, K_1, K_2, aerodynamic resistances R_x, R_1, R_2 and fan characteristics $f(X)$:

$$\begin{cases} X = Y_1 + Y_2; \\ K_x \frac{dX}{dt} + R_x X |X| + K_1 \frac{dY_1}{dt} + R_1 Y_1 |Y_1| = f(X); \\ K_x \frac{dX}{dt} + R_x X |X| + K_2 \frac{dY_2}{dt} + R_2 Y_2 |Y_2| = f(X). \end{cases} \qquad (3)$$

Simulation-model of NDOCP:

$$\begin{cases} X = Y_1 + Y_2; \\ \frac{d}{dt}\left(Y_1 + \frac{K_x}{K_1} X\right) = \left[f(x) - R_x X |X| - R_1 Y_1 |Y_1| \right] / K_1; \\ \frac{d}{dt}\left(Y_2 + \frac{K_x}{K_2} X\right) = \left[f(x) - R_x X |X| - R_2 Y_2 |Y_2| \right] / K_2. \end{cases} \qquad (4)$$

By the method of implicit functions, we obtain the BO-specification of the simulation-model in the form of the structure of functional blocks, which are necessary to find the unknown variables X, Y_1, Y_2 of the system of Eqs. (4) (Fig. 3, BO-simulator).

The analysis shows that the functional block of the BO modeling language (Fig. 2) can be associated with a MIMD process that performs the operation of the block and is programmed by a similar algorithm (Fig. 4): reading the Vector Elements (VE) input data, calculating the output variable $Y = F(VE)$, possible Y-replication for further parallel use and output to the scheme of communications between processes. The principle of solving systems of equations in BO-language corresponds to MIMD-parallelism and can be interpreted as a virtual meaning "Functional block - MIMD-process" (Fig. 5): each block of the BO language is assigned a MIMD process that precisely performs the operations of the block; we get a set of n processes that are connected with each other by a communication graph, which is synthesized by basing on the connection diagram between the outputs and inputs of the BO-simulator blocks (Fig. 3).

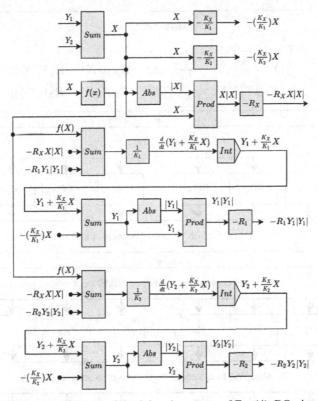

Fig. 3. Structure of blocks for solving the system of Eq. (4), BO-simulator.

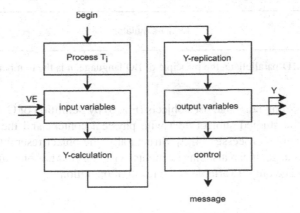

Fig. 4. Scheme of a MIMD-process, similar to the functional block.

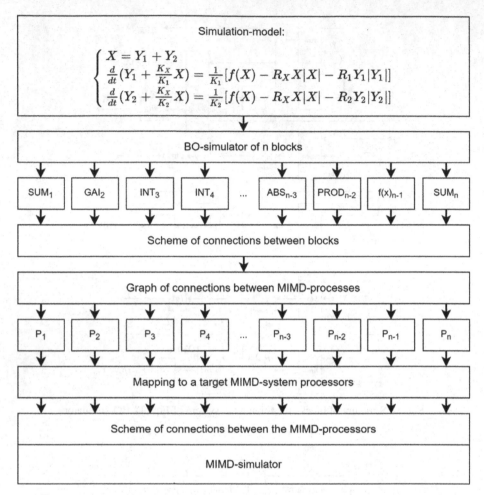

Fig. 5. MIMD-parallelism, the principle of BO-language, n is the number of blocks.

The OO-modeling language uses objects (Fig. 6) by definition of OO-programming and objects of the studied subject area with physical content and the corresponding equations of dynamic processes [4, 5]. Structurally, the object resembles a functional block of BO-language, it can also have n inputs ($X_1,\ldots, X_n$), it has one output and inputs for coefficients. The output variable is the result of operation:

$$Y = O(X_1, X_2, \ldots, X_n, a_1, a_2, \ldots, a_k) \tag{5}$$

The specification of the OO simulator is performed in the form of a structure of objects that execute mathematical operations that are necessary to solve the system of

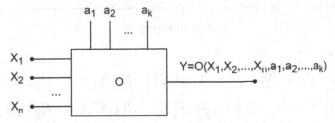

Fig. 6. Object of OO-modeling language.

equations of the simulation-model. The OO approach expands the possibilities of building simulators by manipulating objects according to the principles of object-oriented programming, namely, inheritance, polymorphism, communication between objects by sending messages, dynamic binding, etc. Thus, inheritance allows you to build multi-level hierarchical structures of objects that correspond to the models of complex dynamical systems. Also, thanks to inheritance, polymorphism and communication between objects by sending messages, it is possible to replicate objects and their structures in order to speed up data exchange due to the parallel organization of sending/receiving. Due to this, the OO approach allows the specification of the simulator to be approximated to the structure of the dynamical system which should be modeled. Thus, the objects of OO-language can structurally and functionally reflect the branches of the graph NDOCP (Fig. 7). If an object of an OO-language (Fig. 6) is associated with a MIMD-process (Fig. 4), then an analogy will appear between the principles of operation of a sequential OO-language simulator and its possible MIMD implementation (Fig. 8): the OO principle of solving a system of equations corresponds to MIMD parallelism and can be considered as a virtual "object-process" assignment. The operator of the equation-oriented (EO) modeling language [6] (Fig. 9), which is implemented by software, is an analogy of the MIMD-process: the operator can have n inputs, the output variable is the result of the OP operation.

$$Y = OP(X_1, X_2, \ldots, X_n) \tag{6}$$

A specification of the simulator by EO-language ACSL [6] is a program text of a FORTRAN syntax, names and operator actions that are used.

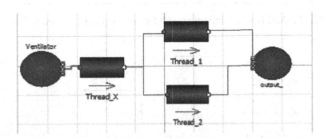

Fig. 7. Object-oriented model for solving the system of Eq. (4), OO-simulator.

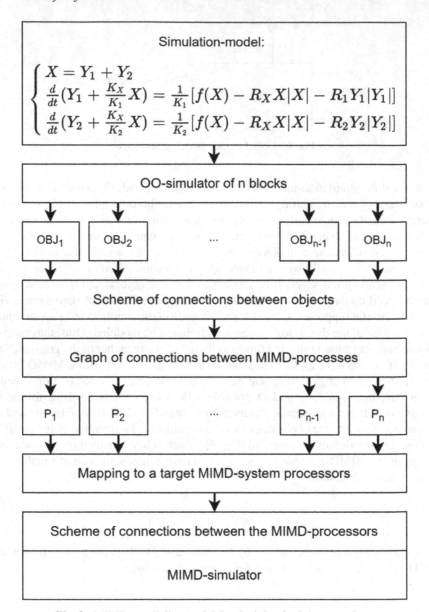

Fig. 8. MIMD-parallelism and OO-principle of solving equations.

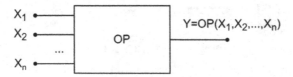

Fig. 9. The operator of the EO-modeling language.

EO-language operators are significantly smaller in terms of computational volume than BO-language blocks and OO-language objects. These volumes can correspond to MIMD-processes of minimum granularity and the EO-specification is transformed into a virtual MIMD-simulator with the number of processes, which significantly exceeds the number of processors of the target MIMD-systems.

3 Transformation of BO-, OO- and EO-Simulator Specifications into Virtual Parallel MIMD-Simulators

Virtual parallel MIMD-simulator is the structure of MIMD-processes, which is based on the considered analogies between BO-, OO- and RO-specifications and MIMD-parallelism in the relations "block-process", "object-process" and "operator-process". The following approach to the transformation of BO-specification into a virtual structure of MIMD-processes is proposed. Let the sequential BO-simulator of a dynamic system consist of n blocks, which in the MIMD-simulator must correspond to n analogous processes.

A vector of compounds for the T_i process is introduced:

$$VST_i = (S_{i1}T_1 S_{i2}T_2 \ldots S_{ik}T_k \ldots S_{in}T_n), \tag{7}$$

where i is the process number, $i = 1, 2, \ldots, n$; S_{ik} - switching parameter: $S_{ik} = 1$ - if there is a connection between the processes $T_i \leftrightarrow T_k$ and $S_{ik} = 0$ - if there is no connection $T_i \leftrightarrow T_k$. In the case $k = i$, we have $S_{ii} = 1$, since the intermediate result of the i-process is used in it for further calculations. The vector VST_i characterizes the virtual process T_i: one output and n inputs, to which the outputs of other processes are connected via S_{ij}. The set of vectors VST_i for the general structure of the BO-simulator is as follows:

$$\begin{cases} VST_1 = (S_{11}T_1 S_{12}T_2 \ldots S_{1k}T_k \ldots S_{1n}T_n); \\ VST_2 = (S_{21}T_1 S_{22}T_2 \ldots S_{2k}T_k \ldots S_{2n}T_n); \\ \qquad \cdots \\ VST_k = (S_{k1}T_1 S_{k2}T_2 \ldots S_{kk}T_k \ldots S_{kn}T_n); \\ \qquad \cdots \\ VST_n = (S_{n1}T_1 S_{n2}T_2 \ldots S_{nk}T_k \ldots S_{nn}T_n). \end{cases} \tag{8}$$

The simulation-model of the studied dynamic system is described by a system of equations, each of which is an implicit function that defines an unknown variable and is solved by the corresponding block and by analogy - the MIMD-process T_i. This variable $VART_i$, being the initial value of the process T_i, is the result of a certain operation on a set of variables that are fed to the inputs of the T_i process according to the equations of the simulation-model. In general case, the $VART_k$ variables are the output values of all other processes, therefore the virtual specification of the MIMD simulator with all possible connections between processes is the following set of variables:

$$
\begin{cases}
VART_1 = FUNT_1(S_{11}VART_1 S_{12}VART_2 \ldots S_{1n}VART_n); \\
VART_2 = FUNT_2(S_{21}VART_1 S_{22}VART_2 \ldots S_{2n}VART_n); \\
\quad\quad\quad\quad\quad\cdots \\
VART_k = FUNT_k(S_{k1}VART_1 S_{k2}VART_2 \ldots S_{kn}VART_n); \\
\quad\quad\quad\quad\quad\cdots \\
VART_n = FUNT_n(S_{n1}VART_1 S_{n2}VART_2 \ldots S_{nn}VART_n),
\end{cases}
\tag{9}
$$

where $VART_i$ – input resulting variables of the processes T_i, $i = 1, 2, \ldots, n$; $FUNT_i$ – operations of T_i processes on input variables that are supplied from the outputs of all other processes participating in solving the equation system of the simulation-model.

For further actions to transform the specifications, a virtual switching matrix is needed

$$
KM = \begin{pmatrix}
S_{11} & S_{12} & \cdots & S_{1(n-1)} & \cdots & S_{1n} \\
S_{21} & S_{22} & \cdots & S_{2(n-1)} & \cdots & S_{2n} \\
 & & & \vdots & & \\
S_{k1} & S_{k2} & \cdots & S_{k(n-1)} & \cdots & S_{kn} \\
 & & & \vdots & & \\
S_{n1} & S_{n2} & \cdots & S_{n(n-1)} & \cdots & S_{nn}
\end{pmatrix},
\tag{10}
$$

that formally describes all the connections between the blocks of the BO simulator and between the processes of the MIMD simulator. The matrix $MZM = KM * DT$ of the state of the simulator is obtained as a result of the operation:

$$
MZM = \begin{pmatrix}
S_{11} & S_{12} & \cdots & S_{1(n-1)} & \cdots & S_{1n} \\
S_{21} & S_{22} & \cdots & S_{2(n-1)} & \cdots & S_{2n} \\
 & & & \vdots & & \\
S_{k1} & S_{k2} & \cdots & S_{k(n-1)} & \cdots & S_{kn} \\
 & & & \vdots & & \\
S_{n1} & S_{n2} & \cdots & S_{n(n-1)} & \cdots & S_{nn}
\end{pmatrix} * \begin{pmatrix}
T_1 & 0 & \cdots & 0 & \cdots & 0 \\
0 & T_2 & \cdots & 0 & \cdots & 0 \\
 & & & \vdots & & \\
0 & 0 & \cdots & T_k & \cdots & 0 \\
 & & & \vdots & & \\
0 & 0 & \cdots & 0 & \cdots & T_n
\end{pmatrix}.
\tag{11}
$$

Here DT is the diagonal matrix of processes. Formal methods (5) ... (9) can be used to transform OO- and EO-simulators into corresponding virtual MIMD simulators.

4   Devirtualization of Specifications of Virtual MIMD-Simulators

Devirtualization is a transformation of the specifications of virtual MIMD-simulators, which determines the implementation of simulators on a given Target Parallel Computing System (TPCS) and requires a solution of the following main theoretical and practical problems:

1. Development of programs of MIMD-processes, which are analogs of blocks, objects and operators of the considered modeling languages. The main element that determines the efficiency of solving systems of differential equations in modeling languages (speed, accuracy, convergence, stability, ability to solve rigid systems, etc.) is the integrator, in which computational methods are implemented programmatically. Analysis shows that in MIMD simulators it is advisable to implement integrators based on parallel block computational methods, which have significant advantages over known sequential methods [7]. It will also allow integrating with the subsystem of the solvers of the equations of the Distributed Parallel Simulation Environment (DPSE) [1, 7].
2. Synthesis of virtual communication switches between MIMD-processes - analogues according to BO-, OO-, EO-specifications and their display in real communication systems of TPCS with use of message exchange functions of MPI- and OpenMP-libraries.
3. A priori analysis of the specifications of virtual MIMD simulators, taking into account the synthesized switches for compliance with the following criteria:

   a. Load balancing of MIMD processes.
   b. Minimizing the volume of data exchange between load balanced MIMD processes.
   c. The presence of the expected acceleration of the parallel implementation of simulation-models in comparison with sequential simulators.
   d. Possibility of implementation in TPCS according to the "process-processor" principle.

4. Proposals for the transformation of BO-, OO-, EO-specifications taking into account the results of a priori analysis and possible approaches to parallelization and levels of parallelism of virtual simulation-models of the subject area.
5. Architecturally relevant software implementation.
6. Integration with functional subsystems of DPSE [1, 8].

5 Conclusions

Growing requirements of subject areas to methods and approaches of modeling of Complex Dynamic Systems with Lumped (CDSLP) and Distributed (CDSDP) Parameters stimulate application of high-performance parallel computers of existing and future MIMD-architectures and cause new theoretical and practical problems of parallel modeling technologies (ParSimTech-problematics). One aspect of the problems in parallel computing systems friendliness to subject matter experts is the transition from programming parallel simulators to their construction by means of modeling languages. The proposed concept for the development of parallel modeling languages is based on the analogy between MIMD processes and the main functional elements of sequential modeling languages. The implementation of the concept is a promising direction of development and research in the field of parallel modeling of CDSLP, CDSDP.

References

1. Feldmann, L.P., Resch, M., Svjatnyj, V.A., Zeitz, M.: Software-Architektur für parallele Simulationsumgebungen. In: Plenarvortrag am ASIM'2014-Symposium Simulationstechnik. Tagungsband, Berlin (2014)
2. Schmidt, B.: Simulations Systeme der 5. Generation, pp. 5–6. SiP, Heft 1 (1994)
3. Angermann, A., Beuschel, M., Rau, M., Wohlfarth, U.: Matlab-Simulink-Stateflow. 6th edn. Oldenbourg, Munich (2009)
4. Modelica – A Unified Object-Oriented Language for Physical Systems Modeling. Language Specification. Version 2.0 (2002)
5. Akessona, J., Ekmanb, T., Hedinc, G.: Implementation of a Modelica compiler using JastAdd attribute grammars. Sci. Comput. Program. **75**, 21–38 (2010)
6. Advanced Continuous Simulation Language (ACSL). Reference Manuel, 4th edn. Mitchel and Gauthier Associates, Concord (1986)
7. Kushnarenko, V., Resch, M., Svjatnyj, V., Wesner, S.: Zur Entwicklung des Gleichungslöser-subsystems der verteilten parallelen Simulationsumgebung. In: ASIM 2014, pp. 357–363. ARGESIM Berlin, Tagungsband, Vienna (2014)
8. Svjatnyj, V., Kushnarenko, V., Shcherbakov, O., Resch, M.: Dekomposition der verteilten parallelen Simulationsumgebung. Probl. Mod. Autom. Des. Sci. Works DonNTU **1**(10)–**2**(11), 227–234 (2012)

Security

Real-Time Monitoring and Scalable Messaging of SCADA Networks Data: A Case Study on Cyber-Physical Attack Detection in Water Distribution System

Seda Balta[1]([✉]) [ID], Sultan Zavrak[2] [ID], and Süleyman Eken[1] [ID]

[1] Kocaeli University, 41001 Kocaeli, Turkey
{seda.balta,suleyman.eken}@kocaeli.edu.tr
[2] Duzce University, 81620 Duzce, Turkey
sultanzavrak@duzce.edu.tr

Abstract. SCADA networks, which are widely used by governments around the world to run computers and applications that perform a wide range of important functions and provide critical services to their infrastructure, are becoming increasingly popular among organizations. Because of their critical role in the infrastructure, as well as the fact that they are a potential target for cyberattacks, they must be secured and protected in some way at all times. In this study, we propose a topic-based pub/sub messaging system based on Apache Spark and Apache Kafka for real-time monitoring and detection of cyber-physical attacks in SCADA systems, which can be used in conjunction with other currently available systems. There are a variety of traditional machine learning approaches used in conjunction with a deep learning encoded decoder algorithm to create the mechanism for attack detection. The performance results demonstrate that our system outperforms the current state of the art described in the literature in this field.

Keywords: Real-time data processing · Pub-sub pattern · SCADA networks security · Data streams · Industrial control systems · IoT

1 Introduction

Real-time data processing is a problem that has been worked on since the 1990s. There is a demand for platforms that satisfy these objectives as the volume of data created has expanded, along with the development of increasingly complicated software solutions. Streaming applications such as fraud detection, network monitoring and electronic trading rely on real-time data processing to ensure that the service provided is deemed correct and reliable. Traditionally, custom solutions were being developed by the companies themselves to address the requirements of real-time processing. This mostly resulted in inflexible solutions with a high development and maintenance cost. Today, however, there exists several stream processing platforms and frameworks [1] that address these requirements to various degrees.

© ICST Institute for Computer Sciences, Social Informatics and Telecommunications Engineering 2022
Published by Springer Nature Switzerland AG 2022. All Rights Reserved
M. N. Seyman (Ed.): ICECENG 2022, LNICST 436, pp. 203–215, 2022.
https://doi.org/10.1007/978-3-031-01984-5_17

Cyber-physical systems (CPS) comprising of Supervisory Control And Data Acquisition (SCADA) systems and Programmable Logic Controllers (PLCs) represent the backbone of managing modern critical infrastructure [2]. In recent years, these cyber-physical systems have seen an increase in adoption throughout many industries such as fossil fuel extraction, power plants, transportation, manufacturing, water, and waste management, agriculture, and so on. The critical nature of this infrastructure makes the threat of cyber-attacks a major concern [3]. It is of utmost importance to rigorously test the SCADA systems for any vulnerabilities and develop cyber-attack detection and prevention techniques to minimize the risks and limit the attack vector and possible damages. There are several studies on the issue of cyber-security of SCADA systems in the literature. To the best of our knowledge, there is no study on real-time monitoring and scalable messaging of SCADA network data.

Following paragraphs give related works on cyber-security of SCADA networks and data streaming in ICS (Industrial Control System). Firsly, we focus on cyber-security of different SCADA networks. Huang et al. [4] presented a Bayesian network-based approach for assessing cyber-security risk levels in SCADA networks in a dynamic and quantitative manner. The simulation results showed that the suggested technique for analyzing SCADA security threats is effective. Nazir et al. [5] explored various techniques and tools to reveal SCADA system vulnerabilities. The applicability of these techniques and tools together with the selected approaches was examined. Finnan and Melrose [6] offered several defense recommendations for SCADA systems against security attacks. These defense proposals consist of six parts: ensuring physical security at remote sites, updating legacy systems, using network identification, training staff, protecting network traffic data, using existing cyber-security resources. Lamba et al. [7] mentioned the applicability of many security methods to vulnerable systems such as SCADA. In their study, real world attacks were mentioned and security vulnerabilities were discussed over these events. Basic security issues were identified for ICS and current solutions. Lakhoua [8] made a comprehensive review and explained how SCADA systems should be designed more securely. In their study, the stages of cyber-security in SCADA systems were mentioned as identify, protect, detect and react, respectively. Different aspects to consider in order to design a safer SCADA system were discussed. To protect vital infrastructure, new standards were introduced, including the usage of encryption and authentication for SCADA systems.

Zhou et al. [9] examined the standards, guidelines and practices for cybersecurity within the scope of three different topics which were broadcast time, geographical location and target audience. Abokifa et al. [10] developed a system to detect abnormal behavior of various components of a water distribution system within the scope of the Batadal project. Multi-layer architecture was used in the system. The first layer of the system, which is implemented using artificial neural networks, aims to detect outliers in the data set. The second layer, also uses an ANN, detects anomalies in the system. The third layer provides the classification of the obtained sensor measurements into the first subsection as normal and abnormal. Almehmadi [11] designed an attack detection system to find anomaly in SCADA network traffic. Using the attack-based system, SCADA network traffic was collected for 30 days and then the network was attacked using a (DoS) attack, message spoofing attack, and man-in-the-middle attack. They evaluated different classifiers. Teixeira et al. [12] investigated the feasibility of using machine learning algorithms to detect cyber-attacks in real time. The test environment was built using equipment used in real industrial environments. In order to gain a better knowledge of attacks and their effects in SCADA environments, advanced attacks were conducted in the test environment.

Alhaidari and AL-Dahasi [13] proposed a new approach using machine learning techniques to prevent DDoS attacks on SCADA systems. Algorithms were trained on the KDDCup99 dataset including a wide variety of intrusions. According to the results, the Random Forest algorithm was chosen as the most successful model in detecting attacks with a success rate of 99.99%. Pliatsios et al. [14] provided an overview of SCADA architecture with a detailed review of SCADA communication protocols. Specific high-impact security events, targets, threats and attacks on SCADA systems were discussed. Protocols were compared in terms of network infrastructure, topology, data rate and maximum distance. Various security recommendation approaches were proposed to prevent these attacks. Phillips et al. [15] looked at how machine learning techniques could be used to detect emerging security concerns in SCADA systems and the Modbus protocol.

Upadhyay and Sampalli [16] described various potential SCADA vulnerabilities by covering real events. Each type of vulnerability was examined, along with recommendations for improving SCADA security systems. The vulnerabilities were examined under four main topics which were product/software vulnerabilities, system configuration vulnerabilities, network vulnerabilities, flaws in SCADA protocols. Khodabakhsh et al. [17] examined cyber-security gaps and vulnerabilities that have emerged through the digitization of substations. Although firewalls and/or encryption partially solves the problem of cyber-attacks, they are not the only solution and attacks are still possible. Ferrag et al. [18] explored various cyber-security system solutions. They divided these solutions into four groups based on their security requirements and vulnerabilities.

Secondly, we give data streaming based works involved in industrial control in the literature. Real-time data, according to [19], has a short life cycle. As a result, the database used in a SCADA system has a specified time limitation. Features of a good database were suggested and the basic principles of real-time database were introduced. Stojkovic and Vukasovic [20] proposed a new upgraded SCADA system to open the old SCADA system open to future changes and innovations. For the first time in an Electricity Company in South East Europe, this system features 19 new Remote Terminal Units (RTU), ICCP data interchange with remote centers, and web-based real-time electricity demand measurement. Gajipara and Ahire [21] developed a real-time SCADA system with LabVIEW and microcontroller to monitor performance by obtaining and controlling physical parameters such as temperature, humidity, soil moisture, and light intensity. Wu et al. [22] developed a real-time urban water distribution network simulation system based on a SCADA system that communicates via OPC.

Tomic et al. [23] received signals from the sensors in real time and analyzed the measured data and then recorded the results in the database. They tried to estimate the concentration of pollutants in the air by performing a statistical analysis of the measured data via the monitoring station using smart SCADA system. Zaev et al. [24] developed a system that provides real-time monitoring and warning of water quality and quantity parameters. This SCADA system provides continuous real-time monitoring of various physical, chemical, and biological parameters. Saravanan et al. [25] proposed a new SCADA system that integrates with Internet of Things (IoT) technology for real-time water quality monitoring. Using the GSM module and Arduino Atmega 368, they aimed to detect water contamination, leakage in the pipeline, as well as automatic measurement of parameters (such as temperature, flow, color) in real time. SCADA captures real-time accurate sensor values via GSM communication.

Babunski et al. [26] proposed a real-time system that allows remote data monitoring for the quality of drinking water. A possible methodology was proposed for the control, reduction and optimization of water loss in the common water supply system with the efficient use of modern SCADA systems. Mercaldo et al. [27] proposed a real-time method to detect attacks targeting SCADA systems. Tank level measurements were taken into account by using the data published within the Batadal project. According to the water levels in the tanks, it is determined in whether there is an attack on the network. The proposed approach consists of two main stages, model building and model validation. As a result, when a total of 20 cases with and without attacks are examined, the proposed technique results in correct classification. Wakti et al. [28] mentioned that the current SCADA meter has several disadvantages. Due to which, the obtained state estimation has low accuracy and is not real-time. In their study, they suggested eliminating the disadvantages by installing a phasor measurement unit (PMU) device. At the Department of Electrical and Energy Engineering at Sapienza University of Rome, Kermani et al. [29] presented a new real-time energy management architectural model based on SCADA system duties in an educational facility with an MG Laboratory test environment named LAMBDA. The goal of the LAMBDA application was to make DIAEE smart in order to save energy. As a consequence, LAMBDA MG LAB's entire SCADA system deployment resulted in a 98% decrease in energy costs. It was also observed that the average monthly electricity bill was reduced by 87% for only local LAMBDA loads. Zavrak and Iskefiyeli [30] used unsupervised deep learning algorithms with a semi-supervised learning strategy to detect abnormal network traffic (or intrusions) using flow-based data. The following is a summary of the study's key contributions:

– This study concentrates on real-time monitoring and scalable messaging of SCADA networks data using topic-based messaging middleware. With the developed system, it is possible to access sensor data (as normal and anomaly) on a topic-based basis in real-time.
– A case study on detection of cyber-physical attacks in water distribution systems is given based on anomaly-based approach using traditional machine learning and deep learning methods.

The remainder of this paper is organized as follows. In Sect. 2, proposed architecture for real-time monitoring and scalable messaging of SCADA networks data is given. In Sect. 3, we compare conventional methods and deep networks based model for BATADAL dataset. The last section concludes the paper and gives future works.

2 Materials and Methods

This section firstly present reproducible research on SCADA network then give details of the proposed real-time monitoring system with pub/sub messaging, and its sub-components as shown in Fig. 1.

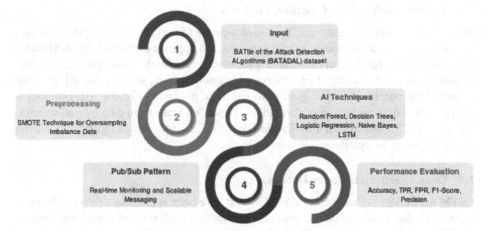

Fig. 1. Sub-components of the proposed system.

2.1 Apache Spark

The amount of data being processed when streaming SCADA network data, commands large amounts of computing power that cannot be provided by solely scaling up a single machine. Instead, it can be achieved by scaling out through distributing the computation across multiple machines [31]. Spark manages this scaling out by abstracting these machines as so-called execution nodes (worker nodes, slave nodes), on which programs (tasks), called spark jobs, are run. These abstract execution nodes can also be separate processes on a single machine, efficiently utilizing multiple cores. Apache Spark can run in stand-alone settings, as well as on some popular platforms (e.g., Kubernetes [32], Mesos, and Hadoop YARN).

The distribution of tasks to these nodes, and the collection of results from them, is managed by the master node (driver node). It utilizes an HDFS (Apache Hadoop Distributed File System) to persist data across these nodes [33]. Furthermore, both Spark and Kafka are developed by the Apache Software Foundation, which means they work well together.

2.2 Apache Kafka

Apache Kafka (version 2.11) distributed streaming platform is used in this study for real-time and large-scale data streaming. It has a topic-based pub/sub architecture and can handle a high number of concurrent consumers and producers. Apache Kafka excels in managing real-time data streams as a unified, high-efficiency, highthroughput, low-latency platform. The storage layer is simply a"distributed transaction log" structured as a "highly scalable message queue". Kafka optimizes the process further by implementing parallelism through the use of partitions and brokers. Furthermore, it has built-in fault tolerance.

2.3   Traditional Machine Learning Methods

In machine learning (ML), the goal is to learn the rules of the program using its input data. The ML program can use the data from experience to improve on the task by maximizing the performance. In this part of the study, we in particular look at one approach for ML, namely supervised learning. In a supervised learning setting, we give the ML program its input and output data. The goal is to learn the parameters of the ML program to map the input data to the output data. In this paper, we learn from data by mainly using supervised ML methods such as Random Forest, Decision Tree, Logistic Regression, Naive Bayes, and LogitBoost.

2.4   Deep Learning Encoder Decoder

LSTM networks [34] are recurrent models that have been applied to a range of learning tasks, including handwriting recognition, and emotion analysis, and speech recognition. A LSTM-based encoder is utilized to turn an input series into a vector with constant dimensionality. The decoder is another LSTM network which produces the desired sequence by means of these vectors. Malhotra et al. [35] suggests an Encoder-Decoder (EncDecAD) LSTM-based methodology for the detection of time series anomalies. In this architecture, the encoder creates a vector representation of the input time series, which is then used by the decoder to reconstruct the time series. The EncDecAD has been taught to reproduce "normal" time series in which the output reflects the input. The likelihood of anomaly at that point is then calculated using the reconstruction error. An encoder-decoder model trained with just normal sequences is shown to be capable of detecting a multivariate time series abnormality. During the training phase, the encoder-decoder has only seen and grasped normal examples of the training data. In contrast to normal sequence reconstruction errors, the trained model fails to reproduce an anomalous sequence well, resulting in larger reconstruction errors.

3   Results and Discussion

3.1   Experimental Setup

The proposed system is written in Python 3 and tested on a local PC. In Pytorch, we created an LSTM network model and its layers.

3.2   BATADAL Datasets

In this study, the attack detection mechanism was verified on an aggregation of three datasets of hourly SCADA readings for 43 system variables: An attackfree dataset (Dataset 1), a labeled attacks dataset (Dataset 2), and an unlabeled cyber-attacks dataset (Dataset 3). The datasets were featured in a competition on cyber-security [36].

3.3 Performance Comparison for Cyber-Physical Attack Detection

We evaluate the success/failure of the cyber-physical assault detection using several metrics obtained from the confusion matrix, such as accuracy, TPR, FPR, precision, and recall, as indicated in equations below:

$$Accuracy = (TP + TN)/(TP + FP + TN + FN) \tag{1}$$

$$FPR \text{ (false possitive rate)} = FP/(FP + TN) \tag{2}$$

$$Precision = TP/(TP + FP) \tag{3}$$

$$TPR \text{ (recall)} = TP/(TP + FN) \tag{4}$$

$$F_1\text{-score} = (2 \times Precision \times Recall)/(Precision + Recall) \tag{5}$$

Table 1. Performance results for traditional machine learning algorithms.

Algorithm	TPR	FPR	Precision	F_1-score	Accuracy	AUROC
Random Forest	0.99	0.004	0.99	0.99	0.99	1
Decision Tree	0.97	0.02	0.97	0.97	0.97	0.98
Logistic Regression	0.91	0.08	0.91	0.91	0.91	0.96
Naïve Bayes	0.75	0.32	0.82	0.72	0.75	0.84
LogitBoost	0.86	0.16	0.86	0.86	0.86	0.94

Table 1 shows performance results of traditional machine learning algorithms on BATADAL. Firstly, SMOTE balancing is done to prevent unbalanced class distribution in the dataset. Also, some pre-processing steps such as string indexer and vector assembling are operated on features. Dataset is split into training/testing ones. Finally, predictions are obtained on test set and compared predictions with underlying labels. Random Forest gives the best performance among traditional machine learning algorithms.

Table 2 shows performance results of EncDecAD on BATADAL. The dataset is partitioned into training and test subsets. To construct a normal profile of network traffic using the semi-supervised learning (SSL) paradigm, the training phase uses only the labeled dataset having normal data characteristics. The testing phase uses an unlabeled data set that includes both normal and attack data characteristics. It's worth mentioning that when computing assessment measures in this study, the labels in the test dataset are taken into account. Because the approaches employed in this research are parameterized, the performance of the models should be computed using the appropriate parameters. The cross-validation operation cannot be performed in the hyperparameter optimization

Table 2. Performance results for EncDecAD.

Test dataset	Window size	Dimension	TPR	FPR	Precision	F_1-score	Accuracy	AUROC
Dataset 2	3	128	0.79	0.012	0.89	0.84	0.96	0.93
	6	128	0.72	0.008	0.91	0.80	0.95	0.94
	1	96	0.64	0.005	0.94	0.76	0.95	0.91
	12	96	0.64	0.02	0.80	0.72	0.94	0.87
Dataset 3	3	128	0.84	0.027	0.87	0.86	0.94	0.94
	1	128	0.77	0.012	0.93	0.84	0.94	0.92
	6	128	0.76	0.017	0.91	0.83	0.94	0.93
	12	80	0.72	0.02	0.89	0.80	0.93	0.91

since anomalous data is not included in the training process [37]. As a result, the hyper-parameters are mostly selected depending on Malhotra et al.'s recommendations [35]. Afterwards, EncDecAD hyperparameters are determined largely through trial and error.

In the hidden layers of EncDecAD, models were trained and built utilizing various dimensions such as 32, 48, 64, 80, 96, and 128. The layer dimensions of the top performing EncDecAD models were determined through trial and error while keeping the layer count constant. The following parameters are needed to configure the EncDecAD neural network. The learning rate is set at 0.001. The Adam updater is used to avoid the local minimum and to discover better alternatives for the optimization process. In hidden layers, the tanh (hyperpolic tangent) function is employed as the activation function. EncDecAD models are trained for 100 epochs with 16 batch sizes. In EncDecAD models, reconstruction error is utilized as an anomaly score. At first, the samples are normalized using the feature scaling technique to ensure that all values are inside the range [0,1]. To determine the effectiveness of the techniques, different training and test datasets are employed. The models are unsupervise, so the neural network is trained using only normal data. The label in the dataset's last column refers to the attack class that is not utilized during training. The testing procedure includes both normal and attack examples. During the test phase, all attacks that are not "normal" are deemed to be "anomaly". Metrics are calculated for the purpose of evaluating the performance of an attack class using just standard data and attack class-specific data.

Table 3 shows performance comparison with other state-of-art approaches on BATADAL dataset. We compare them in terms of methods, performance metrics, real-time data streaming/monitoring, and scalable messaging. Although some works consider real-time processing, there is no work including scalable messaging. Our study also meets needs of a cyber-attack detection mechanism in considerable way.

Table 3. Performance comparison with other state-of-art approaches.

Paper	Method(s)	Performance metrics	Real-time data streaming and monitoring	Scalable messaging
[38]	Model-based fault detection methodology which utilizes a physically-based water hydraulics simulation model (EPANET)	The performance index is 0.98, 0.97, 0.96 for coefficient of variation of 0.05, 0.15, 0.25, respectively	x	x
[39]	LSTM, CNN	Accuracy = 0.93, precision = 0.9, recall = 0.6, FPR = 0.01 with window = 3	✓	x
[11]	Naive Bayes, SVM, Random Forest	Accuracies for Naïve Bayes is 0.61, SVM is 0.71, Random Forest is 0.99	x	x
[10]	Artificial Neural Networks	TPR = 0.936 and TNR = 0.957	x	x
[40]	Random Forest	Accuracy = 0.99	x	x
[41]	On-line forecasting model, non-linear autoregressive networks with exogenous inputs (NARX)	x	✓	x
[42]	Ensemble model, Deep Learning, Time Series	Accuracy = 0.73 for Datasets 1–2 Accuracy = 0.98 for Datasets 3–4	✓	x
[43]	Model-free optimization based solution	x	✓	x
[44]	Deep Learning Neural Networks, Autoencoders	With window length: 24 h, F1-score = 0.882, recall = 0.897, precision = 0.759	x	x
Our study	Apache Spark Apache Kafka Traditional machine learning and deep learning algorithms	Accuracies for Naive Bayes is 0.75, LogitBoost is 0.86, Logistic Regression is 0.91, Decision Tree is 0.97, Random Forest is 0.99, EncDecAD is 0.96 (window = 3, Dimension = 128)	✓	✓

3.4 Data Stream Processing

This sub-section gives real-time monitoring and scalable messaging of SCADA network data. The producer posts messages to subjects here (normal and anomaly). Subscribers to these topics process incoming messages and deliver an acknowledgement when they're finished.

4 Conclusions

CPS are heterogeneous devices that interact via a network and control and monitor a physical process. Control devices, such as PLCs and RTUs, are designed to get sensor readouts from the physical process on a regular basis and subsequently activate actuators to alter the process's state. CPSs are in charge of a wide range of physical processes, as well as essential infrastructure. CPS attacks may do severe harm to humans and the environment, and securing them is still a work in progress. In this paper we focus on three problems to improve the security of CPS: (i) realtime monitoring, (ii) scalable messaging of SCADA network data, and detection of cyber-physical attacks in water distribution systems.

In this study, we propose a topic-based pub/sub messaging system for real-time monitoring and detection cyber-physical attacks in SCADA systems. It is provided to detect anomalies obtained from SCADA data providers and to send this information to subscribed users on a topic-based basis. For real-time monitoring and messaging, Apache Kafka is used. Besides, Apache Spark is used for the purpose of stream processing. A case study is done on water distribution systems. According to performance results, our system is more successful than the state-art-works in the literature. There are still many open questions and challenges in the field. The networks are not only subject to attack and relatively unsecured, but these systems are also growing in size and increasing in complexity. We will extend our system to cope with this growth and complexity. Also, a real-time reporting tool will be added.

References

1. Van Dongen, G., Van den Poel, D.: Evaluation of stream processing frameworks. IEEE Trans. Parallel Distrib. Syst. **31**(8), 1845–1858 (2020)
2. Lee, E.A.: Cyber physical systems: design challenges. In: 2008 11th IEEE International Symposium on Object and Component-Oriented Real-Time Distributed Computing (ISORC), Orlando, FL, pp. 363–369. IEEE (2008)
3. Zhu, B., Joseph, A., Sastry, S.: A taxonomy of cyber attacks on SCADA systems. In: 2011 International Conference on Internet of Things and 4th International Conference on Cyber, Physical and Social Computing (CPSCom), Dalian, China, pp. 380–388. IEEE (2011)
4. Huang, K., Zhou, C., Tian, Y.C., Tu, W., Peng, Y.: Application of Bayesian network to data-driven cybersecurity risk assessment in SCADA networks. In: 2017 27th International Telecommunication Networks and Applications Conference (ITNAC), Melbourne, Australia, pp. 1–6. IEEE (2017)
5. Nazir, S., Patel, S., Patel, D.: Assessing and augmenting SCADA cyber security: a survey of techniques. Comput. Secur. **70**, 436–454 (2017)

6. Finnan, K, Melrose, J.: Cyber security for pipelines other SCADA systems. Control Eng. (2017)
7. Lamba, A., Singh, S., Balvinder, S., Dutta, N., Rela, S.: Mitigating cyber security threats of industrial control systems (SCADA & DCS). In: 3rd International Conference on Emerging Technologies in Engineering, Biomedical, Medical and Science (ETEBMS), pp. 31–34 (2017)
8. Lakhoua, N.M.: Review on SCADA cybersecurity for critical infrastructures. J. Comput. Sci. Control Syst. **10**(1), 15 (2017)
9. Zhou, X., Xu, Z., Wang, L., Chen, K.: What should we do? A structured review of SCADA system cyber security standards. In: 2017 4th International Conference on Control, Decision and Information Technologies (CoDIT), Barcelona, Spain, pp. 0605–0614. IEEE (2017)
10. Abokifa, A.A., Haddah, K., Lo, C.S., Biswas, P.: Detection of cyber physical attacks on water distribution systems via principal component analysis and artificial neural networks. In: World Environmental and Water Resources Congress 2017, Sacramento, California, pp. 676–691. TRB (2017)
11. Almehmadi, A.: SCADA networks anomaly-based intrusion detection system. In: Proceedings of the 11th International Conference on Security of Information and Networks, Cardiff, UK, pp. 1–4. ACM (2018)
12. Teixeira, M.A., Salman, T., Zolanvari, M., Jain, R., Meskin, N., Samaka, M.: SCADA system testbed for cybersecurity research using machine learning approach. Future Internet **10**(8), 76 (2018)
13. Alhaidari, F.A., AL-Dahasi E.M.: New approach to determine DDoS attack patterns on SCADA system using machine learning. In: 2019 International Conference on Computer and Information Sciences (ICCIS), Aljouf, Saudi Arabia, pp. 1–6 (2019)
14. Pliatsios, D., Sarigiannidis, P., Lagkas, T., Sarigiannidis, A.G.: A survey on SCADA systems: secure protocols, incidents, threats and tactics. IEEE Commun. Surv. Tutor. **22**(3), 1942–1976 (2020)
15. Phillips, B., Gamess, E., Krishnaprasad, S.: An evaluation of machine learning-based anomaly detection in a SCADA system using the modbus protocol. In: Proceedings of the 2020 ACM Southeast Conference, Tampa, FL, USA, pp. 188–196. ACM (2020)
16. Upadhyay, D., Sampalli, S.: Scada (supervisory control and data acquisition) systems: Vulnerability assessment and security recommendations. Comput. Secur. **89**, 101666 (2020)
17. Khodabakhsh, A., Yayilgan, S.Y., Houmb, S.H., Hurzuk, N., Foros, J., Istad, M.: Cybersecurity gaps in a digital substation: from sensors to SCADA. In: 2020 9th Mediterranean Conference on Embedded Computing (MECO), Budva, Montenegro, pp. 1–4 (2020)
18. Ferrag, M.A., Babaghayou, M., Yazici, M.A.: Cyber security for fog-based smart grid SCADA systems: solutions and challenges. J. Inf. Secur. Appl. **52**, 102500 (2020)
19. Wu, J., Cheng, Y., Schulz, N.N.: Overview of real-time database management system design for power system SCADA system. In: Proceedings of the IEEE SoutheastCon 2006, Memphis, Tennessee, pp. 62–66. IEEE (2006)
20. Stojkovic, B., Vukasovic, M.: A new SCADA system design in the power system of montenegro-ICCP/TASE. 2 and web-based real-time electricity demand metering extensions. In: 2006 IEEE PES Power Systems Conference and Exposition, Atlanta, GA, pp. 2194–2199. IEEE (2006)
21. Gajipara, N.D., Ahire, P.L.: Design of SCADA for real time system with labview and microcontroller. Int. J. Innov. Res. Adv. Eng. (IJIRAE) **1**(7), 85–90 (2014)
22. Wu, W., Gao, J., Yuan, Y., Zhao, H., Chang, K.: Water distribution network real-time simulation based on SCADA system using OPC communication. In: 2011 International Conference on Networking, Sensing and Control, Delft, Netherlands, pp. 329–334. IEEE (2011)
23. Tomić, J., Kušljević, M., Vidaković, M., Rajs, V.: Smart SCADA system for urban air pollution monitoring. Measurement **58**, 138–146 (2014)

24. Zaev, E., Babunski, D., Tuneski, A.: SCADA system for real-time measuring and evaluation of river water quality. In: 2016 5th Mediterranean Conference on Embedded Computing (MECO), Bar, Montenegro, pp. 83–86. IEEE (2016)

25. Saravanan, K., Anusuya, E., Kumar, R.: Real-time water quality monitoring using internet of things in SCADA. Environ. Monit. Assess. **190**(9), 1–16 (2018)

26. Babunski, D., Zaev, E., Tuneski, A., Bozovic, D.: Optimization methods for water supply SCADA system. In: 2018 7th Mediterranean Conference on Embedded Computing (MECO), Budva, Montenegro, pp. 1–4. IEEE (2018)

27. Mercaldo, F., Martinelli, F., Santone, A.: Real-time SCADA attack detection by means of formal methods. In: 2019 IEEE 28th international conference on enabling technologies: infrastructure for collaborative enterprises (WETICE), Napoli, Italy, pp. 231–236. IEEE (2019)

28. Wakti, M.H., Putranto, L.M., Hadi, S.P., Yasirroni, M., Marsiano, A.F.D.: PMU location determination in a hybrid PMU-SCADA system. In: 2020 12th International Conference on Information Technology and Electrical Engineering (ICITEE), pp. 245–250. IEEE (2020)

29. Kermani, M., Adelmanesh, B., Shirdare, E., Sima, C.A., Carnì, D.L., Martirano, L.: Intelligent energy management based on SCADA system in a real microgrid for smart building applications. Renewable Energy **171**, 1115–1127 (2021)

30. Zavrak, S., Iskefiyeli, M.: Anomaly-based intrusion detection from network flow features using variational autoencoder. IEEE Access **8**, 108346–108358 (2020)

31. Wolke, A., Meixner, G.: TwoSpot: a cloud platform for scaling out web applications dynamically. In: Di Nitto, E., Yahyapour, R. (eds.) ServiceWave 2010. LNCS, vol. 6481, pp. 13–24. Springer, Heidelberg (2010). https://doi.org/10.1007/978-3-642-17694-4_2

32. Kubernetes Apache spark contributors. https://kubernetes.io. Accessed 11 Feb 2021

33. Zaharia, M., et al.: Apache spark: a unified engine for big data processing. Commun. ACM **59**(11), 56–65 (2016)

34. Hochreiter, S., Schmidhuber, J.: Long short-term memory. Neural Comput. **9**(8), 1735–1780 (1997)

35. Malhotra, P., Ramakrishnan, A., Anand, G., Vig, L., Agarwal, P., Shroff, G.: LSTM-based encoder-decoder for multi-sensor anomaly detection (2016)

36. Taormina, R., et al.: Battle of the attack detection algorithms: disclosing cyber attacks on water distribution networks. J. Water Resour. Plan. Manag. **144**(8), 04018048 (2018)

37. Nicolau, M., McDermott, J.: Learning neural representations for network anomaly detection. IEEE Trans. Cybern. **49**(8), 3074–3087 (2018)

38. Housh, M., Ohar, Z.: Model-based approach for cyber-physical attack detection in water distribution systems. Water Res. **139**, 132–143 (2018)

39. Erba, A., et al.: Constrained concealment attacks against reconstruction based anomaly detectors in industrial control systems. In: Annual Computer Security Applications Conference, Austin, USA, pp. 480–495 (2020)

40. Aghashahi, M., Sundararajan, R., Pourahmadi, M., Banks, M. K.: Water distribution systems analysis symposium–battle of the attack detection algorithms (batadal). In: World Environmental and Water Resources Congress 2017, Sacramento, California, pp. 101–108 (2017)

41. Brentan, B.M., et al.: On-line cyber attack detection in water networks through state forecasting and control by pattern recognition. In: World Environmental and Water Resources Congress 2017, Sacramento, California, pp. 583–592 (2017)

42. Chandy, S.E., Rasekh, A., Barker, Z.A., Campbell, B., Shafiee, M.E.: Detection of cyberattacks to water systems through machine-learning-based anomaly detection in SCADA data. In: World Environmental and Water Resources Congress 2017, Sacramento, California, pp. 611–616 (2017)

43. Giacomoni, M., Gatsis, N., Taha, A.: Identification of cyber attacks on water distribution systems by unveiling low-dimensionality in the sensory data. In: World Environmental and Water Resources Congress 2017, Sacramento, California, pp 660–675 (2017)
44. Taormina, R., Galelli, S.: Deep-learning approach to the detection and localization of cyber-physical attacks on water distribution systems. J. Water Resour. Plan. Manag. **144**(10), 04018065 (2018)

Author Index

Printed in the United States
by Baker & Taylor Publisher Services

Printed in the United States
by Baker & Taylor Publisher Services

Printed in the United States
by Baker & Taylor Publisher Services